Shrines in Africa

AFRICA: MISSING VOICES SERIES

Donald I. Ray, general editor

ISSN 1703-1826

University of Calgary Press has a long history of publishing academic works on Africa. *Africa: Missing Voices* illuminates issues and topics concerning Africa that have been ignored or are missing from current global debates. This series will fill a gap in African scholarship by addressing concerns that have been long overlooked in political, social, and historical discussions about this continent.

No. 1 · **Grassroots Governance?: Chiefs in Africa and the Afro-Caribbean** Edited by D.I. Ray and P.S. Reddy · Copublished with the International Association of Schools and Institutes of Administration (IASIA)

No. 2 · **The African Diaspora in Canada: Negotiating Identity and Belonging** Edited by Wisdom Tettey and Korbla Puplampu

No. 3 · **A Common Hunger: Land Rights in Canada and South Africa** by Joan G. Fairweather

No. 4 · **New Directions in African Education: Challenges and Possibilities** Edited by S. Nombuso Dlamini

No. 5 · **Shrines in Africa: History, Politics, and Society** Edited by Allan Charles Dawson

Shrines in Africa

HISTORY, POLITICS, AND SOCIETY

UNIVERSITY OF
CALGARY
PRESS

EDITED BY ALLAN CHARLES DAWSON

© 2009 Allan Charles Dawson

University of Calgary Press
2500 University Drive NW
Calgary, Alberta
Canada T2N 1N4
www.uofcpress.com

No part of this publication may be reproduced, stored in a retrieval system or transmitted, in any form or by any means, without the prior written consent of the publisher or a license from The Canadian Copyright Licensing Agency (Access Copyright). For an Access Copyright license, visit www.accesscopyright.ca or call toll free 1-800-893-5777.

LIBRARY AND ARCHIVES CANADA CATALOGUING IN PUBLICATION

Shrines in Africa : history, politics, and society / edited by Allan Charles Dawson.

(Africa, missing voices series, 1703-1826 5)
Includes bibliographical references and index.
ISBN 978-1-55238-246-2

1. Shrines–Africa–History. 2. Shrines–Social aspects–Africa. 3. Shrines–Political aspects–Africa. 4. Land tenure–Africa. 5. Africa–Religion. I. Dawson, Allan Charles, 1973- II. Series: Africa, missing voices series 5

BL2400.S57 2008   200.96   C2008-907231-6

The University of Calgary Press acknowledges the support of the Alberta Foundation for the Arts for our publications. We acknowledge the financial support of the Government of Canada through the Book Publishing Industry Development Program (BPIDP) for our publishing activities. We acknowledge the financial support of the Canada Council for the Arts for our publishing program.

This book has been published with the help of a grant from the Canadian Federation for the Humanities and Social Sciences, through the Aid to Scholarly Publications Programme, using funds provided by the Social Sciences and Humanities Research Council of Canada.

Cover design, page design and typesetting by Melina Cusano

TABLE OF CONTENTS

Introduction.
    Allan Dawson (McGill University/STANDD)   vii

1. Pots, Stones, and Potsherds: Shrines in the Mandara Mountains (North Cameroon and Northeastern Nigeria)
    Judith Sterner (Alberta College of Art and Design)
    Nicholas David (University of Calgary)   1

2. The Archaeology of Shrines among the Tallensi of Northern Ghana: Materiality and Interpretive Relevance
    Timothy Insoll (University of Manchester)
    Benjamin Kankpeyeng (University of Ghana, Legon)
    Rachel MacLean (University of Manchester)   41

3. Earth Shrines and Autochthony among the Konkomba of Northern Ghana
    Allan Charles Dawson (McGill University/STANDD)   71

4. Shrines and Compound Abandonment: Ethnoarchaeological Observations in Northern Ghana
    Charles Mather (University of Calgary)   95

5. Constructing Ritual Protection on an Expanding Settlement Frontier: Earth Shrines in the Black Volta Region
    Carola Lentz (Johannes Gutenberg University, Mainz)   121

6. Moroccan Saints' Shrines as Systems of Distributed Knowledge
    Doyle Hatt (University of Calgary)   153

Index   205

Introduction

ALLAN CHARLES DAWSON

There is a clear West African bias to the papers in this volume. Much of the reason for this is the influence of Peter Lewis Shinnie on the life and careers of a number of the researchers presented here. Peter passed on in the summer of 2007, but his voice still echoes in these pages.

*****

Shrines, in the African context are cultural signposts that help us understand and read the ethnic, territorial, and social lay of the land. Just as the church steeple in Europe once marked the centre of a community whose boundaries lay at the point where the rising spire came into view or the tolling of the bells could be heard, shrines on the African landscape help shape and define village, community, and ethnic boundaries. Shrines are physical manifestations of a group's claim to a particular piece of land and are thus markers of identity – they represent, both figuratively and literally, a community's 'roots' in the land they work and live upon. The shrine is representative of a connection with the land at the cosmological and supernatural level and, in terms of a community's or ethnic group's claim to cultivable territory, serves as a reminder to outsiders that this is – in very real terms – 'our land.'

Shrines are vessels in two important senses. They can act as containers in a literal sense for the spirits of ancestors and deities who must be regularly placated and petitioned for blessings, requests for intercession, and divine sanction. These spirits or entities must be venerated with pilgrimages, offerings such as money, food, beer and hard alcohol, and sacrifices of fowl, small stock and cattle. Spiritual intercession from ancestors and deities is sought for a wide range of events, including but not limited to: births, marriages and funerals; the appointment of a new chief; the building of a new home or compound; political or military success; protection against witchcraft; a safe journey; and, perhaps most importantly, the planting or harvesting of a season's agricultural produce. Indeed, supplication to a shrine is motivated by the same reasons that a Christian might use to go to church or a Hindu might offer for supporting their local temple to Ganesh. Shrines are also *symbolic* vessels and reference points for knowledge about the social universe within which different African communities must live. Shrines serve to demarcate areas of territory and thus provide members of a community with a way to assert rights of cultivation over land. In those parts of Africa where internal migration and movement is commonplace, shrines form part of a system or network of boundary markers that say to outsiders: "we got here first."

AUTOCHTHONY

Recent anthropological literature that looks at autochthony and citizenship explores assertions of origin from and connectedness with the land (Ceuppens and Geschiere 2005; Comaroff and Comaroff 2001; Geschiere and Jackson 2006; Geschiere and Nyomnjoh 2000; Leonhardt 2006). Autochthony literally means 'of the soil' or 'of the earth,' and for the societies under scrutiny here, these concepts are of particular relevance. Each of them is engaged in the process of legitimating not only their claim upon a territory but also their existence as a distinct group with rights to institutions such as paramount chiefs and representation in national political bodies. These groups are active in proclaiming their rights over the land in a language that at once evokes both essentialized notions of 'belonging' to the land and linkages with the 'soil' and also overt references to those who do not 'belong' – foreigners. We need only look to Rwanda, Darfur, and Côte D'Ivoire for clear examples of this kind of rhetoric. Moreover, these kinds of processes are not unique to Africa. All over of the world, the march towards ever more integrated forms of globalization seems to also invite renewed struggles over who is 'of the land' and who is a 'stranger.' The language of autochthony, again, in the African context, differs from that of indigenousness as it implicitly accepts that societies can move or migrate into new areas. Claims of autochthony do rest on something of a quasi-mystical attachment to the land, much like those of indigineity, but are distinguished by two important points: firstly, that societies, communities, bands of pioneers, kin groups, etc., have continued to move around and stake out new territory on the African landscape; and secondly, that upon the establishment of a compound, homestead, village or community, these pioneers – through the establishment of an earth shrine that symbolically represents their existence as cultivators and as societies that practice ancestor veneration – become inextricably linked with the land they occupy. This linkage becomes a major component of the representation, projection, and management of group – whether regional or ethnic – identity. Indeed, those societies that practice earth and ancestor veneration, and a number of them are discussed in this volume, typically employ a very elaborate vocabulary of primordial interconnectivity with the land in their ethnic discourse, and the shrine, whether a baobab tree or a piece of pottery, is the ultimate symbolic manifestation of this link – the shrine is autochthony made real.

Although, with one notable exception, the papers in this volume focus on West African societies, all of the authors seek to demonstrate how an understanding of shrines can shed light on patterns of settlement and migration in Africa. An overarching theme that can be found in all of the papers is that societies interact with objects of ritual devotion – shrines – in differing ways based on their distance from metropoles of power and how a particular group symbolically constructs the earth on which it resides. This idea owes much to Igor Kopytoff's notion of an internal African frontier that exists in the "open areas nestling between organized societies": what might be called an "interstitial frontier" or institutionally open-space where new social processes might develop and unfold (Kopytoff 1987:9). Into this space are sent 'frontiersmen,' first-comers and founders; migrants sloughed off by their own society due to dwindling cultivable land, populations fleeing from slave-raiders and conflict, or rural farmers escaping the influence of a growing urban environment (Kopytoff 1987).

For Kopytoff, the primary problem for African societies pushed out into the open spaces – into hinterlands or the 'bush' – was the construction and legitimation of authority over their new territory, over existing populations or over late arrivals to a newly staked-out area (1987). Often, new settlements placed non-kin or competing ethnic groups in close proximity and frontiersmen were forced to reinterpret ideas of kinship and authority. The authors of the papers in this volume contend that within these newly created social spaces the shrine comes to signify and represent claims to ownership, rights of usage and residence, and fluctuating assertions of ethnic and religious distinctiveness. Further, the shrine, by symbolically representing a new settlement's connection with the spirits of the land and with ancestors, serves to reinforce or to reorganize internal forms of solidarity and identity. Shrines act as important symbols of group membership and collective identity – ethnic, religious, and regional. From the West African savannah to montagnard Morocco, shrines serve to culturally demarcate the landscape, asserting origin, ownership, and historical connectedness with a piece of earth.

ETHNIC IDENTITY

Over the past two decades, anthropology and cognate disciplines have come to view ethnic identity not as bounded and stable, especially in areas like the West African savannah, but as mutable and flexible and as an instrument to be used to further a collective's goals (Fardon 1996; Jenkins 1997; Lentz 1994; Murphy and Bledsoe 1987; Royce 1982; Smedley 1999; Stahl 1991). The belief that all African societies exist in neat little ethnic boxes, persuasively and richly described by an ethnographer/biographer, was very much a product of a particular period of British social anthropology. Kopytoff writes:

> Occasionally ... African societies ... do not fit the tribal model.... Such a society does not quite hang together. It presents a mishmash of regional cultural traits.... The legitimacy of its political institutions comes periodically into question, as does its independence from nearby polities who may dispute the very territory it occupies. (1987:4–5)

To be sure, there are some African societies that more obviously fit this description than others. However, I would argue that anyone familiar with the internals of African social organization and local discourses about ethnic identity in groups both large and small in Africa will find that these kind of ambiguities exist within the marginalized groups of the savannah – historically, the so-called *acephalous* societies of the Sahel – and the mighty chiefdoms and kingdoms of regions like the Guinea coast and the

Horn. For example, recent scholarship about the origins of the Yoruba in Nigeria points to significant regional differences between the Òyó, Ègbá, Ègbádò, Ìjèsà, and other component Yoruba chiefdoms in their overall relationship with Ilé-Ifê as the Yoruba traditional centre and capital (dare we say shrine?), and in the belief of descent from the same founding hero – Odùduwà (Matory 2005). Histories of slavery, conquest, and expansion among larger groups such as the Gonja and Asante of West Africa also call into question the stability of ethnic categories, as subjected peoples often slipped in-and-out as members of the dominant ethnic group, based on contingency and circumstance (Staniland 1975; Wilks 1961; Wilks et al. 1986).

Autochthony, as the Comaroff's write, elevates "to a first-principle the ineffable interests and connections, at once material and moral, that flow from 'native' rootedness, and special rights, in a place of birth" (2001: 635). Claims of autochthony are implicit in Kopytoff's model of migration on the African frontier. They form the basis for arguments about group identity formation in a fragmented landscape of changing kin and ethnic affiliations. In the context of the post-colonial African state, autochthony now serves as the most 'authentic' way to assert not only a group's roots in a particular territory but also, more importantly, the rights and status of a group as citizens of the nation state. In this sense, the shrine, as a symbolic nexus for concentrating and honing ideas about a collective's unity, mirrors the unpredictability and malleability of group membership within the African state.

TAXONOMIES OF 'SHRINES'

Shrines, like collectives, are not immutable and their meaning within the society fluctuates as the morphology of the collective changes. Groups can be expelled from the territory that they claim to have founded and where their earth shrine dwells, and consequently new earth shrines can be established or proxies in new territories can serve old, inaccessible shrines. In cases where another ethnic group takes over a territory from its former occupants, local discourse about an important physical feature of the landscape considered an earth shrine or ritual locale is modified or adjusted to support the claims of the new inhabitants to the territory. Shrines can be modified, rebuilt, renovated, relocated, forgotten, re-legitimized, and forgotten once again.

African shrines can be material objects such as ceramic pots, shaped stones, constructed buildings, houses, tombs, gravesites, or assemblages of rocks. They may also be natural features of the landscape such as mountains, ponds, lakes, rivers, or other water features and embody a specific or localized representation of a larger supernatural force. The famous rock shelter of *Tongnaab*, Lake Bosumtwi in the Ashanti region of central Ghana, and the various forms of the *Adansonia* genus of tree found throughout the African savannah – the Baobab – all fall into this category.

Elizabeth Colson (1997) distinguishes between two kinds of shrines or foci of ritual activity among the Tonga of Zimbabwe, and this taxonomy of shrines is, I believe, of use in our review of the discussions presented in this volume. For Colson, "shrines of the land" are those constructed by human hands – they embody spirits that once existed on the earthly plain and require offerings from their descendants or kin group (1997:52). Contrasting these more local shrines exist "places of power," which are typically permanent landscape features regarded as intrinsically sacred or powerful. They are associated with named spirits from mythology, essences of nature such as the 'goddess of the sea' or the 'god of the mountain' or with the founding heroes or apical ancestor of an ethnic group, region or state (Colson 1997:52). As Mather notes, "'shrines of the land' encode local histories … while 'places of power' express histories transcending human actors and local communities" (2003:26).

The distinction Colson makes hinges on local and regional bodies of knowledge about history and identity. Shrines of the land correspond to local ideas about identity that operate along the cleavages between immediate neighbours both at the intra-ethnic level – between kin-groups, clans, or neighbouring communities – and at the inter-ethnic level between neighbouring groups. These interactions are certainly important for understanding the internal placement of kin-groups on the ground and on local boundary disputes between ethnic groups. However, their importance as cultural signposts flows from the discourse that exists around 'places of power.' These higher-level foci for ritual activity articulate ideas about identity and group cohesion that operate at the regional and, crucially, at the state level. In an era where ethnic competition within the state increasingly incorporates primordial ethnic language and the vocabulary of autochthony, issues of citizenship and rights over land hinge on authenticity and legitimacy. Ethnic groups are often forced to respond to the accusation of rivals that they are 'foreigners,' 'interlopers, or 'invaders' (Marshall-Fratani 2006) and so 'places of power' come to symbolically represent the ethnic unity of a group and their rightful place within the territorial boundaries of the state.

CONTRIBUTORS

Two of the contributions in this volume focus specifically on the first-comer–latecomer dynamics of political authority in Africa as they pertain to earth shrines. Carola Lentz's *Constructing Ritual Protection on an Expanding Settlement Frontier: Earth Shrines in the Black Volta Region* focuses on the Dagara in the area between the Volta Rivers of northern Ghana and southern Burkina Faso. This paper seeks to explore the dynamics of migration and movement of Dagara-speaking groups in the Black Volta region of West Africa into thinly settled areas of the savannah. Lentz focuses on the discourse of earth shrine creation in local histories about Dagara expansion and competition with neighbouring groups. For Lentz earth shrines serve, in some ways, as a deed or title to land and the ability to serve a shrine signifies a group's ownership of a particular territory.

Allan Charles Dawson's *Earth Shrines and Autochthony among the Konkomba of Northern Ghana* also deals with one of the so-called acephalous peoples of West Africa, the Konkomba. Dawson's work explores how claims of autochthony by this ethnic group to a former settlement and its associated earth shrine are representative of attitudes towards chieftaincy and embody articulations of ethnic identity. For the Konkomba, asserting their autochthony and their right to venerate the earth shrine of their ancient capital means more than just a claim to land. Right of access to the shrine of Yendi is an important step, many Konkomba argue, in their quest to gain a paramount chief in Ghana's national House of Chiefs. Although the Konkomba openly scorn the institution of chieftaincy and generally regard the office of earth priest in their villages with much more respect, this move needs to be understand in the context of regional movement to re-legitimize chieftaincy in Ghana and elsewhere in Africa. The discourse of development workers, non-governmental community agencies, and scholars in Ghana and indeed throughout much of Africa has, in the past decade, started to emphasize a renewed role for chiefs and traditional authority in African governance – economic development and the expansion of democratic ideals in Africa must include, is it argued, Africa's original forms of political authority (see Ray 1996 and Skalnik 1996). For the Konkomba, the attainment of paramount status, concomitant citizenship in the community of traditional leaders, and their place as an autochthonous people of northern Ghana are all linked to their claims to the earth shrine of Yendi.

Doing archaeological research in tropical Africa presents its own array of unique difficulties. With a nod to methodology, Charles Mather, in *Shrines and Compound Abandonment: Ethnoarchaeological Observations in Northern Ghana amongst the Kusasi* demonstrates that in instances of compound abandonment in northern Ghana by the Kusasi where curation of useable material culture has not taken place, shrines often stand a good chance of being output into the archaeological record. This paper examines the likelihood of shrines being output into the archaeological record and provides suggestions about the strategies archaeologists can employ to discover shrines at abandoned compound sites.

In African history and anthropology there is perhaps no better-known shrine than the *Tongnaab* shrine of the Tallensi of northern Ghana, brought to prominence, ethnographically speaking, by the seminal work of Meyer Fortes (1945; 1949). *Tongnaab* is very much a 'place of power' for the Tallensi people, but also represents a body of knowledge about the history of the Tongo Hills and the Tallensi people that permeates the entire Voltaic cultural landscape. From Dagara country in the East, to Asante in the South, to the Mossi plains across the border in southern Burkina Faso, *Tongnaab* is recognized as one of the most important shrines in West Africa. Upon my first visit to *Tongnaab* in 2001, my Konkomba friends asked me if I would petition the shrine for them. "But you are Konkomba; how can you ask that shrine for anything?" I asked them. My friend responded, "Well, our ancestors were related to the Tallensi and anyway, that is one of the most important and powerful shrines in all of Ghana; even the Asante fear it! Its strong!" It is commonly held in Ghana that the Tallensi and the people of the Voltaic highlands retreated into the hill country to escape the attacks of mounted slave raiders from the south. That the Konkomba, also a people that were historically subject to slave raiding, should mark – at the level of exoteric knowledge about the region – *Tongnaab* as a shrine that represents the unity of the Tallensi and a history of Tale resistance to slavery is significant. Ritual locales such as *Tongnaab* in their service of collective identity help express more than just an ethnicity but can also help articulate a broader political message of unity and resistance. In *The Archaeology of Shrines among the Tallensi of Northern Ghana: Materiality and Interpretive Relevance*, Timothy Insoll, Benjamin Kankpeyeng, and Rachel MacLean seek to supplement the anthropological material and the apparent dearth of archaeological data on the Tallensi shrines of the Tongo Hills, including *Tongnaab*, by reconstructing the history of movement and settlement and the sequence of occupation in this part of northern Ghana through excavation.

Judith Sterner's and Nicholas David's *Pots, Stones, and Potsherds: Shrines in the Mandara Mountains (North Cameroon and North-western Nigeria)*, present a number of case studies that demonstrate how an understanding of the various types of shrines found in these montagnard communities throws light on the nature of regional diasporas and migration. The study of shrines, the authors suggest, not only provides information about the roots of political authority in the Mandara region but also illuminates the importance of considering shrines when trying to understand historical process in general.

Finally, Doyle Hatt's paper in this volume, *Moroccan Saints' Shrines as Systems of Distributed Knowledge*, is concerned primarily with what Moroccan saints' shrines mean in both the local and in the broader national context. The focus of this paper is on how a shrines' 'external' meaning is part of a category of phenomena situated within an overall system of knowledge about landscape and space within the wider culture. Hatt, like Colson, differentiates between shrines that represent bodies of knowledge about the local landscape and local history and shrines that operate at a national level and embody a discourse about the history of the Moroccan people and state. All of the shrines discussed by Hatt are of the material culture type in that they are, even at the most basic level, constructed by human action in some way. Hatt distinguishes between different forms of *marabout* or saint shrine on the basis of the differential meanings and bodies of knowledge that locals and visitors attach to them and the extent to which the shrines transact ideas about the local and the national. In this sense, small saint shrines that represent ideas about the community and landscape that are highly localized and esoteric very much conform to Colson's idea of a 'shrine of the land' – To understand what these shrines represent, individuals and groups need to tap into local knowledge and local meanings. At the broader regional level exist the shrines of well-known *marabouts* and patron saints and at the national level, the tombs of sultans Mulāy Idrīs I and Sdī Muhammad V. These broader-level shrines are very much 'places of power' in that they are signifiers of collective identity and are associated with mythical founder heroes who embody what it means to be Moroccan.

REFERENCES

Ceuppens, Bambi, and Peter Geschiere. "Autochthony: Local or Global? New Modes in the Struggle over Citizenship and Belonging in Africa and Europe." *Annual Review of Anthropology* 34, no. 1 (2005): 385–407.

Colson, Elizabeth. "Places of Power and Shrines of the Land." *Paideuma* 43 (1997): 47–57.

Comaroff, Jean, and John L. Comaroff. "Naturing the Nation: Aliens, Apocalypse and the Postcolonial State." *Journal of Southern African Studies* 27, no. 3 (2001): 627–51.

Fardon, Richard. "'Crossed Destinies': The Entangled Histories of West African Ethnic and National Identities." In *Ethnicity in Africa: Roots, Meanings and Implications*, edited by Louise de la Gorgendière, Kenneth King, and Sarah Vaughn, 117–46. Edinburgh: Centre of African Studies, Edinburgh, 1996.

Fortes, Meyer. *The Dynamics of Clanship among the Tallensi, Being the First Part of an Analysis of the Social Structure of a Trans-Volta Tribe*. London: International African Institute, 1945.

———. *The Web of Kinship among the Tallensi; the Second Part of an Analysis of the Social Structure of a Trans-Volta Tribe*. London: International African Institute, 1949.

Geschiere, Peter, and Stephen Jackson. "Autochthony and the Crisis of Citizenship: Democratization, Decentralization, and the Politics of Belonging." *African Studies Review* 49, no. 2 (2006): 1.

Geschiere, Peter, and Francis Nyamnjoh. "Capitalism and Autochthony: The Seesaw of Mobility and Belonging." *Public Culture* 12, no. 2 (2000): 423–52.

Jenkins, Richard. *Rethinking Ethnicity: Arguments and Explorations*. Thousand Oaks, CA: Sage, 1997.

Kopytoff, Igor. "The Internal African Frontier." In *The African Frontier: The Reproduction of Traditional African Societies*, edited by Igor Kopytoff, 3–84. Indiana: Indiana University Press, 1987.

Lentz, Carola. "'They Must Be Dagaba First and Any Other Thing Second ...': The Colonial and Post-Colonial Creation of Ethnic Identities in Northwestern Ghana." *African Studies* 53, no. 2 (1994): 57–91.

Leonhardt, Alec. "Baka and the Magic of the State: Between Autochthony and Citizenship." *African Studies Review* 49, no. 2 (2006): 69–94.

Marshall-Fratani, Ruth. "The War of 'Who Is Who': Autochthony, Nationalism, and Citizenship in the Ivoirian Crisis." *African Studies Review* 49, no. 2 (2006): 9–43.

Mather, Charles. "Shrines and the Domestication of Landscape." *Journal of Anthropological Research* 59, no. 1 (2003): 23–45.

Matory, J. Lorand. *Black Atlantic Religion: Tradition, Transnationalism, and Matriarchy in the Afro-Brazilian Candomblé*. Princeton: Princeton University Press, 2005.

Murphy, William P., and Caroline H. Bledsoe. "Kinship and Territory in the History of a Kpelle Chiefdom (Liberia)." In *The African Frontier: The Reproduction of Traditional African Societies*, edited by Igor Kopytoff, 123–47. Bloomington: Indiana University Press, 1987.

Ray, Donald I. "Divided Sovereignty: Traditional Authority and the State in Ghana." *Journal of Legal Pluralism and Unofficial Law* 37–38 (1996): 181–202.

Royce, Anya Peterson. *Ethnic Identity: Strategies of Diversity*. Bloomington: Indiana University Press, 1982.

Skalnik, Peter. "Authority Versus Power: Democracy in Africa Must Include Original African Institutions." *Journal of Legal Pluralism and Unofficial Law* 37–38 (1996): 110–22.

Smedley, A. "Race and the Construction of Human Identity." *American Anthropologist* 100, no. 3 (1999): 690–702.

Stahl, Ann B. "Ethnic Style and Ethnic Boundaries: A Diachronic Case Study from West-Central Ghana." *Ethnohistory* 38, no. 3 (1991): 250–75.

Staniland, M. *The Lions of Dagbon: Political Change in Northern Ghana*. Cambridge: Cambridge University Press, 1975.

Wilks, Ivor. *The Northern Factor in Ashanti History*. Legon: Institute of African Studies, University College of Ghana, 1961.

Wilks, Ivor, Nehemia Levtzion, and Bruce M. Haight. *Chronicles from Gonja: A Tradition of West African Muslim Historiography*. Cambridge: Cambridge University Press, 1986.

Pots, Stones, and Potsherds: Shrines in the Mandara Mountains (North Cameroon and Northeastern Nigeria)

JUDITH STERNER (ALBERTA COLLEGE OF ART AND DESIGN)
AND NICHOLAS DAVID (UNIVERSITY OF CALGARY)

ABSTRACT

In pre-colonial times the Mandara mountains were home to numerous small-scale societies practising varied economies and at varying levels of social complexity. Case studies that monitor varieties of shrines and their uses in the petty chiefdom of Sirak, in a larger Sukur chiefdom that specialized in iron making, and in Gudur, which we interpret as a ritual paramountcy, show that the division of ritual labour tracked but did not parallel that of labour in general. In a religious context characterized by a distant high god and omnipresent spirits and in an environment subject to repeated but unpredictable natural disasters and, in recent centuries, exposed to raiding by plains states, ritual specialists came to serve multiple communities. One cluster of communities, created by a diaspora from Gudur, relied on a chief, Bay Gudal, for protection from natural disasters and to ensure their fruitfulness and that of their animals and crops. Study of Gudur shrines and traditions throws light on the nature of the diaspora and indicates that this chief's roles included those of priest, rainmaker, and diviner but that his power was limited in practice, if not in the perception of diasporan communities whose distance favoured its mythical exaggeration. The study of shrines not only documents the familial roots of political power and the importance of considering shrines' congregations for understanding historical process, but, in a reversal of received views, reveals Gudur as a less complex ritual and political entity than Sukur.

Keywords: Sirak, Gudur, Sukur, Mandara mountains, Cameroon, ancestors shrines.

> Les pratiques religieuses de la plupart des populations non-islamisées du *Mādara* [Mandara], sont caractérisées par un trait commun : la représentation par des pierres polies et des *bourmas* (ou poteries) d'êtres auxquels on rend un culte. [de Lauwe 1937:54][1]

INTRODUCTION

It is not surprising to anyone who has walked the paths of the Mandara mountains that de Lauwe's attention was drawn to sacred pots. For these pots are not all kept in the darkened recesses of a shrine room or beneath a granary: some are left upon the tombs of their former owners; some are tucked into rock outcrops to protect against dangerous spirits, and others are reused for secular purposes or abandoned. Nearly seventy years after de Lauwe's visit to the region, the tradition of sacred pots, potsherds and stones continues even though diminished by the influences of Islam and Christianity. In this paper we follow de Lauwe's lead in analyzing in a regional and comparative perspective those artefacts and ecofacts that are the "material focus of religious activities" and thus are shrines according to van Binsbergen's minimal definition (cited by Colson 1997:47).

The region with which we deal is not the Mandara mountains as a whole but that part of it within which communities are found that, in whole or in part, claim connections usually of descent to Gudur, reputedly a major religious centre (Fig. 1). In discussing Gudur we make use of Kopytoff's (1987) concept of the internal African frontier, considering Gudur as, in his terms, a "metropole," but in a broader sense the whole Mandara mountain area can be considered as a frontier within which, as innumerable oral traditions insist, people have for centuries been migrating at various scales to found new communities and to merge and abandon old ones. It is this frontier process that underlies the cultural similarities that we have earlier described in terms of montagnard participation in

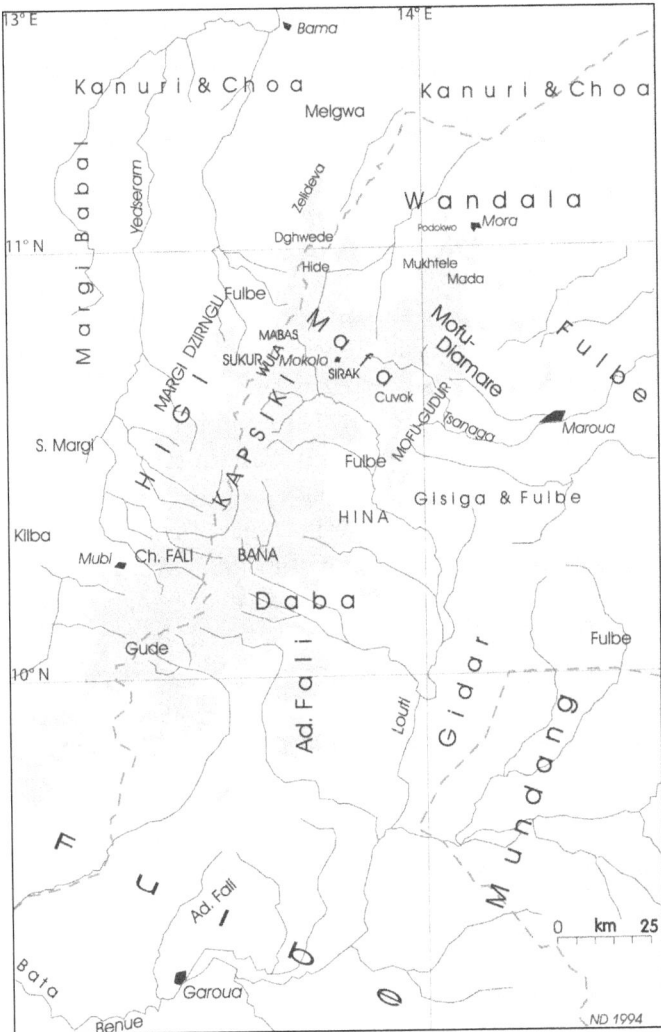

Fig. 1. Map of the Mandara mountain area of Nigeria and Cameroon showing selected communities and ethnic groups, towns and rivers. Capital letters indicate those groups of which a substantial part claims descent from Gudur. While certain Mafa chiefs and rainmakers including those of Soulede, Vreke, and Mudukwa claim Gudur descent, this does not appear to be generally true of this large ethnic group. The same can be said of the Daba and Gude.

a common symbolic reservoir (David and Kramer 2001:206–18; Sterner 1992).

We shall argue first that in the numerous small-scale montagnard societies of the region the division of ritual labour is closely related to that of labour in general and to social complexity. However before proceeding we should clarify the context of our observations. By the late twentieth century an earlier system of interaction with the spirit world had become much attenuated by "modernization," the growth of markets and towns populated by practitioners of Islam and Christianity, and the mission-based spread of Christianity to the countryside in which the majority of the population continues to live. Nonetheless, despite the competition of world religions, local religions and ritual, though practised now primarily by those, mainly elders, who have not been exposed to Western-style education, survive and, together with the historical evidence provided by ethnographers and others, provide a substantial basis for inference. Thus we can state that, in the pre-colonial period, which here ends in 1902, Mandara montagnards practised a religion that combined belief in a distant high god and numerous spirits with whom they established contact through various material foci, stones and pots being the most common. The spirit world was populated by ancestors and a vast variety of other spirits: of places, those of mountains and water points (wells, springs, pools) being among the most important, of crops, diseases, of one's own doppelganger soul, and many others. Contact with these spirits, which often took the form of an offering or sacrifice and a negotiation in the general manner described by Kopytoff (1971), took place both according to a ritual calendar and on other occasions when need arose. In both situations divination was often practised, sometimes by the person responsible for the cult but often by specialists. Divination determined an auspicious time for the ritual, if necessary the spirit to which the ritual should be addressed, and the nature of the offering and form of the rites, which often comprised a magical component. Thus divination, communication with spirits through shrines, and magic were inseparably linked. It was only in the period following World War II and especially since independence in 1960 that this system of beliefs and practices was seriously challenged by the extension of the power of the state and the modernizing influences noted above.

The original field material presented here is drawn mainly from Sterner's research at Sirak (between 1986 and 1990) and that of Sterner and David at Sukur (between 1991 and 1996) and most recently at Gudur

(2004). An earlier paper (David and Sterner 1999) sketches the nature of the Sirak and Sukur polities and these are described in greater detail by Sterner (2003), and Sukur also by David and Sterner (1995, 1996). Gudur is best known from the work of Seignobos (1991a), a human geographer with long and wide experience of northern Cameroon, and Jouaux (1989, 1991). In an ethnographic present located in the late nineteenth and early twentieth centuries, Sirak is best described as a petty priest-chiefdom and Sukur as a chiefdom committed to a village iron-smelting industry. Seignobos characterizes Gudur as a theocratic chiefdom and Jouaux hesitates between chiefdom and kingdom. Our recent research there led us to identify it rather as a form of ritual paramountcy exercised by the chiefdom of Gudal over a group of petty chiefdoms mostly speaking the same *mofu-gudur* language and collectively known as the Mofu-Gudur (David in press). Despite these differences and although, unlike Sirak, both Sukur and Gudur exerted, to a lesser and greater extent respectively, an influence over certain of their neighbours, the cultures of all three polities resemble each other much more than they differ.

In what follows we have omitted much ethnographic detail on ceramics that can be found in our earlier publications (David 1990; David et al. 1988; Sterner 1989a,b, 1992, 1995, 2002, 2003; Sterner and David 2003) and those of others (e.g., Barreteau, Sorin and Mana 1988).

SIRAK

Before there were pots, the ancestors 'resided' in stones and when beer was offered to them it just rolled off their backs. But in a pot the beer remained just like in a person's stomach.[2]

Sirak, while considerably smaller than Gudur and most other Mandara mountain communities, comprises the same basic elements: there is a chief and six clans whose ancestors came from different settlements, Gudur being one, and decided to be "as brothers." And as at Sukur, Gudur and among many other groups, there are two castes – farmers and smith/potters (Sterner and David 1991). Men of the latter caste are responsible for funerals and other ritual activities, including a near monopoly on divination; the women monopolize pot-making and may be engaged in the rituals associated with the vessels they produce.

Some twenty-one distinctively named and differently decorated pot types are made for use as shrines. The categorization of shrine types below, developed in cognizance of Mather's (1999:79) classification of Kusasi (Ghana) shrines, emphasizes the nature of the spirits and of the social entities or "congregations" that serve and are served by the shrines.

Household shrines

Shrines held within households have diverse associations and functions. They contain potent and dangerous spirits, including those of the household's ancestors and others that are the "property" of or are associated with individual family members.

Ancestor shrines

The most common shrine pots at Sirak are those made after the end of the period of mourning to contain the spirit of an ancestor (Fig. 2). The holder or custodian of such a pot must have living siblings or descendants on whose behalf he or she makes specified sacrifices. When a man dies it is his eldest surviving son (or daughter if there are no sons) who will have this responsibility. A senior man will serve the cult of his father, his father's father, and his father's mother, all represented by pots that are kept in a special small room in his house.[3] A youngest son (or daughter) keeps the pot of his mother in his senior wife's kitchen. Annual sacrifices, as well as sacrifices undertaken upon the advice of a diviner who is a member of the smith/potter caste, are made at these ancestor shrines on behalf of the descendants. Children who do not inherit responsibility for their parents' shrines may use a piece of quartz or a potsherd to make their own offerings.

It is not uncommon for an immigrant of many years to participate in the ceremonies of his new community, but to continue within the confines of his home to use the ancestor pots of his natal village and conduct the rituals in the style of his former home. This and other evidence indicates that montagnard emigrants also take their ancestor pots and certain other shrines with them when they emigrate to found new communities or join others already established.

Fig. 2. Sirak shrines: from right to left, father, father's father, and damaged father's mother pots, left in their small room in an abandoned house.

Other potent spirits

The most common shrine in this category is that of the spirit associated with millet and sorghum. This shrine consists initially of a piece of quartz usually kept beneath the head of household's primary granary. The householder makes sacrifices at this shrine several times a year, often after consultation with a diviner who may recommend the sacrifice of a particular animal or for a granary pot to be made to house the spirit.

Pot shrines relating to hunted leopards and the spirits of men killed in war represent another category of potent spirits that require placation; these exist now only as heirlooms and memories.

Upon the birth of twins, who are regarded as both fragile and dangerously potent, a set of pots comprising a small beer jar and a bowl is made for each twin.[4] After a first sacrifice, others must be made annually in conjunction with the village-wide purification ceremony. On this occasion the parents, the twins and other close relatives assemble in the kitchen. Beer is poured into each twin pot and bowl, and over the twins themselves. This is essential not only for the well-being of the twins and their family but for the entire community.

Personal shrines

Unlike among the Mafa, Sirak do not possess a personal soul pot. However, the placenta is conceptualized as the baby's double and as having a soul that requires some attention. Placentas are buried beneath an upturned pot, pierced for the passage of the spirit. A woman's flour storage pot is used for a girl baby's placenta and a man's tripod meat cooking pot (legs removed) for a boy's.[5] These pots, located behind the mother's room and outside the house wall, are left in place so long as the compound is occupied.

Gawula, the biennial male initiation ceremony, commemorates the attainment of elder status. Not every man will be initiated, for he must already be married, he must have another candidate as a partner, and his older brother(s) must have already been initiated. Each initiate receives a large jar used to serve beer to the other initiates once it has been consecrated with an offering of flour and water. When the owner dies it is placed on his tomb with a hole knocked in the base.

Many heads of households possess a pot known as the "shrine of tears" that is used to maintain harmony in the household. After an initial offering overseen by the smith/diviner, beer from this pot is shared with the household head's children; subsequent offerings are made after consultation with a diviner. The wife of an elder may have an equivalent vessel.

Clan shrines

As the generations pass, male ancestors cease to be pots but are replaced by potsherds or pieces of quartz placed in clan sites, thus becoming elements in collective shrines served by the senior clan elder. The chiefly clan has a shrine atop the mountain where members of this clan formerly lived – it consists of pots that contain the spirits of leopards and enemies slain by clan members. In this shrine there were the remains of several such vessels, fragments of small bowls that had originally covered their mouths, and bones of sacrificial animals. In theory each clan has such a shrine.

Some, perhaps once all, clans also have (or had) pot shrines to protect their members against disease.

Both types of clan shrines occupy permanent sites. Sacrificial animals are killed, prepared, and eaten at the site, and cooking pots may be left nearby.

Nature spirit shrines

Some "wild" or nature spirits are localized, being associated with water points, trees, rock outcrops, mountains, or other sites. These spirits and the shrines associated with them are called *halalay*. Such spirits are easily offended, for example by persons committing adultery in their vicinity, and require placation. If a person falls ill after cutting down a tree, a diviner may recommend that a pot be made. The afflicted person then returns to the tree with the diviner and the potter. After drinking some beer, a mixture of beer and ground sesame is put in the pot, which is left beneath a rock. Another type of *halalay* keeps the water in wells from leaving. Before a new well is lined with granite slabs, the neighbourhood elder responsible makes a sacrifice that is subsequently repeated annually. *Halalay* sites may be further marked with upright stones.

Shrines that protect against spirits of disease are usually made for an individual and are not localized, although there is one shrine where pot necks are left and offerings made by those suffering from ear problems. Once near a path Judy Sterner came across a pot with an anthropomorphic head like a Mafa God pot that had been made for someone who had suffered a seizure.

Community shrines

It is characteristic of Sirak that community shrines are few and little emphasized. Judy Sterner knows of, but has not visited, one to which the chief goes to sacrifice to the spirit of the mountain on behalf of the larger community. Another elder prays for rain on behalf of the people of Sirak, and it would seem reasonable to describe the focus of his rites as a community shrine, but Judy Sterner has no personal knowledge of the shrine nor of him and his practice. In case of serious drought, appeal used to be made to the chief of Gudur.

Discussion

What is most characteristic of Sirak and many other smaller montagnard polities, including Mafa settlements (Müller-Kosack 2003), is that heads of households, while they may be assisted by diviners (generally of the smith/potter caste), are for the most part ritually self-sufficient and that individuals take considerable ritual responsibility for themselves. Clan rituals are not emphasized. In the annual rites of purification, it is not priests but the parents of twins whose ritual acts, undertaken independently within their scattered households, sum to provide protection for the community as a whole.

The consequences of (a) this substantial ritual self-sufficiency, and (b) a tendency – inferred rather than documented – for smith/potter caste diviners to suggest that their clients invest in a suitable pot through which to engage the spirit responsible for their situation, include a greatly elaborated set of shrines, here for the most part materialized as ceramic vessels, numerous examples of which are present in most households and can be found distributed widely through the community territory.

SUKUR

Sukur has the same social and cultural building blocks as Sirak and other communities – a chief, several clans, a potter/smith caste, and the use of pots and stones as shrines. But there are significant differences, for Sukur specialized in industry and trade and was in part dependent upon its neighbours for the raw materials necessary for iron-making. It has a chief with a reputation and influence extending beyond his community but at the same time relies for its rain upon a ritual specialist resident in neighbouring Wula. There are twenty-one clans, some including that of the chief with claims to Gudur origin, and an extended set of titleholders. The chief of Sukur initiates important ceremonies after divination by himself or another diviner – several past chiefs of Sukur were renowned diviners – however sacrifices and other offerings are made on his behalf by priestly titleholders.

Household shrines

Sukur ancestor pots are far less elaborate than those of Sirak; they are very small and normally undecorated, or may not even be pots. A small usually plain jar is the model for ancestor and most other shrine pots, and the process whereby it comes to represent the ancestor is somewhat different from at Sirak, here beginning in a vessel given to a young man at his initiation into adulthood. The general term for such shrines is *suku*, a term also applied to ancient lower grindstones (*tson*), commonly believed to be made by God, used for similar purposes (David 1998).

In theory ancestor shrines are served very much as at Sirak, but we have a strong impression that the cult of ancestors is less elaborate and is practised less frequently. A shrine that, by its name, *suku juk*, refers to a collectivity of lineage ancestors, may well not exist in actuality. If there are clan shrines at Sukur, we are not aware of them. As at Sirak the spirits of twins are considered powerful and potentially dangerous. The associated pots are nearly identical to those at Sirak, but rituals practised by the parents of twins do not, when summed together, protect the community.

Placentas are buried beneath upturned pots behind the mother's room and within the compound wall. A woman's first child receives a small plain jar. Every year during the purification ceremony, the mother offers a chicken and beer on the shrine. When the next child is born, the pot is passed on and is finally abandoned when all the children are grown and no longer in need of protection.

As at Sirak there are shrines for the spirits of men and leopards violently killed, but at Sukur these are not kept in the compound or in a clan shrine but rather in the owner's field outside the compound walls. Such shrines serve to protect the owner's farm and possessions from theft and other misfortunes. Every year the owner makes an offering of flour at planting, harvesting, and threshing. If a family member is ill or other misfortunes strike, a diviner may advise the sacrifice of a red cock. The potency of the spirits associated with such shrines is such that they are dangerous to pregnant women. For this and other reasons, an owner may decide to destroy it, an act that requires a sacrifice.

Nature spirit shrines

The nature spirits of Sukur are much like those described for Sirak. They are usually found at water points (springs, wells), rock outcrops, or craggy

Fig. 3. Grindstone-mortars of the kind frequently used as shrines at Sukur. These are located next to the council chamber in the northern sector of the chief's residence.

mountain tops, trees, or groves. These are the dwelling places of *hri*, a term referring both to the spirit and its shrine, which may include a pot or pots or one or more stones. *Hri* shrines are immovable in geographic space, whereas *suku*, even if rarely moved, are localized only in social space. Seven of the most potent are the sites of annual sacrifices that protect the entire community in a manner described below.

Community shrines

Zoku, the annual purification ceremony at Sukur, takes place at several locations and initiates a ritual cycle that takes place over subsequent months at a number of *hri* shrines served by titleholders with priestly functions. The cycle begins with sacrifice of a bull (nowadays a small goat) at a shrine at the base of great gate-like natural granite pillars atop Mixyrux hill. Although this is not made explicit, the Mixyrux shrine constitutes the religious heart of Sukur. The sacrifice is addressed both to the *genius loci* and to God. A free translation goes as follows:

> This offering is for God, may it bring health to the people, may they become as numerous as grains of magnetite ore. There, O spirit, is your food; the offering is the responsibility of my patriline, handed down by my father. The things that enter our houses through holes in the wall, let them be not as snakes but as earthworms on the path at our children's feet. Spirits, take your food, and bring health and prosperity to the people. Let the grains of millet be as grains of sand so that all may eat. Spirit of this high rocky place, drive evil things away from us, the people. So be it.

One of the priestly functionaries holding the *Mbesefwoy* title is responsible for this sacrifice. On the evening of the same day, two other titleholders leave the chief's house and walk through Sukur calling the ancestors to come. They carry a small pot of beer to a shrine on Muva mountain (the highest point in Sukur) where they make an offering to ancestors. The following day the spirits of the dead and those of impurity and disease are driven off beyond Sukur's borders by a ritual war party of titleholders.

Zoku is the first of seven sacrifices that take place over the next three months at different nature spirit shrines. They are made by *Mbesefwoy* and other priestly titleholders on routes into and out of Sukur, at sites where powerful nature spirits reside.[6] Strips of goatskin are hung across the paths to bar the entry of evil forces. Upon completion of the cycle, Sukur is ritually sealed against spirit and other attacks.

Chiefly shrines

There are several shrines in and around the chief's house. Some of these take the form of small beer jars while others are grindstones and others again are gateways or gateway elements. These are all associated in various ways with the chieftaincy (see Smith and David 1995). One set of pots, for example, represents previous chiefs and is served by a titleholder, *Tlisuku*, who acts as the chief's chaplain.

A shrine named *Yawal De'ba* is associated with and has perhaps been appropriated by the chief of Sukur. *Yawal* is a ceremony held in February after the millet harvest at intervals decided by the chief. It celebrates his power and that of his clan but also the acquiescence and integration of past dynasties, representatives of which perform rituals at the shrine. This consists of three newly made pots, the principal being a tall narrow neckless storage vessel with three small horn-like spikes below the rim, which are set in a stone-lined pit.

Another shrine, located within the chiefly residence, celebrates Sukur's ritual seniority amongst its neighbours. This consists of a grindstone-mortar containing a number of ancient upper grindstones of an elongate shape quite unlike those used today. It is called the *tson vwad* or grindstone-mortar altar of the hairlocks. "Each of its stones represents one of the chiefdoms in the region to which the *xidi* [chief] sends ... the *tlagama* title-holder to braid into the new chief's hair a lock ... of his predecessor's" (Smith and David 1995:454).[7] This custom at one and the same time symbolizes the continuity of the chieftaincy and the ritual seniority accorded to Sukur by up to nine of their neighbours, including Gulak (Margi), Kamale (Higi), Wula and Mabas.

Although the Sukur rely primarily for their rain on the prayers of *Tluwala*, a rainmaker living in Wula with whom the chief deals through emissaries, there is a rain shrine in Sukur located not far from the chief's residence and close to *Yawal De'ba*. It is called the *suku yam* (shrine of water) and appears to serve as a first line of defence in the event of interruptions in the rains. Its story and the associated ritual practices relate it

Fig. 4. A priestly titleholder offers beer at the Yawal De'ba shrine in Sukur.

to Gudur and may indicate that it is a community shrine that has been subsumed under the chief's authority.

While there are other shrines associated with the chief, they can all be comprehended within the framework developed above, except for *hri Mcakili*, a stone (perhaps a grindstone-mortar) kept hidden beneath a granary cap. *Mcakili* (or *Mpsakali*) is the Sukur name for Gudur. The shrine is located next to the chief's megalithic throne in the ceremonial area outside his residence. Every year, before the main harvest in December, the chief makes an offering here. It is said that long ago if locusts and leopards were a problem this offering consisted of beer and a sorghum paste, the latter obtained from Gudur.[8] Thus this shrine is a material statement of the chief's claim to Gudur descent and a special relationship with its chief. Such ritual legitimation of his authority is all the more needed in view of the long sequence of depositions and abdications of Sukur chiefs (see http://www.sukur.info/Soc/Xidis.htm).

Discussion

Sirak and Sukur share essentially the same belief system but at Sukur, while heads of households and lineages retain ritual responsibility for their ancestors, specialists, in the form of priestly titleholders such as the six *Mbesefwoy*, act on behalf of the community in the purification and in other ceremonies, including initiation, and the chief's ritual responsibilities are devolved to *Tlisuku*. Ceramics are less important as shrines at Sukur than at Sirak, partly because the wives of smiths, who worked with their husbands to fine bloomery iron for sale at Sukur's iron market, produced pots in lesser quantities and lower quality. Diviners rarely suggest that their clients commission pots and far more frequently advise their clients to place various kinds of offerings, some of which they provide, at crossings of ways. Thus, although there may be as many shrines per person as at Sirak, ceramic ones are certainly fewer.

Community-wide ritual action is always initiated by the chief and is never achieved incrementally by the additive actions of individual householders. Unlike the similar Sirak *halalay*, several of the Sukur *hri* shrines combine, in a cycle coordinated by the chief, to protect the entire community. Delicate political adaptations are evident; the chief cannot dismiss the *Mbesefwoy* and other priestly titleholders responsible for the ritual defence of the polity.

A dimension not present at Sirak is evident in the *tson vwa'd* shrine that links Sukur to its neighbours while claiming a ritual seniority that, at least until very recently, appears to have been generally acknowledged though not, according to our sources, on the basis of a Gudur origin of Sukur's chiefly dynasty. However this may be, a legitimacy based on Gudur descent is claimed by the present clan Dur chiefly dynasty in the rituals associated with the *suku yam* rain shrine and, more forcefully, in the *hri Mcakili* shrine, where the appellation *hri* seems to insist on a direct connection between Gudur and Sukur mediated by a nature spirit.

GUDUR

Gudur is not as easily defined as Sirak or Sukur and has meant many things to many people at different times. The name can refer to a clan, a physical space, a regional shrine, the single small chiefdom of Gudal, or a more complex chiefly entity comprising the chiefdoms of, from north to south, Ndeveley, Kilwo, Mambay, Gilvawa, Gudal, Minglia (Mangezla), Mokong, Katamsa, Dimeo, Mofu (Mafaw), Mosso (Maaca'b), Zidim, and Njeleng, this last being the only unit that is not *mofu-gudur*-speaking (Fig. 5). Masakal in the northeast and Mawuldal to the west are usually included within Gudur, and Mowo, to the east, is also closely associated. These three communities speak *mofu-gudur* but have strong links respectively with the Mofu-Diamaré, the Cuvok, and the Gisiga. The larger Gudur political entity is characterized by Seignobos (1991a) as a theocratic chiefdom, by Jouaux (1989) as something between a chiefdom and a kingdom, and by ourselves as a group of small chiefdoms that acknowledge one of their number, Gudal, as ritually paramount.[9] We all agree that at some time or times in the past Gudur was the point of origin of a diaspora that reached across the Mandara mountains and even down onto the edges of the plains to the west (Fig. 1). Seignobos (2000a:46) now sees this movement, which he regards as part of a much larger pattern of northeast to southwest migration (Seignobos 1991b), as dating to the eighteenth century and involving Gudur colonization of lands to the west.[10] Jouaux is noncommittal about both date and process. We differ from Seignobos and argue that the main diaspora from Gudur westwards took place in the mid-nineteenth century as a result not of an *expansionist policy* but of the substantial *defeat* of Gudal and its neighbours by the Fulbe, then engaged in the jihad initiated by Usman Dan Fodio. With the hills in Mofu-Gudur territory already densely populated, Gudur, and particularly Gudal, occupants of the plains and lower slopes would have been especially at risk and liable to flee before the onslaught of Fulbe cavalry. It is possible to place this process in the 1830s–1840s on the evidence of Mohammadou's (1988:125–27) history of the Fulbe chiefdom of Gazawa (east of Gudur) who (re-)established themselves at Gazawa around 1820, from which time on Gudur would have been under more or less continuous attack until its various elements were either defeated or had come to an accommodation with the Fulbe.[11]

Igor Kopytoff's *African frontier* thesis provides a framework for understanding Gudur's regional significance, for many of the polities of the Mandara mountains constitute a

> local frontier, lying at the fringes of the numerous established African societies. It is on such frontiers that most African

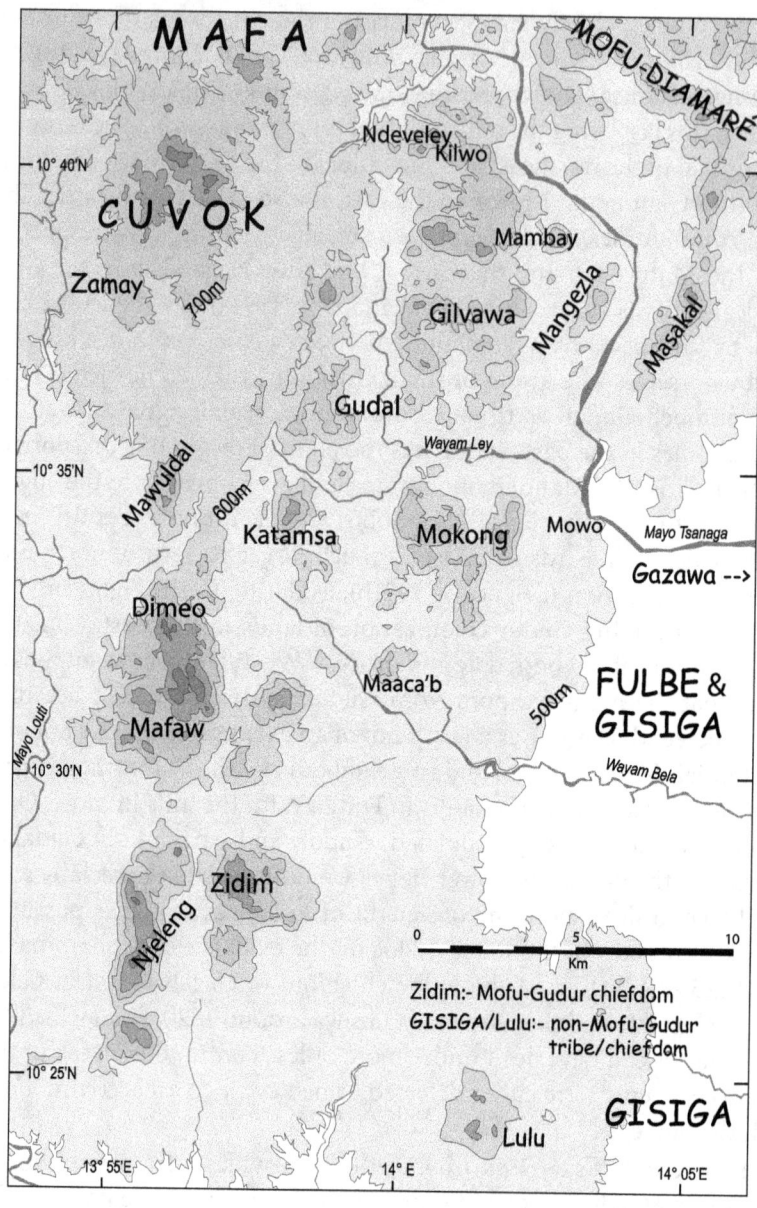

Fig. 5. Gudur, showing its component chiefdoms [and nearby communities mentioned in the text].

polities and societies have, so to speak, been 'constructed' out of the bits and pieces – human and cultural – of existing societies. This posits a process in which incipient small polities are produced by other similar and usually more complex societies. (1987:3)

Following Kopytoff (1987),[12] we can consider Gudur as a centre or "metropole" from which the frontier process began with the creation of "frontiersmen," people who because of Fulbe attacks and locusts (Lavergne 1943) left their home settlement on the advice of "Ngom," supposedly the ninth chief of the Gudal line but in fact the first who can be solidly situated in history. This placed them in an "institutional vacuum" where they "begin a process of social construction that, if successful, brings into being a new society" (Kopytoff 1987:25). This "re-institutionalization" takes place on a frontier that is not necessarily a geographical vacuum, for the immigrants often encounter others that share many similarities in culture, language, and material culture. The immigrants either join an existing group on the frontier or establish their own society, one that is constructed "not out of whole cloth but from a cultural inventory of symbols and practices that were brought from a metropole and that pre-dated any particular society being observed" (1987:34).

In the present instance, Gudur migrants, moving in small contingents towards the west, would have risked capture and enslavement by other montagnards. The Mayo Tsanaga valley and that of its tributary, the Mayo Goudoulou, offered the easiest axis of penetration by Fulbe raiders, and so the inhabitants of these valleys, disproportionately Gudal and of Gudal clan, would have been the most likely to have been displaced westwards. When seeking refuge amongst the inhabitants of the area, it would have been very much in their interest to emphasize their value as warriors and farmers, and to talk up their connections with a chief possessing the power to control plagues and other misfortunes and to ensure the fertility of humans and their stock. Rather than founding their own settlements, they frequently joined others, whence the widespread existence at Sirak, Sukur, and among the Kapsiki, Higi and other groups, of clans that claim Gudur origins and others that do not. The lack of Gudur metropolitan knowledge of the diaspora fits well with this reading of history, as does the absence of Gudal participation in the installation of chiefs of the diaspora polities and the general lack of special relationships between diaspora communities.

The new and growing communities so formed would have had, according to Kopytoff, to validate themselves to themselves as well as to other polities in the region. Self-validation in the discourse of the Mandara implies establishing ancestry, in this case exotic but nonetheless honourable. Validation vis-à-vis others entails having a "charter that drew upon widespread regional values, themes and traditions, and upon historical events and memories that carried prestige in the region as a whole" (Kopytoff 1987:72). The migrants from Gudur would have worked hard to advance the claims of Gudur to embody such a charter. And so many clans came to claim direct or indirect Gudur descent and to believe that their communities' well-being might be ensured by their leaders' access to the powers of Gudur's chief. As van Beek (1981:118) astutely observed "one can claim a Gudur origin on account of the ritual importance of that village, and not because one really is of Gudur stock." It was not enough, however, just to claim a Gudur origin; it was also necessary – at least in theory – to return on occasion to "recharge" rain-making paraphernalia, receive new medicines, or seek protection from locusts or renewed fertility and fecundity. Such journeys to Gudur are better remembered on the periphery than at the centre.

At both Sirak and Sukur we were told of envoys who had journeyed to Gudur bearing gifts for the chief of Gudal, in return for which they obtained protection from leopards, disease, drought, and especially locusts. Indeed, it was in the 1930s, during a catastrophic set of locust invasions, that the last envoys went from Sukur to Gudur. What was it that they found? What shrines did they visit?

Household, clan, community and nature spirit shrines

Little has been written of these shrines at Gudur, and during our two-month stay we learned of them only incidentally. The range of ancestor pots described by Barreteau et al. (1988) is similar to that of Sirak, and, as at Sirak, a special room in the compound is built to house them. On Gilgam mountain we visited a collective shrine where chiefly ancestors of the Masacavaw clan were represented by decorated jars (Fig. 6). There and elsewhere our attention was drawn to *halalay*, which here are clan shrines – perhaps with aspects of nature spirit shrines – usually located in sacred groves. We know also of shrines where the earth priests, often but not always members of clans considered as autochthonous that have lost or ceded political leadership to later-comers, carry out sacrifices on behalf of the community. Thus the present *Maslaslam*, earth priest of the Ngwadaama clan, informed us that his ancestor had ceded the chieftaincy of what was to become Gudal to Biya (otherwise known as Bi Dilgam or Nguéleo), the first Bay (chief of) Gudal, who had arrived from Mowo bringing with him salt, a common symbol of civilization (see also Seignobos 1991a:237). Mowo, located only eight kilometres to the east, appears to have been an earlier magico-religious centre that, likely under pressure from the plains states of Wandala and Bagirmi, lost its ritual pre-eminence, its shrines and ritual being dispersed, some to Gudal and others to Mofu-Diamaré settlements (Seignobos 1991a, 1995).

All in all it would seem that the household, clan, and community shrines at Gudur – and in other chiefdoms of the group – differ only in details from those of Sirak and Sukur. We are ignorant as to the functions of nature spirit shrines, which surely exist. However, our limited investigation of titleholders' duties does not suggest that there are any equivalents to the *Mbesefwoy* or *Tlisuku* nor anything comparable to the ritual circumscription of Sukur, sealing it against exterior physical and spirit attack.

Chiefly shrines and chiefly divination

When Biya arrived from Mowo by a roundabout route dictated by his bull, he brought with him rain stones. These, like the bull, had been bequeathed to him by the chief of Mowo whom he had been serving since he had arrived there as a boy from Wandala some years before. There are two types of rain stones: one kind brings rain and the other, named after the rainbow, stops it falling. These stones are kept in the chief's house in a tripod pot covered with the skin of a hyrax. The rain sacrifice for Gudal begins after divination by the chief of the smiths and an antelope has been hunted. It is inaugurated by four of the titleholders in the chiefly cemetery, one of whom addresses the ancestors. The party then moves to the chief's house where he sacrifices the animal in the presence of the rain stones, quite possibly anointing them with its blood. We were told by our Gudur assistant that the last time this had happened was in the late 1950s.

Whereas this ritual has all the aspects of one carried out on behalf of the community by and under the auspices of the chief, sacrifices for rain on behalf of other communities would appear to have been conducted by the chief in his house either alone or at least without the formal

Fig. 6. The Masacavaw clan ancestor shrine on the small Gilgam massif (Gudal chiefdom).

participation of titleholders. In such cases the chief was, we suggest, not acting as chief of Gudal or of Gudur, but either as a particularly powerful diviner or a rain-maker, a *"sorcier"* in the words of de Lauwe (1937), one of the first Europeans to meet Bay Takwaw II, chief of Gudal from 1930 until his death in 1980. The shrines described by de Lauwe are *kuley*, pots specially made for that purpose.[13] In a photograph of the chief (de Lauwe 1937:plate IV:2), a *kuley* pot is visible in the background.

It is not possible from de Lauwe's account to sort out which sacrifices are for the chief's lineage, and thus like sacrifices carried out by other household heads, which others are for Gudal, which, if any, are for Gudur in general, and which are for clients from more distant places. In 2004 we asked chiefs and titleholders of nine of the fifteen chiefdoms commonly assigned to what we regard as the Gudur paramountcy how they obtained their rain. Only two, Katamsa and Mofu, informed us that they had never relied on Gudal. Katamsa has, we were told, been going to Mowo "since the time of the whites" and Mofu has its own rain-makers. And only Mofu admitted ever going to Gudur to seek protection against locusts. It would seem therefore that the chief of Gudal never carried out sacrifices or any other ritual on behalf of the entire set of Gudur chiefdoms that acknowledge his ritual pre-eminence – those in which "Toute la tradition est commandée par Gudur," as we were told by the chief of Zidim, Chef de Canton de Mofu-Sud.

The shrines and rituals described by de Lauwe were all located within the chiefly residence, one small room containing the pots representing the chief's father, father's father (FF), and father's father's father (FFF). Whether acting on behalf of his household, his community, or as a diviner, the ritual ingredients (beer, animal, flour, etc.) and pots are often the same or very similar. Individuals came with offerings in order to obtain a cure for disease or have children, while others came as emissaries to seek benefits – rain and fertility being pre-eminent – for their villages and to stave off misfortunes of many kinds including leopards, caterpillars that destroy the millet, and locusts. How successive chiefs of Gudal acquired these other powers is unclear, and they did not in fact control locusts but, as described below, only access to those who carried out the sacrifices.

De Lauwe does not mention two of the most important shrines at Gudal, the first of which is a small room without doors and windows located at Yideng Bay, the original residence of Gudal chiefs, on the spot where Biya's bull sank into the ground (Fig. 7). How precisely this shrine is served and its mysterious contents used are unknown to us: like the *hri Mcakili* at Sukur, its prime function would seem to stand as a guarantor of the legitimate authority of the chief.[14] The second shrine is that of the locusts, to which we now turn.

The locust shrine

While the chief of Gudal conducted the rain sacrifices himself, he did not control the locust shrine himself nor carry out the requisite sacrifices. Instead the shrine, located in the eastern Usa (or Wusa) quarter of Gudal but in fact almost as close to Mowo as to Bay Gudal's residence, was operated by the senior member of the Masuwa clan. There is convincing evidence in the form of oral traditions (e.g., Barreteau 1999 [collected in 1986] and a tradition collected by us from the son of the present elder responsible) that control over this shrine was on at least one occasion contested by the chief of Gudal but that, ultimately unsuccessful, he had to accept the Masuwa's authority over it. He nonetheless controlled outsiders' access to it, from which he no doubt derived economic benefit.

According to Beauvilain (1989:116–17, 129) locust invasions in the greater region are reported for the 1880s, 1893–1900 and 1930–39.[15] The severe famines of the 1930s that resulted from successive locust infestations are well-documented and still remembered by the elderly. The famine of 1931 was particularly severe in the Mandara mountains: "Les montagnards gardent encore un souvenir très vif de la dernière grande famine de ce genre, survenue en 1931" (Boutrais 1987:25). Some Mafa preferred to hand over their children to Fulbe rather than to see them starve. De Lauwe makes no mention of the chief of Gudur's powers over locusts, despite his presence in the region while their invasions were still occurring. The most detailed descriptions of the response to locust infestations and of Gudur's role in it come from British mandated territory.[16] At the start of the locust invasions in 1930, the chief of Sukur, described by Assistant District Officer MacBride (1937:3) as the "sole accredited agent for the Priest of Gudur," collected a tax to construct an iron vessel to contain "all the locusts of the world."[17] Kulp, an American missionary in the region at the same time as MacBride and Shaw, was informed that part of the chief of Sukur's power was due to the belief that he had

Fig. 7. The room lacking a door in Yideng Bay, former residence of the chiefs of Gudal. The chief is said to have received visitors and dispensed justice under the tree at the top left of the picture.

> ... the power to drive out the locusts which have been destroying so much of the crops in the last seven years or more. But since a part of the rite which must be performed to drive out the locusts is the sacrifice of two virgins, it is reported that fear of British officials has operated to prevent him carrying out the rite, hence the locusts still are in the country. (Kulp 1935:17)

Although it would be surprising if locust invasions at Sukur were not combated by ritual action, we know of no Sukur shrine dedicated to this purpose and have never heard of any sacrifices there involving virgins of either sex. But perhaps Kulp's mention of virgin sacrifice does indirectly explain why de Lauwe learned nothing of the locust shrine; Bay Gudal would not have wished to advertise a ritual activity likely to have been severely sanctioned by the French.

It is possible that the locust shrine in Usa quarter dates back to the period of Mowo ritual pre-eminence. According to Seignobos (1991a:247), the Masuwa are responsible for the locust sacrifice, a position they had previously held at Mowo. They discovered the shrine site: an open tomb from which locusts were emerging and spilling out over the fields. They warned the chief of Gudur who gave them the responsibility for the sacrifice to be carried out in his name.[18] But if indeed the Masuwa had, as Barreteau's (1999) tradition suggests, brought their expertise in dealing with locusts with them from Wandala territory further north, then it seems as likely that they maintained this role when Mowo disintegrated as a dominant polity, and that the options open to the chief of Gudur were only to acknowledge or, as we have already seen, to challenge their stewardship.

The site on the small Mabasa massif, five kilometres west of Mowo and four kilometres east of Gudur's chiefly quarter, is in a natural amphitheatre amidst a grove of *Sterculia setigera* trees.[19] When we visited it in July 2004, it was much overgrown (Fig. 8) compared with Seignobos' (1991a:244–45) sketch of the site in the dry season. There are many upturned pots, all with holes deliberately made in the bases. Our guide informed us that each sacrifice required three – a tripod meat pot and two large storage pots, one "male" and the other "female." It was our impression that pots generally occur in such sets, of which we were able to identify between thirteen and fifteen, a total that should represent the minimum number of sacrifices.[20]

Fig. 8. The locust shrine in the Usa quarter of Gudal. Note the large upturned pots.

Following an account of the conflicted relationship between the chief of Gudal and the head of the Masuwa clan, known as "No locusts in Wandala," Barreteau's tradition, recorded it seems from a non-Masuwa source, provides a detailed description of the locust sacrifice:

> All returns to normal, but the following year as they are cultivating the millet, the locusts appear once more. The chief [of Gudur] consults the diviner – the sacrifice of a man is required. People in other villages consult diviners as well. They come to see the chief of Gudur who tells them that a man and a woman must be sacrificed. A messenger is sent to the chief of Gidar [other sources indicate Hina] who, having many people [perhaps a reference to slave raiding], provides the victims. The victims and a billy goat are taken to Wusa. The Masuwa pray before the altar of "No locusts in Wandala" and sacrifice the goat. The meat is cooked and left in a container with porridge. There are two openings for the locusts, one male and the other female. The man who makes the sacrifice lays a mat over the holes. The male victim seats himself above the male hole, the female victim above the female hole. They are served the meal. As they eat the locusts come up and eat away the mat. As the mat falls into the hole the victims are pushed in. The hole is closed with leaves of the blood plum [*Haematostaphis barteri*, a tree that bleeds red] and earth. The locusts will return no more. If they do the Whites will know what to do. There are no longer people to make the sacrifice. (1999:158–64)

We obtained an almost identical description of the locust sacrifice from our Masuwa guide. Seignobos' (1991a:248–49) description, also obtained from Masuwa informants, is very similar (and cf. Jouaux 1989:277–78). Seignobos (1991a:243) comments on the difference between details of the Masuwa version of the locust sacrifice and those he obtained from informants at Wula, Gili, and Udah on the western margins of the Mandara mountains. The former describe a tomb or hole in the ground, the latter a rock cleft or room containing locusts, closed with doors of iron. Strümpell (1922/23:56–58) learned in 1906 or 1907 from the Kapsiki of a pot kept at Gudur in a special hut with doors of iron that contained a magical liquid. If these doors were opened or damaged by an unauthorized person, calamity would strike the region; epidemics would wipe out humans and animals, whirlwinds would destroy villages, and locusts would devour the crops in the fields. He also mentions offerings sent to Gudur by the chief of Sukur that include a virgin girl and a black horse.[21] In the early 1990s we recorded a range of similar stories at Sukur.

All these accounts except Strümpell's refer to the 1930s, when the last remembered journeys to Gudur took place. We were told by the son of Sukur's last emissary, who travelled with representatives from nearby Wula Mango, Kurang, and Damay, that they variously took: a horse, a gown, and six slabs of iron with four legs each; a slab of iron with four legs to stop the locusts; eight men with nine sheets of iron to seal the hole from which the locusts came, and a horse as a gift for the chief of Gudur. During the same period the people of Sirak are said to have sent the chief of Gudur a young girl, a bull, or grain for protection from locusts.

Reading the shrine is problematical: the thirteen- to fifteen-pot clusters presently visible could all represent sacrifices carried out in the 1930s on behalf of Gudur itself and non-Mofu-Gudur. Since that time, there have been no acridian invasions. However Strümpell's account is indicative of the activity of the locust shrine at least as far back as the invasions of the late nineteenth century. The various accounts of the sacrifice contain elements of cliché. For example, the treacherous seating of a person on a mat that then collapses beneath them occurs in Fulbe stories, and the containment of a misfortune behind or within an iron door or cauldron is a western Mandara element with resonance far south among the Chamba, where "worn out hoes were used to block the hole from which locusts would otherwise emerge to ravage their crops" (Fardon 1990:74–75). But this is not enough to discredit the general truth of these accounts, and it would seem likely that on at least one occasion humans were sacrificed, an event almost without parallel in the region and indicative of the depth of the people's despair. Other victims seem sometimes to have been acceptable: according to Podlewski (1966:89) Bay Takwaw II of Gudal recalled the sacrifice of a young couple at the locust shrine when he was young and told him that he had sacrificed a horse there.[22]

What does seem certain is that the locust shrine served a clientele that, besides Gudal itself, consisted primarily of diasporan communities. Of the other chiefdoms of the paramountcy, we know of only two that admit to have ever relied on the locust shrine, while five deny having made use of it at any time. As in the case of rain, it was groups from beyond the Mofu-Gudur that came to Gudur for protection against locusts.

Discussion and conclusions

If Gudur was indeed a polity larger and more complex than Sukur, then we would expect greater specialization of ritual labour, but this seems not to be the case. As noted above, household, clan, community, and nature shrines are, to the best of our knowledge, not significantly different in structure from those of Sirak and Sukur and closer to Sirak in terms of their materialization as ceramics. Whether at Gudal or in other of the Gudur chiefdoms, there were no priestly titleholders comparable to the *Mbesefwoy* of Sukur. Nor, while the chief of Gudal initiates the cycle of annual purification ceremonies that bring in the new year in most, if not all, the Mofu-Gudur chiefdoms, is there anything comparable to the Sukur shrines involved in celebration of the chief's rule of his community and his ritual seniority among the neighbour chiefs. While the chief of Gudal was held in considerable awe and enjoyed some privileges and benefits in his own and the other Gudur chiefdoms (Jouaux 1989), his pre-eminence seems to have been very largely limited to the ritual sphere, where it served in our view primarily to provide a charter for a Mofu-Gudur social world that, transcending the microcosms of the petty chiefdoms, facilitated the conduct of social, political and economic life on a broader and more sustainable scale – not unlike, in its way, the potlatch institution of the northwest coast of North America.

Thus, in terms of its shrines and of its economy, which unlike Sukur's did not involve the integration of neighbouring communities in specialist production, Gudur appears less rather than more complex a political entity than Sukur. On the other hand, as the result (we argue) of historical circumstances peculiar to the Fulbe jihad, chiefs of Gudal were able to extend the range of their divining practice to a remarkable degree, attracting a clientele that, albeit drawn mainly from communities of the Gudur diaspora, was more widely dispersed than that of any other diviner we know of, past or present. We must distinguish here between the chief's priestly role in carrying out purification and perhaps other ceremonies on behalf of Gudal, his role as a rain-maker for Gudal, some other Mofu-Gudur and some outsiders, and his use of the same material – his ancestral shrines and the rain stones legitimately inherited by his forebear from the chief of Mowo – when acting as a diviner and purveyor of medicine on behalf of outsiders in search of fecundity of humans, animals, and crops, and of protection from natural disasters.

Although the scale of Bay Gudal's divining practice was exceptional both in its geographic scale and in the powers attributed to the medicines offered his clients, its pattern accords with Mandara norms. Strümpell (1922/23:57) states that Sukur and Kapsiki communities (many of whose clans claim Gudur origins) made contributions to Gudur's "powerful priest" in order to obtain his goodwill, for even powerful Sukur relied upon the favour of the Bay Gudal. Outsiders who sought Bay Gudal's aid appear to have regarded him with a degree of awe and perhaps fear that, unlike in the case of some powerful Mofu-Diamaré chiefs (Vincent 1991:333ff.), was not backed up by the threat of physical force but only by his purported ability to either bring or withhold the rains or to unleash plagues of locusts. For example, van Beek's (1981:118) Kapsiki informants stated that representatives of the Bay Gudal visited the villages of those dependent upon Gudur to see if they "followed the ancestors." Although it is improbable that such visitations ever occurred (van Beek, pers. comm. 2004), it was claimed that the sanction for not doing so was locust-induced famine. Thus Bay Gudal was to be feared more by outsiders than by his neighbours because, as Jouaux (1989:283) suggests, following de Heusch (1962:1470), "L'éloignement du chef [et donc 'perte de contact direct avec le peuple'], renforcé par divers tabous, est favorable à une exagération mythique." However, even within Gudur, Jouaux (1989:280) states that the overriding attitude towards the chief derived from her extensive interviews with inhabitants of the many Mofu-Gudur chiefdoms could best be summed up as follows: "on avait peur du chef de Gudur car il pouvait bloquer la pluie ou envoyer les criquets." It must be stressed that these fears relate not to the powers inherent in shrines served by the Bay Gudal but rather to those, analogous to those of a sorcerer (as de Lauwe so astutely recognized), possessed by him as a person.

It is indeed ironic that, despite his great reputation, Bay Gudal's control of the most renowned shrine was at best indirect. For the locust shrine at Usa is the only Gudur shrine that can be described as both regional and tied to a particular place rather than to a particular person, although even this characterization requires qualification.[23] Although the shrine may well predate the Gudur ritual paramountcy and have been inaugurated in the period of Mowo's ritual ascendance, it appears from the evidence at hand to have primarily served diaspora communities. In this sense it is hardly a regional shrine but rather one that came to attract a widely dispersed clientele that had in common their socio-political link to Gudur. It is noteworthy, for example, that so far as we know, none of the Mofu-Diamaré polities located only a few kilometres to the north ever sought the protection of the Usa locust shrine; nor did they regard Bay Gudal with any particular respect.

The locust shrine, guaranteed as genuine by its historical link to Mowo, is in fact only one of the ritually charged remnants of that polity's dissolution. There is another locust shrine at Gabaka in Mofu-Diamaré territory that also derives from Mowo and which is also served by a Masuwa priest. Similarly, besides those rain stones inherited by the first Bay Gudal from Mowo, others from the same source went to Morley in Mofu-Diamaré territory. Each of these last-named shrines – and there are others – attracts clients from a considerable area and could be described as "regional shrines." But it would be more accurate and productive to view this from a different perspective and to regard each and every shrine as having a clientele, or more precisely a congregation. Thus, the congregation of the Catholic shrine of Lourdes in the French Pyrenees may be said to extend to Australia but does not include Protestants or Muslims living in the village. The areal extent of the congregation is less interesting than the processes that have produced the distribution. In the case of the locust shrine and of the rain stones, we have offered an interpretation of those processes. As regards Gabaka, Morley, and similar shrines, much more of the kind of research initiated by Seignobos (1995) into the history of Mowo and its descendant communities is required for their congregations to be understood in historical terms.

The classification of shrines used in this paper relates on the one hand to their congregations, varying from a single individual, to a household, a lineage, a clan, a whole community, or a larger entity united by history, most commonly in this study the Gudur diaspora. Another dimension involves the referent of the shrine. This includes: a single (or group of) human spirit(s); God (as in Mafa Zhikile pots but not present in Sirak, Sukur, or Gudur); nature spirits tied to place; and spirits that relate to entities of the experienced world, as of disease or of sorghum. Rain stones – glossed as "the children of water/rain" among the Mofu-Diamaré (Vincent 1991:621) – would seem to have as their referent unlocalized nature spirits, and the referent of the locust shrine would appear to be the locusts themselves or rather their collective spirit.

Shrines are served by persons acting as priests on behalf of the shrine's congregation. Family rituals provide the model for rituals on larger scales that invoke human, and particularly ancestral, spirits, God and nature spirits also. Thus, when the chief of Gudal makes offerings and prays to his *kuley* on the occasion of the purification ceremony, he is doing so as the father of his community, as do the individual heads of households. This is so common throughout the world as to be almost a truism (see, e.g., Walker and Lucero [2000] on the Pueblos of the American Southwest and on the Maya). As these authors state (2000:143), rituals never leave the home but are appropriated for political purposes.

The other strong elements in Mandara ritual, of divination and magic, were also extrapolated from the familial to the scale of the polity or regional congregation. While diviners most commonly (in our limited experience) advise their clients regarding the nature of the offering or sacrifice they should make to a particular spirit, they may also provide herbal or other remedies, some of which can be classed as magical. Similarly, when Bay Gudal divined for envoys from a distant community, he would advise as to what beasts should be sacrificed or other offerings made and provide them with a magical liquid or more probably the dried dregs of beer consumed at the ceremony. This they would take home with them, dilute, and distribute to part or all of the community in order to regenerate failing fertility or for some other purpose. Such potions are also said to have regenerated the powers of the Fali rain-makers (Wade 1997) and of the chief of Vreke (Müller-Kosack 2003:349).[24]

Finally we wish to emphasize that, since the division of ritual labour and the degree of socio-political complexity are closely related, the study of shrines offers an avenue for the elucidation of political arrangements. It is clear that, at Sirak, heads of households are for most purposes ritually independent, even if they are commonly tutored by smiths. Whereas at Sirak during the New Year's purification ceremony it is all parents of twins who separately but concomitantly defend their community against misfortunes, at Sukur a specialized set of priestly titleholders, serving *hri* shrines and communicating through them with God, fulfil a similar function. The chief also delegates his ritual functions to a chaplain, *Tlisuku*. But when we turn to Gudur, which has until now been universally regarded as the most complex montagnard polity of precolonial times, we find no comparable specialization of priestly roles. On the contrary, the individual Gudur chiefdoms are in their familial and other religious observances much more like Sirak than Sukur, and the specialization of the chief of Gudal partakes not so much of the role of priest chief as of diviner and rain-maker, roles that are more often segregated than combined in Mandara societies (Sterner 2003:198–227).

ACKNOWLEDGMENTS

The fieldwork for this paper was undertaken between 1986 and 2005 in the context of the Mandara Archaeological Project and was supported by the Social Sciences and Humanities Research Council of Canada (SSHRC) and by a grant to Judith Sterner from the University of London in 1992. It was authorized by the Ministry of Culture, Cameroon, and by the National Commission for Museums and Monuments, Nigeria. We wish to thank the many local authorities and communities amongst and with whom we have worked, and particularly our assistants, Kodje Dadai, John Tizhe Habuga, Philip Emmanuel Sukur, Markus Ezra Makarma, the late Isnga Dalli Sukur and Alioum Baya Mana. We dedicate this paper to the memory of Isnga and of two much regretted long-term colleagues, Eldridge Mohammadou and Daniel Barreteau, whose historical, ethnographic, and linguistic researches continue to serve as a foundation for our own (and others') studies, especially in relation to Gudur.

NOTES

1. "The religious practices of the majority of the un-Islamized peoples of the Mandara are characterized by a common trait: the representation by polished stones and bourmas [pots] of beings to whom worship is offered" (our translation).

2. Interview with Zera Huvdub ta Zayag (19-07-89).

3. In the past a finial was placed on the roof of this room; it proclaimed to all who passed by that this man was the head of a minimal lineage. If the custodian is a married daughter, the ancestor shrine room will be built some distance from her husband's house.

4. The category of twins in the Mandara mountains includes other multiple births, breech births, and sometimes other "abnormal" births.

5. Sirak midwives are frequently of the smith/potter caste; some smiths are specialist midwives.

6. One of these routes has the additional protection provided by six pots buried in the path. These are to ward off attacks from enemies coming from the north.

7. Several of the rain stones used by Mofu-Diamaré chiefs to bring or withhold rain are shaped like elongated upper grindstones (Sterner 2003:211n.36).

8. The last time Sukur emissaries went to Gudur was during the locust invasions of the 1930s. No one we met at Sukur has ever been to Gudur.

9. Since the 1930s there has been a tendency in both the anglophone and francophone literatures to attribute to Gudur a political and religious importance that we regard as unjustified. Description of Gudur as a "pagan Mecca" (Shaw 1935) or of the clients of Bay Gudal as "pilgrims" invokes a model that is fundamentally misleading – but we cannot argue this in detail here (David in press).

10. Seignobos (1991a:254) places the apogee of Gudur considerably earlier at the end of the sixteenth and start of the seventeenth century. No reason is given for the change in Seignobos (2000a).

11. We do *not* claim that all those clans and communities that claim a Gudur origin necessarily form part of the nineteenth century diaspora that resulted from the Fulbe conquest. Migration, often at a micro-scale, is a normal process in and around the Mandara mountains, and some Gudur-descended groups to the west of Gudur may have been there considerably longer. Historical research is required to define the situation more precisely. It would, for example, seem likely that the Gudur connections claimed by groups located to the south and east of Gudur (Gisiga, Mundang, and others) mostly antedate the nineteenth-century diaspora.

12. See Sterner (2003) for further discussion of Kopytoff's frontier thesis.

13. The term also means ancestor or spirit or a sacrifice to ancestors (Barreteau 1988). Podlewski (1966:89) also witnessed Bay Takwaw pray to his ancestors for rain.

14. Whether in fact this room is a "focus of religious activities," as we believe is the case, or rather a Pandora's box remains uncertain. The chief of the northern Mafa Vreke polity, who claims Gudur descent, possesses a similarly closed room, which he informed Nicholas David was "full of snakes and diseases." In either case, its ideological significance is clear.

15. Seignobos (2000b:111, 112) mentions shortages and famines in northern Cameroon in the years: 1890–93, 1903–04, 1912–14, 1921–27; the locust invasion of 1933 was the most devastating in forty years.

16 The region had been part of German Kamerun until 1916. In 1919 it was partitioned between Great Britain and France. The League of Nations Mandate did not formally come into effect until 1922 (Barkindo 1985:37).

17 J. Hunter Shaw (1935) also states that in 1931 contributions were made at Sukur to make an iron door to shut in all the locusts. Other communities (Fali, Cheke, Margi, and Kilba) contributed. In 1934 the chief of Sukur collected one penny from all adult males to be sent Gudur to drive out the locusts (Kulp 1935). MacBride (1937:3–4) also wrote of the "sacrifice of thanksgiving" initiated by the chief of Sukur in 1936 when the locust invasions were coming to an end: "a cock to be killed for every male and an egg to be crushed between thigh and belly by every woman. This sacrifice was performed in most of the villages of the Mandara District and in many of the Mubi villages as well.... The result was an unprecedented shortage of eggs and chickens during the first six months of 1936."

18 Jouaux (1989:277–78) discusses the locust sacrifice (*kuley nga jaray*) in reference to the relationship between Masuwa and the chief of Gudur. While, for her, the latter is the uncontested "master" of the locust sacrifice, the Masuwa of Gudal's role in carrying it out is crucial; the Masuwa of Zidim provide the sacrificial victims.

19 Podlewski (1966:89) states regarding the site: "il faut s'enfoncer bien loin au coeur de massifs caparaçonnés d'immenses dalles désertiques (les cultures y sont interdites); là se trouvent des excavations, aujourd'hui celées et surmontées de poteries, qui auraient été le point de départ des invasions d'acridiens locales."

20 Seignobos (1991a:247–48) states that there are some twenty upturned pots – he is referring to the large beer brewing and storage jars – amongst a "chaos" of potsherds and tripod pots. The larger storage pots (those with bodies flaring from a narrower base) are made by the wives of the Mogura smiths. Mogura are a clan of the smith/potter caste affiliated with the Masuwa (Seignobos 1991a:253).

21 Strümpell's account conflates the doorless room at Yideng Bay, the medicine given by Bay Gudal to envoys from other communities, and the protection offered by the sacrifice at the locust shrine.

22 It seems more probable that the chief sent the horse for sacrifice as it is elsewhere stated that the chief of Gudal never visits the locust shrine.

23 The ancestral shrines and the rain stones of Gudal have been housed successively at Yideng Bay, a chiefly residence on the mountain above it and now in the small compound below where Bay Takwaw's successor as customary (but not administrative) chief lives.

24 The practice may be regarded as magical in that the liquid was believed to have a physical effect. In this it was more comparable to a homeopathic medicine in which the active ingredient is diluted to an infinitesimal amount than to the wine distributed at a Christian communion.

REFERENCES

Barkindo, Bawuro Mubi. 1985. "The Mandara Astride the Nigeria-Cameroon Boundary." In *Partitioned Africans: Ethnic Relations across Africa's International Boundaries 1884–1984*, ed. A. I. Asiwaju, 29–49. London: C. Hurst & Co.

Barreteau, Daniel. 1988. *Description du Mofu-Gudur: Langue de la famille tchadique parlée au Cameroun. Livre I – Phonologie; Livre II – Lexique*. Paris: ORSTOM.

———. 1999. "Les Mofu-Gudur et leurs criquets." In *L'homme et l'animal dans le bassin du lac Tchad*, ed. Catherine Baroin and Jean Boutrais, 133–69. Paris: Éditions IRD.

Barreteau, Daniel, Liliane Sorin, and A. Bayo Mana. 1985. La poterie chez les Mofu-Gudur: des gestes, des formes et des mots. Mimeo Mss, Paris: ORSTOM.

Beauvilain, Alain. 1989. *Nord-Cameroun: Crises et peuplement*, 2 vols. Alain Beauvilain.

Boutrais, Jean. 1987. *Mbozo-Wazan : Peuls et montagnards au nord Cameroun*. Paris: ORSTOM.

Colson, Elizabeth. 1997. "Places of Power and Shrines of the Land." *Paideuma* 43:47–57.

David, Nicholas. 1990. *Vessels of the Spirits: Pots and People in North Cameroon*. 50 mins. Calgary: Department of Commmunications Media, University of Calgary.

———. 1998. "The Ethnoarchaeology and Field Archaeology of Grinding at Sukur, Adamawa State, Nigeria." *African Archaeological Review* 15, no. 1:13–63.

———. In press. "La chefferie de Gudur (Monts Mandara, Cameroun) : une hypothèse minimaliste." In *Migrations et mobilite spatiale dans le bassin du lac Tchad (Actes du 13ᵉ Colloque Méga-Tchad, Maroua, 31 octobre – 2 novembre, 2005)*, ed. Henry Tourneux.

David, Nicholas, and Carol Kramer. 2001. *Ethnoarchaeology in Action*. Cambridge: Cambridge University Press.

David, Nicholas, and Judith Sterner. 1995. "Constructing a Historical Ethnography of Sukur, Part I: Demystification." *Nigerian Heritage* 4:11–33.

———. 1996. "Constructing a Historical Ethnography of Sukur, Part II: Iron and the 'Classless Industrial' Society." *Nigerian Heritage* 5:11–33.

———. 1999. "Wonderful Society: the Burgess Shale Creatures, Mandara Chiefdoms and the Nature of Prehistory." In *Beyond Chiefdoms: Pathways to Complexity in Africa*, ed. Susan K. McIntosh, 97–109. Cambridge: Cambridge University Press.

———. 2005. "The Dur Xidis of Sukur." Web page. Available at http://www.sukur.info/Soc/Xidis.htm.

David, Nicholas, Judith Sterner, and Kodzo B. Gavua. 1988. "Why Pots are Decorated." *Current Anthropology* 29, no. 3:365–89.

de Lauwe, Paul-Henri. 1937. "Pierres et poteries sacrées du Mandara (Cameroun)." *Journal de la Société des Africanistes* 7:53–67 (+ plates).

Fardon, Richard. 1990. *Between God, the Dead and the Wild: Chamba Interpretations of Ritual and Religion*. Washington: Smithsonian Institution Press.

Jouaux, Catherine. 1991. "La chefferie de Gudur et sa politique expansionniste." In *Du politique à l'économique : Études historiques dans le bassin du lac Tchad*, ed. Jean Boutrais, 193–224. Collection Colloques et Séminaires. Paris: ORSTOM.

Jouaux, Catherine. 1989. "Gudur: chefferie ou Royaume?" *Cahiers d'études africaines* 114, no. 29-2:259–88.

Kopytoff, Igor. 1971. "Ancestors as Elders." *Africa* 41:120–42.

———. 1987. "The Internal African Frontier: The Making of African Political Culture." In *The African Frontier: The Reproduction of Traditional African Societies*, ed. Igor Kopytoff, 3–84. Bloomington: Indiana University Press.

Kulp, H. Stover. 1935. "Notes Taken on a Tour in Madagali District in Company with the Touring Officer, Mr W.R. Shirley, June 14–22." National Archives of Nigeria, Kaduna, Yolaprof J21.

Lavergne, Georges. 1943. "Rapport sur 5 tournées N°173." 1943. APA 11876/J, Archives nationales, Yaoundé.

MacBride, D.F.H. "1937. Mandara District: Village Histories." National Archives of Nigeria, Kaduna, Yolaprof J21.

Mather, Charles M. 1999. An Ethnoarchaeology of Kusasi Shrines, Upper East Region, Ghana. PhD dissertation, Calgary: University of Calgary.

Mohammadou, Eldridge. 1988. *Les lamidats du Diamaré et du Mayo-Louti au XIXe siècle (Nord Cameroun)*. Tokyo: Institute for the Study of Languages and Cultures of Asia and Africa.

Müller-Kosack, Gerhard. 2003. *The Way of the Beer: Ritual Re-Enactment of History among the Mafa, Terrace Farmers of the Mandara Mountains (North Cameroon)*. London: Mandaras Publishing.

Podlewski, André M. 1966. *La dynamique des principales populations du Nord-Cameroun (entre Benoué et lac Tchad)*. Cahiers ORSTOM, Série Sciences Humaines, III, 4. Paris: ORSTOM.

Seignobos, Christian. 1991a. "La forge et le pouvoir dans le bassin du lac Tchad ou du roi-forgeron au forgeron-fossoyeur." In *Forges et forgerons (Actes du 4e Colloque Méga-Tchad, 1988, Vol. 1)*, ed. Yves Moñino, 383–84. Paris: ORSTOM.

———. 1991b. "La rayonnement de la chefferie théocratique de Gudur (Nord-Cameroun)." In *Du politique a l'économique: Études historiques dans le bassin du lac Tchad*, ed. Jean Boutrais, 225–315. Paris: ORSTOM.

———. 1995. "Données historiques." In *Terroir de Mowo : Saturation foncière et émigration*. Olivier Iyébi-Mandjek, and Christian Seignobos, 69–78 (+ figure and table). MINAGRI (Département Paysanal et Gestion de Terroirs)/SODECOTON/ORSTOM, Yaoundé.

———. 2000a. "Aliments de famine : répartition et stratégies d'utilisation." In *Atlas de la province de l'extrême-nord du Cameroun*, compiled by Christian Seignobos and Olivier Iyébi-Mandjek, 111–14. Paris: Minrest, Cameroun, and Éditions de l'IRD.

———. 2000b. "Mise en place du peuplement et répartition ethnique." In *Atlas de la province de l'extrême-nord du Cameroun*, compiled by Christian Seignobos and Olivier Iyébi-Mandjek, 44–51. Paris: Éditions de l'IRD and Minrest, Cameroun.

Shaw, J. Hunter. 1935. "Madagali District." 1935. National Archives Nigeria, Kaduna, NAK 17/3 25073 (3947).

Smith, Adam, and Nicholas David. 1995. "The Production of Space and the House of Xidi Sukur." *Current Anthropology* 36, no. 3:441–71.

Sterner, Judith. 1989a. "Sirak Household Ritual." In *Households and Community*, ed. A. Scott MacEachern, Richard D. Garvin, and David J. W. Archer, 22–27. Calgary: Chacmool.

———. 1989b. "Who is Signalling Whom? Ceramic Style, Ethnicity and Taphonomy among the Sirak Bulahay." *Antiquity* 63, no. 240:451–59.

———. 1992. "Sacred Pots and 'Symbolic Reservoirs' in the Mandara Highlands of Northern Cameroon." In *An African Commitment: Papers in Honour of Peter Lewis Shinnie*, ed. Judith Sterner and Nicholas David, 171–79. Calgary: University of Calgary Press.

———. 1995. "Life and Death in Mandara Ceramics." In *Mort et rites funéraires dans le bassin du lac Tchad (Séminaire du Réseau Méga-Tchad, ORSTOM Bondy, du 12 au 14 septembre, 1990)*, ed. Catherine Baroin, Daniel Barreteau, and Charlotte von Graffenried, 63–74. Paris: ORSTOM.

———. 2002. "Potters of the Mandara Mountains." *Ceramics Technical* 15:14–21.

———. 2003. *The Ways of the Mandara Mountains: A Comparative Regional Approach*. Cologne: Rüdiger Köppe.

Sterner, Judith, and Nicholas David. 1991. "Gender and Caste in the Mandara Highlands: Northeastern Nigeria and Northern Cameroon." *Ethnology* 30, no. 4:355–69.

———. 2003. "Action on Matter: the History of the Uniquely African Tamper and Concave Anvil Pot-Forming Technique." *Journal of African Archaeology* 1, no. 1:3–38.

Strümpell, Kurt F. 1922–23. "Wörterverzeichnis der Heidensprachen des Mandara Gebirges (Adamaua)." *Zeitschrift für Eingeborenen-Sprachen* 13:47–74; 109–49.

van Beek, Walter E. 1981. A. "Les Kapsiki." In *Contribution de la recherche ethnologique à l'histoire des civilisations du Cameroun*, 2 vols., ed. Claude Tardits, 1:113–19. Colloques Internationaux du Centre Nationale de la Recherche Scientifique, 551. Paris: CNRS.

Wade, James H. 1997. "Rainmakers and the Problematics of Power in Fali Society." In *L'homme et l'eau dans le bassin du lac Tchad (Séminaire du Réseau Méga-Tchad, J.W. Goethe-Universität, 13–14 Mai, 1993)*, ed. Herrmann Jungraithmayr, Daniel Barreteau, and Uwe Siebert, 271–84. Proc. Seminar des Internationalen Forschungsnetzes Mega-Tschad, Paris: ORSTOM.

Walker, W. H., and L. J. Lucero. 2000. "The Depositional History of Ritual and Power." In *Agency in Archaeology*, ed. M.-A. Dobres and J. Robb, 130–47. London: Routledge.

The Archaeology of Shrines among the Tallensi of Northern Ghana: Materiality and Interpretive Relevance

TIMOTHY INSOLL (UNIVERSITY OF MANCHESTER),
BENJAMIN KANKPEYENG (UNIVERSITY OF GHANA, LEGON),
AND RACHEL MACLEAN (UNIVERSITY OF MANCHESTER)

ABSTRACT

The material culture of the Tallensi is, comparatively speaking, somewhat analytically neglected in comparison to the wealth of ethnographic material available. The present paper seeks to redress this dearth of archaeological data by focusing on the history of a particular Tallensi shrine in the Tongo Hills of northern Ghana. Shrines, especially in the West African context, appear to serve as symbolic repositories of information and shared understanding about regional social processes, and ethnohistory and archaeological excavation of shrines and associated material culture can reveal much about settlement patterns, resource utilization, and ethnicity.

Keywords: Tallensi, shrines, materiality, Tongo Hills, Ghana.

INTRODUCTION

The Tallensi of northern Ghana are well known via the seminal anthropological studies of Meyer Fortes (e.g., 1967, 1969, 1987). Fortes provides a wealth of detail on, for instance, kinship and aspects of Tallensi religion and ritual practice in relation to ancestor worship and to a lesser extent shrines. However, his functionalist approach means that Tallensi material culture is comparatively neglected, as is the historical dimension of their existence. The net result is that the Tallensi are, to a certain extent, 'fossilized' in time, or as cogently put by Allman and Parker (2005:38–39), "marooned on the margins of a distant hinterland in a timeless ethnographic present." The study by Allman and Parker, just cited, attempts to redress this ahistorical portrait of the Tallensi primarily through the consideration of the history of one shrine, Tonna'ab or Yaane. In so doing, the anthropology of the Tallensi has thus been recently supplemented by historical study.

However, the limitations of the historical record in relation to the Tallensi, as indeed to that of most of the ethnic groups of northern Ghana (and, indeed, in surrounding areas) are obvious, where written history begins almost exclusively with European contacts at the end of the nineteenth to early twentieth century (see Allman and Parker 2005). The occasional reference in Arabic historical sources might exist (Insoll 2003), but not seemingly to the Tallensi, and in overall terms these historical sources are very sparse. Thus it is surprising that, until the start of an ongoing research project begun in 2004 (Insoll et al. 2004, 2005), no archaeological research had been completed in the Tongo Hills, the epicentre of Tallensi settlement, beyond an ethnoarchaeological study of Tallensi house compounds (Gabrilopoulos 1995) and an inventory of cultural heritage completed by one of the present authors (Kankpeyeng 2001).

Partly in an effort to redress this disciplinary imbalance, the archaeological research project described here was begun, with three seasons of excavations and survey completed so far (Insoll et al. 2004, 2005). The primary aims of this research are various and include:

- To reconstruct the sequence of occupation in the Tongo Hills.
- To obtain ceramics that could be compared to those recovered from excavations previously completed in Gambaga, the capital of Mamprugu and currently being prepared for publication (Kense 1992;

K. Fowler pers. comm.).
- To evaluate varying perceptions of landscape as manifest by different interest groups, ages, and genders.
- To evaluate the archaeology of African traditional religions through excavation in extant shrines and via recording of other aspects of Tallensi material culture.

Answers to these research objectives are of course only partial and preliminary. But by way of brief summary, excavations in a rock shelter, Gbegbeya Veug (Hyena's Cave) have provided stratified quartz lithic assemblages without accompanying ceramics (Insoll et al. 2005). This is seemingly indicative of occupation of the Tongo Hills during the Late Stone Age but this occupation as yet remains undated. Obviously, no connection can be or is postulated with the Tallensi for this period. This point is significant for Tallensi oral tradition describes a two-fold division of their society of seemingly comparatively recent origin, with the Talis as the autochthonous inhabitants of the area who, "sprung from the earth itself" (Fortes 1987:43). In contrast, the Namoos, the inhabitants of Tongo, a settlement just northeast of the Tongo Hills, trace their origins to Mamprugu. The latter is an area (and a chiefdom) associated with the Mamprusi ethnic group, situated about thirty kilometres southeast of the Tongo Hills, and on top of the Gambaga Escarpment (see Fig. 1) (Drucker-Brown 1975; Kankpeyeng 2001:23).

The migration of the Namoos and postulated Mamprugu connections in the traditions give rise to the second research objective outlined above. But when exactly this migration occurred is difficult to reconstruct. Archaeology can contribute little until the comparative ceramics analysis made feasible by the large assemblage of ceramics recovered during the recent excavations is complete (see below; Ashley 2006). Fortes (1987:43) records that local traditions suggest the immigration from Mamprugu occurred some fourteen to fifteen generations ago (presumably with a base line of the 1930s–1940s, the era of his primary field research), which perhaps could be construed as constituting a three-hundred-year time-span, allowing twenty years per generation, and thus providing a date of circa the mid-seventeenth century. However, this should be treated with caution.

This paper primarily relates to the final research objective, i.e., the archaeological manifestation of African traditional religions with particular

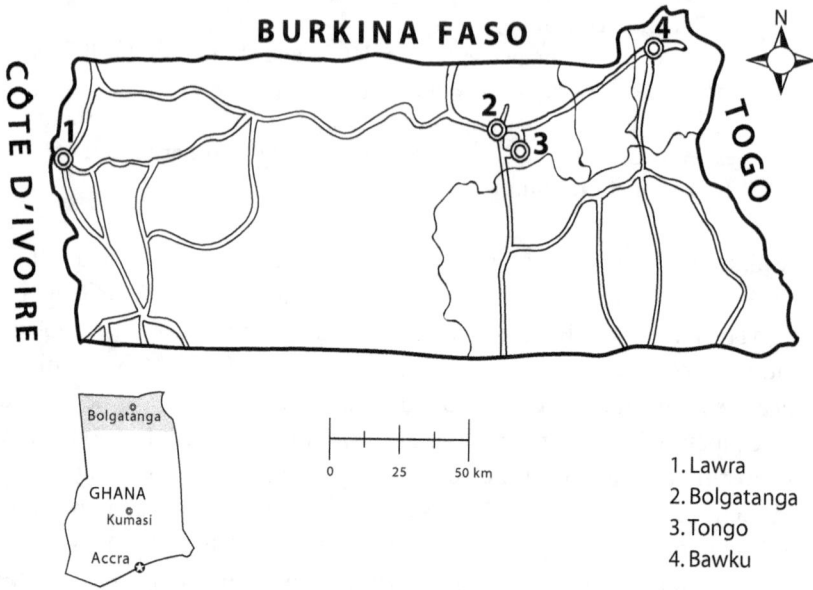

Fig. 1. The location of the Tongo Hills in northern Ghana.

reference here to shrines, but it also connects with the third objective in challenging assumptions that can underpin the meaning of concepts such as 'nature' in archaeological interpretation (Insoll 2007a).

SHRINES, ARCHAEOLOGY, AND THE LANDSCAPE

Shrines dominate the landscape of the Tongo Hills. This domination operates both conceptually in the importance accorded the shrines by the Tallensi, and also practically in the restrictions imposed on their access, which impinges upon the landscape as a whole. In this context it is important to note, before proceeding further, that besides the formal research clearance obtained from the official Ghanaian state research agencies and their representatives, shrine access was also negotiated both with the relevant local communities and with the shrines and their custodians, primarily via the agency of sacrifice.

Innumerable shrines exist in the Tongo Hills, but three shrines dominate: Tonna'ab/Yaane, Bonaab, and Nyoo. Of these Nyoo is perhaps of primary interest to the archaeologist, as shall become apparent, it being a large 'sacred grove' functioning as an earth shrine and of further significance in being used annually as a dancing ground at some point from late February to early April during the pre-agricultural Gologo or Golib festival (Fortes 1987:34; Kankpeyeng 2001:26). It is also, seemingly, the shrine that has been most neglected by other observers, in favour of either Tonna'ab/Yaane (e.g., Allman and Parker 2005), or Bonaab (Fortes 1969). In terms of function of the other two major shrines, Tonna'ab, a rock shelter, is described as "paramount among the earth shrines" by Kankpeyeng (2001:24) but as one of the "great ancestor shrines" or "bo'a" by Allman and Parker (2005:80). Notwithstanding this major difference in opinion as to function, Tonna'ab is of importance as a shrine that abhors evil, is good at identifying witches (Allman and Parker 2005:6), and is both benevolent and curative (Kankpeyeng 2001:24), especially with regard to infertility; hence, its power is widely recognized, and thus it is a shrine that is extensively 'franchised' via the movement of powerful objects such as lithics associated with the shrine (Insoll 2006). Bonaab, however, is essentially another sacred grove and a shrine that is understood to have "benevolent, protective and curative" properties (Kankpeyeng 2001:24).

These shrines represent the two primary strands of Tallensi religion, as described by Fortes (1987), i.e., the earth and ancestral cults. Ancestral worship functions on various levels. Each segment of a Talis composite clan has a lineage shrine to distinguish it from other segments and to which they sacrifice individually (Fortes 1967:6). Contrasting with this, groups of maximal lineages belonging to different clans (but not necessarily united by ties of clanship) collaborate "in the cult of their collective ancestors" (Fortes 1967:6) via joint sacrifice. Materially, the ancestral cult is represented by the ancestral shrine, which can be manifest in various ways, as a household shrine, or in an external shrine such as a sacred grove or cave (Kankpeyeng 2001), but involving ritual practices that have no specialist priests (Fortes 1987:150). The latter, however, are specifically involved in the earth cult, for this is linked with specialist priests, the Tendaana, the "custodian of the earth" (Fortes 1987:43), and is materially manifest through sacred places, *ten*, within which are located the earth shrines, *tengbana*, which the priests serve.

Permission was granted for all three shrines, Nyoo, Tonna'ab, and Bonaab, to be surveyed to varying degrees. The potential for the application of archaeology in further understanding Tallensi shrines was immediately evident, for the results obtained via a survey within Nyoo were striking, as initially, both at a distance and walking within it, the Nyoo shrine seemed like a natural place – albeit a denuded sacred grove. But this was not so, for far-spreading archaeological vestiges visible on the surface clearly indicated that this was in fact an extensive enshrined archaeological site divided into a series of different zones. These included a 'field' of standing stones, an area of stone arrangements with an associated spread of pottery covering some three hundred metres east to west, and an active sacrificial area lacking such overt archaeological features. Furthermore, test excavations completed in 2005 confirmed that this was not a 'natural' sacred grove with, for example, the pottery spread seen to be formed of both complete pottery vessels and shards that had been forced into the ground to a maximum depth of thirty centimetres, and thus seemingly representative of an act of structured 'ritual' deposition (Insoll et al. 2005).

Hence Nyoo was made the focus of two large area excavations completed in July 2006 and undertaken in order to better understand what was represented by these spreads of archaeological material within the shrine, and to further assess whether they had any connection with contemporary Tallensi ritual practices.

NYOO 06 (A). The first of these units was assigned the code NYOO 06 (A) and measured 8m x 4m (N10°40'31.0" W000°48'39.2"). As observed in the 2005 test pit (NYOO 05 [A]), only shallow archaeological layers were encountered with a maximum depth of ca.15–20 cm before sterile deposits were reached. This noted, the matrix that was removed was densely filled with archaeological material, predominantly shards, many from complete vessels apparently broken in situ, but also containing an assemblage of 35 lithic objects comprising predominantly stone grinder–pounder–rubbers, both fragmentary, and complete, but also lumps of quartz. Five small pieces of both vitreous and tap slag, two iron points and one iron finger ring were also recovered. A definite increase in density in pottery present was also evident towards the southern end of the trench, i.e., where it incorporated the test pit, NYOO 05 (A), which had been almost wholly filled with pottery (Insoll et al. 2005) (see Fig. 2).

Fig. 2. NYOO 06 (A). The 2005 test pit is to the left of the photo where the density of pottery is greater (Photo: T. Insoll).

Fig. 3. Demarcated stone arrangements after the pot filled layer was removed (Photo: T. Insoll).

Interspersed amongst the pot-filled deposits were seven stone arrangements (see Fig. 3). Originally, it was thought that these might represent cairns, but this idea was discarded on the basis that the stone arrangements were almost entirely composed of a single layer of stones. There was no significance apparent in the numbers of stones composing the arrangements, which ranged between 16 and 51. However, care had definitely been taken in the arrangements of the stones, possibly with some concern evident as to the colour-patterning of the aplite (fine-grained granite), Bongo granite, and schist present. The colours red, pink, black, and grey were noted, with white represented by smaller fragments of quartz frequently found, as well as by the banding in some of the granite. In so doing, this could potentially be a further manifestation of the oft-noted red–white–black colour symbolism evident in sub-Saharan Africa (Jacobsen-Widding 1979; Turner 1985).

Removal of the stone arrangements and excavation below one of these (SA 1) to a depth of 45 cm produced very little material in comparison to the infill between them – 'Infill' here being the right term to use, as it would appear that the pots were deposited after the stones had been arranged. The dates of neither the stone arrangements nor the pottery filled layer are known, pending the results of thermoluminescence dating in progress at the Oxford University Research Laboratory for Archaeology and the History of Art.

The precise function of the stone arrangements and pot infill is also unclear, though the oft-misused term 'ritual' (Insoll 2004) would here seem entirely justified. Working hypotheses can, however, be proposed. Firstly, the random arrangements of the shards in the infill layer and the inclusion of the smashed complete or nearly complete vessels would seem to preclude their description as potsherd pavements of the type found elsewhere in West Africa (e.g., Shaw 1978). At Ife in Nigeria, for instance, the shards forming the pavement were often set in the ground on their edge in herringbone designs (Shaw 1978), as opposed to the random patterning evident in Nyoo.

Rather, what might be represented by the ceramics (and other materials) in this feature at Nyoo are communal ritual activities, possibly even one deposition event involving a lot of people and pottery. Preliminary indications with regard to the pottery assemblage indicate little variability with a standard range of vessel types found (Ashley 2006), supporting the hypothesis that repeat deposition over a long period of time is not represented. The absence of any contextual difference also supports this idea of a single or at least a rapid deposition event. However, the gradation in density of pottery present (already remarked upon) indicates that a simplistic uniform infilling around the stone arrangements did not take place.

What the deposition of the pot and other materials might represent or be associated with is unclear. Various suggestions can be made, with perhaps the most compelling being that it might broadly function within the framework of commemorating or supplicating the ancestors or deceased, although the absence of funerary remains precludes a direct link with the dead. This interpretation would seem plausible based upon broad parallels elsewhere, less so, perhaps, with Tallensi practices today, but certainly reminiscent of, for instance, the Akan Asensie, or 'place of pots' (Bellis 1982) – a point qualified with the proviso that direct Akan connections are not being proposed, just generic parallels suggested. The deliberate destruction of some of the pots, with holes forced, bored, or chipped in their bases, for example, might support this association with the ancestors or deceased, an interpretation lent further weight by the results of the excavations in NYOO 06 (B) discussed below.

Furthermore, based upon observations of contemporary practices in Nyoo Biil, the shrine associated with the Golib festival, it is possible that the stone arrangements served as meeting or assembly places perhaps utilized during important rituals or festivals. Very similar stone arrangements are used in Nyoo Biil when each elder, chief, or priest has their specific known seating place on one of the stones. Such arrangements are also found outside some contemporary Tallensi compounds, as at the house of Yiran, the caretaker of Yaane. However, the previous hypothesis advanced (Insoll et al. 2005) that NYOO 05 (A) was part of a putative village site (and thus by inference so would NYOO 06 [A] have been) now seems much less probable based on the density of the stone arrangements, the absence of other domestic indicators (in comparison with the settlement site recorded during the survey and described above, for example), and the parallels with contemporary ritual sites just described.

Although it is unwise at this preliminary stage to advance too far in interpretation, it can again tentatively be suggested that, based on contemporary parallels, what might also be represented by the stone arrangements at Nyoo is the residue of movement, perhaps dance. Again, during the ritual activities observed at Nyoo Biil, dance around and between the

Fig. 4. Tallensi elders seated on a similar stone arrangement during dances associated with the Golib/Gologo festival (Photo: T. Insoll).

Fig. 5. NYOO 06 (B). Standing stones and associated pots (Photo: T. Insoll).

stone arrangements was seen to be a key part of the Golib festival (see Fig. 4). That such activities might also have occurred in the area of stone arrangements excavated in Nyoo would not seem inconceivable considering the contemporary parallels with existing Tallensi practices.

NYOO 06 (B). The second unit excavated was likewise placed adjacent to a test pit completed in 2005, NYOO 05 (A). This unit of 6 x 4 metres was situated within the area of Nyoo most densely clustered with standing stones so as to attempt to gain an insight into their meaning and purpose (N10°40'32.8" W000°48'39.8"). In total 12 clusters of either paired or single standing stones were recorded (see Fig. 5). Shallow surface cleaning of 1–2 centimetres depth almost immediately encountered groups of iron bracelets and points that had been placed adjacent to the standing stones. Ultimately, eight complete iron bracelets, seven iron bracelet fragments, one iron finger ring, five iron points, and two fragments of iron strip were recovered. The bracelets were almost uniformly of simple design and their presence was described as representing the interring of 'personal gods' associated with the dead, i.e., intimate personal possessions, possibly following the instructions of diviners to carry out such actions (R. Naatoam pers. comm.).

This would broadly concur with Fortes (1987:267) description of the notion of *sii* and its links with concepts of the person – personhood – and personal possessions. Specifically, "*sii*, therefore, in one of its aspects, is the focus, one might almost say the medium, of personal identity which is objectively represented in possessions characteristic of a person's sex and status" (Fortes 1987:267). Such possessions as described by Fortes (1987) included the individual's clothing, and for a woman her personal ornaments such as brass bracelets and beadwork, and for a man, his tools such as the hoe and axe, or bow and arrow. Iron bracelets would and could certainly constitute such a category of intimate personal possessions, of precise ontological status and association, even if we cannot go so far as to interpret which gender and/or age or initiation status might have been linked with these artefacts.

The function of, and meaning behind, the presence of the iron points is less immediately obvious. They could have served a variety of purposes, but based upon contemporary analogy and the context of discovery, they could also have been used for ritual purposes. This interpretation might be lent support by the ritual pots recovered beneath and adjacent to each of the standing stones (see below). An association between similar pots and

Fig. 6. Iron bracelet and points in situ (Photo: T. Insoll).
Fig. 7. Contemporary diviners supports and pot from NYOO 06 (B) 4 (Photo: T. Insoll).

iron points exists today in certain divining rituals, where the iron points are used as supports for the pots (H. Goldaan pers. comm.).

Interspersed with the iron objects were ceramic shards, and seven either fragmentary or complete granite or schist pounder–rubber–grinders and two white quartz lumps, as well as a small fragment of red ochre, and another of slag. Both the number of pounder–rubber–grinders found and the density of ceramics was less than that recorded in NYOO 06 (A), though the lithics and ceramics were otherwise of the same types. Considering the evidence from both NYOO 06 (A) and NYOO 06 (B) in totality, it would appear that distinct differences in ritual practice are indicated in the various areas of the Nyoo shrine. This is manifest both in the excavated materials recovered and in the surface features previously recorded.

This notion of differential ritual practices across Nyoo is lent further support by two pear-shaped clay objects, broken but still conjoining, which were uncovered in association with a complete pot (NYOO 06 [B] 4 – D4). The standing stone that this pot had almost certainly been associated with no longer survived, though some of its stone packing was still seemingly in place adjacent to and above the pot (see Fig. 8). These clay objects (or object, as they had been joined) had a hole in each of the two pear-shaped segments (see Fig. 9). Again, providing a precise interpretation as to what this object was used for is impossible, and opinions sought from community members varied, though generally consensus existed in that it was:

a) A ritual object.
b) Probably offered libation and/or sacrifice (hence the holes).
c) Functioned as a 'personal god.'

That this object might have functioned within the context, perhaps, of fertility concerns or rituals would be entirely plausible, if unproven. Their actual shape, 'pear-shaped,' being a somewhat neutral description, is reminiscent of a pair of testicles, and, if correct, a fertility association would thus not seem unwarranted. Direct parallels have not been found, though Preston Blier (1987:48) refers to small earthern balls that are produced by the Batammaliba midwife following the birth of a child. These are made around the infant's birth sack "as a symbol of the creative process" (Preston Blier 1987:119). No such meaning is proposed for the Nyoo object, and

Fig. 8. Clay ritual object in context (Photo: T. Insoll).

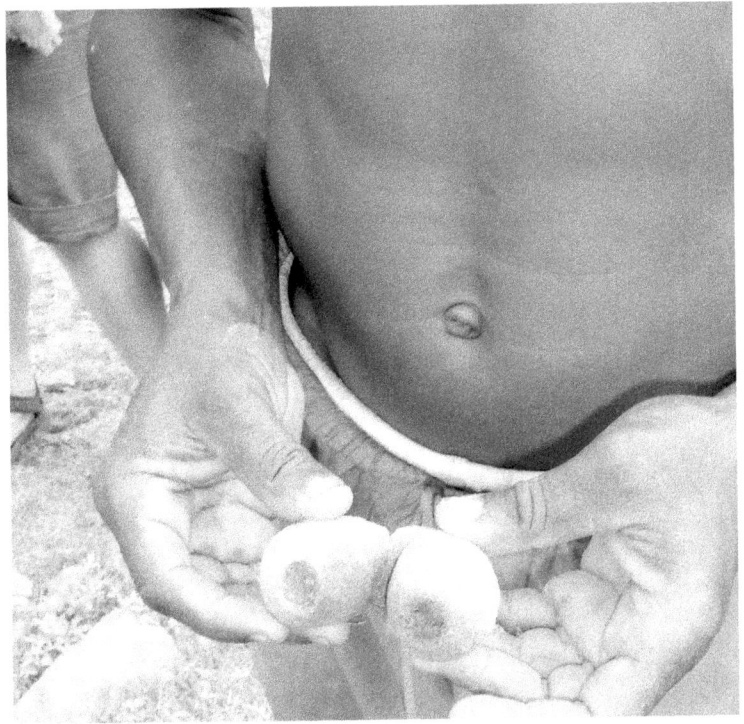

Fig. 9. The clay ritual object (Photo: T. Insoll).

the latter is not even a ball shape, but it does indicate the ritual use of clay to produce generically similar ritual objects by a linguistically related group from Togo.

Ultimately from context NYOO 06 [B] 5, thirteen complete and one partially complete pots were recovered. Fourteen of these were left in situ, below and slightly adjacent to their standing stones, and in three other instances had been removed before this association had become clear, as described (see Fig. 5). Eleven of these vessels were capped with large potsherds forming a sort of lid, and the forms of the vessels varied, indicating that a uniform suite of material culture was not being ritually interred. Of the thirteen complete vessels left in situ, two were Short Collar Necked Jars (see Fig. 10), nine Flared Mouth Bowls, one a Spherical or Flared Mouth Bowl (the lid made precise attribution difficult), and one a Hemispherical

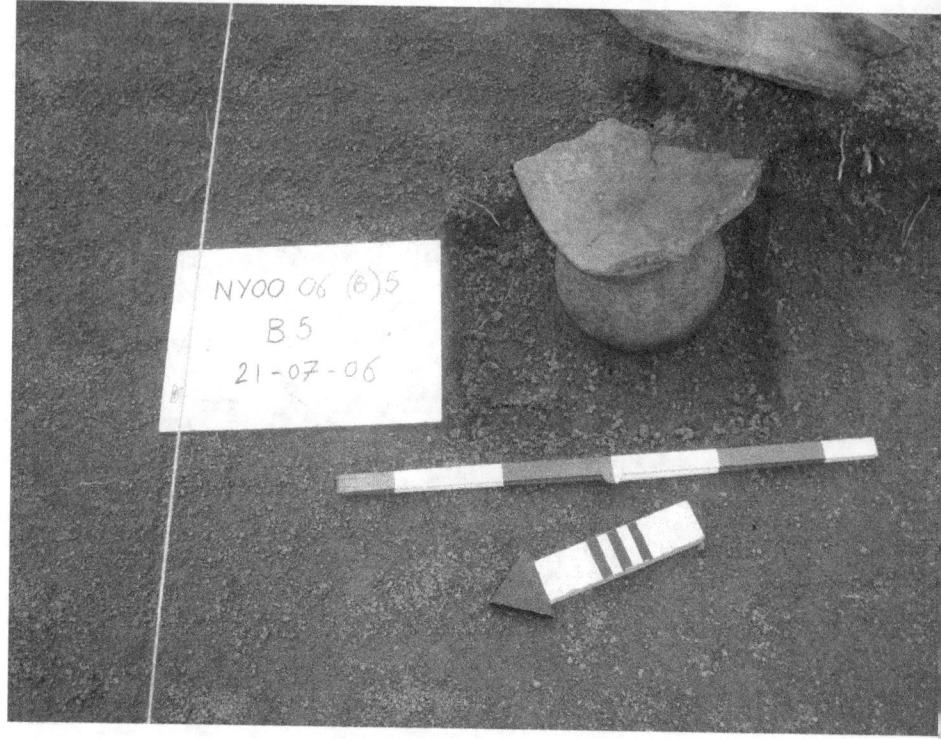

Fig. 10. Example of 'ritual' vessel (Short Collar Neck Jar with lid) (Photo: T. Insoll).

Bowl. No trace of pits associated with the deposition of these pots was found and they were located at a depth (to the top of their lids or rims) from the ground surface of between 12 and 23.5 centimetres. The position of the pots in relation to the standing stones also varied and no meaningful cardinal orientation could be reconstructed, other than, perhaps, a certain propensity for a northern position.

The ritual nature of the deposits in this area of Nyoo was thus firmly indicated by the discovery of these pots – fact confirmed during a visit to NYOO 06 (B) by a group of Tallensi elders led by the Assemblyman, John Bawa Zuure. The ensuing discussion was useful for interpretive purposes in indicating that the specific associations between, for example, the iron bracelets, standing stones, and pots was unknown; they did not resemble contemporary practices, but the general meanings were that they were linked into negotiating destiny via the agency of 'personal gods' and functioned within the framework of ancestral worship, with perhaps the key point being that Nyoo should be considered as the great shrine for all the Tallensi, where worship started and spread from (J.B. Zuure pers. comm.). It could thus in effect be called a reservoir or nucleus of ritual practice and is broadly analogous to the notion of "symbolic reservoirs" as discussed by Sterner (1992:171–72; and see MacEachern 1994), but 'symbol' would here be translated into 'ritual.'

Following the visit of the elders, and in accordance with local wishes, no further pots were removed, and the fourteen vessels left in situ were ultimately reburied when the site was backfilled. However, prior to backfilling in order to assess whether human burials at a greater depth were also associated with the pots and standing stones (this had been thought unlikely by the elders), a test pit was excavated. No archaeological material was recovered from below a depth of 40 centimetres (and no human remains), and only a few shards of pottery from above this, again demonstrating the shallow nature of deposits across the site.

Tonna'ab and Bonaab

Thus the archaeological importance of Nyoo was well attested to by the results of the excavations in clearly indicating complex ritual activities no longer practised within the shrine. Yet its past importance is at variance with its contemporary position in terms of, for example, external revenue generation, which is little or nothing in comparison to Tonna'ab and to a lesser extent Bonaab. As already noted, Tonna'ab is a source of considerable revenue, being known as "Nana Tongo" to southern, e.g., Akan, pilgrims (Allman and Parker 2005:154–63), for reasons described previously. However, Tonna'ab has, again in contrast to Nyoo, a much lesser archaeological fingerprint, being formed of a rock shelter with an associated range of ritual paraphernalia (see Fig. 11). Thus the complexity of the shrines is indicated in their evident differences, and in the fact that size does not necessarily correlate with greater importance. But the recurring element shared between Nyoo and Tongnaab (the situation in Bonaab is less clear for full access was not permitted to the central area of this shrine) is that both shrines involve relationships with the past, i.e., with archaeological sites and associated material culture.

This has already been described for Nyoo. At Tonna'ab such a relationship is evident in the use of the rock shelter as the shrine, part of a gallery of such shelters running along the low hill in which the shrine is situated. Within the rockshelter, the inclusion of, for example, a large thickly potted storage vessel, not of a type used today and linked with the 'ancestors' by general consent, again implies this relationship. This was also noted during a survey of the rock outcrop, Kudoro, southeast of Gbegbeya Veug – an outcrop surveyed for two reasons: firstly, because of its proximity to Hyena Cave with its possible early occupation evidence (see above), and, secondly, for its potential associations with the Golib Festival, Kudoro being located immediately behind the place occupied by the Santeng Tengdana for the duration of the festival. Of interest here is another shrine, Gobal (located at N10°40'14.8" W000°49'01.3"). Access to this shrine was restricted, and hence it could only be viewed from a distance, but the shrine itself was apparently formed of a rock-shelter set within a natural bowl-shaped 'amphitheatre' below the summit of Kudoro, the latter riddled with numerous rock shelters containing spreads of potsherds. Thus, if analogy with the latter is correct, it would seem that Gobal again represents the process of enshrining archaeological sites, in so doing indicating a complex awareness of the past and relationships therewith (Insoll 2006).

Similarly, in much smaller shrines, such as household shrines, lesser shrines associated with festivals, or purpose-specific shrines linked with medicinal or healing uses, recurrent potential relationships with archaeological materials were again noted. Such observations were gained from examining two shrines composed of portable lithic objects; a shrine associated with the Bo'araam harvest festival and formed of quartz spheres, which is located near the house of the caretaker of Tonna'ab, Yiran, and the other a shrine with medicinal properties incorporating various schist, possible grinding stones–pounders, at the entrance to the Bonaab sacred grove.

The question as to what degree human agency was involved in the production of the latter objects is intriguing, for at first sight these would all seem to be human-produced grinders–rubbers–pounders. However, a survey of the northeastern slopes of the Tongo Hills indicated that identical types of stones to these schist 'grinders–rubbers–pounders' are frequently seen scattered in fields and forming clearance boundaries at the

Fig. 11. Interior of the Tonna'ab shrine illustrating sacrifice area, sacrificer, and associated equipment and residues (Photo: T. Insoll).

Fig. 12. Medicinal shrine associated with the Bo'araam festival (Photo: T. Insoll).

Fig. 13. Field clearance boundary formed of schist 'grinders/rubbers/pounders' (Photo: T. Insoll).

base of the hills in such profusion that this would seem to preclude their human 'origin' (see Fig. 13). However, analysis of samples of these objects also recovered from the excavations in Nyoo is underway to address this issue. In contrast, the anthropogenic origin of the quartz spheres is seemingly much more certain (B. Baneong-Yakubo pers. comm.) but cannot be confirmed by microscopic analysis as ritual prohibitions do not allow their handling. Hence overall, it would again seem that the Earth and/or ancestors are ostensibly being appropriated via tangible material culture of possible archaeological provenance.

At Bonaab, the potential relationship between shrines, the past, and archaeological materials is more difficult to infer, not necessarily for its absence but because, as noted, access to the central area of the shrine was restricted in comparison to Nyoo (the easiest) and Tonna'ab. This was apparent in the prohibition, for example, on taking metal objects such as the survey equipment into this part of the shrine. Moreover, extraneous factors pertinent to archaeology complicate the issue with respect to Bonaab. Specifically, that as part of the aftermath of the British pacification of the Tongo Hills in 1911, the Bonaab shrine was destroyed using axes, fire, and dynamite (the latter unsuccessfully [Allman and Parker 2005:76–77]), the importance of this information being obviously that such destructive action would affect the archaeological record as well. Thus our understanding of Bonaab is much more incomplete, even if its botanical inventory has been surveyed (see below) and its perimeter planned.

DISCUSSION

This research into the archaeology of shrines in the Tongo Hills is potentially of a greater epistemological significance than that pertaining to its regional archaeological value alone. This perhaps grand-sounding claim is made in comparison to the archaeological study of other religions in Africa – Christianity (Finerran 1992) or Islam (Insoll 2003) – that of African traditional religions has been surprisingly neglected (De Maret 1994). Thus the archaeology of shrines, the focus of this paper, is little understood in comparison to, for instance, the development of the mosque in West Africa (Prussin 1986; Insoll 1996, 1999, 2003), or churches in Ethiopia and the Sudanese Nile Valley (Adams 1996; Phillipson 1998).

The suggested reasons for this lacuna are various and potentially include, for example, the correlation of written history with the archaeology of Islam and Christianity, their links (presumed at least) with external trade networks, and the often-greater (presumed at least) material imprint of their associated architectural traditions, etc., upon the archaeological record. To these can also be added the potential factor of an element of disinterest by many archaeologists in the material signatures and correlates of African traditional religions such as shrines, as opposed to material culture associated with world religions (Insoll 2001, 2003, 2004). Of course, some notable exceptions exist, as represented, for example, in West Africa by Nic David (e.g., David 1992) and Judith Sterner (e.g., Sterner 1992; and see David and Sterner this volume), and their students (e.g., Mather 1999,

2003; and see this volume). Similarly, relevant high-profile sites of shrines in West Africa, such as various locations in Ife (Garlake 1974; Willett 1967), have attracted archaeological attention, but in general it is reasonable to note that a state of neglect by archaeologists exists. Selected West African examples have been chosen here for it is the focus of this paper, but analogous points could equally be made for East Africa, as in the imbalance evident in archaeological research on Islam on the East African coast (e.g., Horton 1996; Horton and Middleton 2000), as opposed to the Kaya settlements and shrines of the coastal hinterlands (Mutoro 1994).

In interdisciplinary terms, this stands in contrast to the interests of anthropologists where the study of shrines in African traditional religions have been given a much greater prominence (e.g., Awolalu 1979; Goody 1959; Morris 2000; Zahan 1974). This is something archaeologists, both those working in sub-Saharan Africa and elsewhere, could do well to heed. For the insights gained from understanding the processes by which shrines are created, franchised, evolve, mutate, or are neglected or reactivated, for instance, have a resonance across large parts of the archaeological record, both temporally and geographically. Similarly, as one of us has recently discussed (Insoll 2006, 2007a), the marrying of insights gained from archaeology to the fortunate position of situating interpretation within relevant living religious traditions and ritual practices as of those of the Tallensi can lead to the necessary questioning of interpretive assumptions in relation to the presumed existence of universal concepts such as 'nature' (Insoll 2007b) or universal notions of materiality.

For the latter, the prominence accorded rock within Tallensi notions of materiality has been recently explored, and it was seen to be a material of special power and significance (Insoll 2006). This was evident in:

1. The potential importance ascribed rock as a direct product of the Earth.
2. The pre-eminent role accorded to rock shelters such as the Tonna'ab shrine.
3. The use of rock within shrine-franchising processes seemingly as a physical link to places of power, and potentially as an initiator of this power.
4. The seeming absence of rock art as a possible means to avoid altering the rock.
5. The recurrence of rock in ritual contexts such as shrines.

This in turn was suggested as of possible analogical value (Insoll 2006:233–36), albeit indirectly, for understanding how shrines were franchised and created in the Neolithic of the British Isles. As represented, perhaps, by the inclusion of 'exotic' rocks within the famous sites of Stonehenge (the Welsh sourced bluestones [Bradley 2000:95]) or by the quartz from the Dublin/Wicklow Mountains used at Knowth and Newgrange in the Republic of Ireland (Cooney 2000:136).

Further important data on the importance of rock in shrine-creation processes was also gathered during the recent excavations in Nyoo, as an adjunct to which a full survey of the standing stones previously mentioned was completed. This survey encompassed both mapping the positions of the 143 whole or fragmentary stones recorded and identifying their petrography and provenance. What this indicated was that a variety of locally available rock types were being used in the production of the standing stones. These included Bongo granite, amphibole-chlorite schist, metachert, and Leocratic granite (Baneong-Yakubo et al. 2006). Initially, it was thought that, excluding the Bongo granite, these rocks had been brought into the Nyoo shrine from significant distances. However, survey of the northeastern down slope of the Tongo Hills, already referred to, indicated that these rock types, though not seemingly immediately available on the plateau, were being sourced from the slopes of the Tongo Hills as well as, potentially, the lowlands below. This is of interest for a statement was obviously being made not only through the erection of the standing stones themselves but also through the materials they were made of, i.e., not only the Bongo granite immediately to hand. What the potential significance of this may have been, though, is not known, for such standing stones are not erected in the Tongo Hills today and thus any specific associations that might have existed with specific rock types have been lost.

Similarly, the 'unnatural' constitution of the botanical inventory of the supposedly 'natural' shrines was also of interest and again holds potentially far-reaching interpretive implications for archaeology. A recurrent pattern indicated by survey was that all the shrines considered, Bonaab, Nyoo, and Tonna'ab, to varying degrees, were far from unaltered places (Insoll 2007a). For instance at Bonaab the ethnobotanical survey indicated that this was a 'natural' sacred grove only insofar as the expected dominant tree species *Anogeissus leiocarpus* was present (Abbiw 2005). But this is also a species extensively used for fuel wood and making charcoal. Hence, although prohibitions exist on exploiting trees at Bonaab today, we do not know if such prohibitions existed in the past and thus *Anogeissus* might have been encouraged to grow for this purpose, and remains today as a vestige of such arboriculture (Insoll 2007a).

Likewise at Nyoo, besides the presence of the obvious archaeological remains, the 'natural' element of this 'sacred grove' was further diluted once the botanical inventory was completed. Here, in contrast to Bonaab and Tonna'ab, the dominant species were *Detarium microcarpum* (Tallow tree), *Annona senegalensis* (Wild Custard Apple), and *Combretum ghasalense*. Furthermore, almost without exception, the trees, shrubs, and plants present had been interfered with by human action (D. Abbiw pers. comm.) and were there because humans allowed them to be. Their presence was not due to natural 'selection' or activity as such, and those trees and shrubs that survived were there primarily because they also have some useful purpose (Insoll 2007a).

At Tonna'ab, natural vegetation does exist, but it is primarily there because of prohibitions on the exploitation of the trees in the vicinity of the shrine. This means that its surroundings are protected and the vegetation present can be classified as *Edaphic Climax* and is not human-altered (Abbiw 2005). It did not suffer the same fate as Bonaab, surviving in its 'natural' form as it was unknown to the British (see Allman and Parker 2005:80). Thus the dominant tree surrounding the shrine is *Bombax buonopozense* (Red-flowered Silk Cotton tree), along with *Diospyros mespiliformis* (West African Ebony) and *Trychoscypha arborea* (Abbiw 2005) – in its preservation it becomes almost what could be described as 'monumental' in an area otherwise heavily exploited (Insoll 2007a).

Here the wider archaeological resonance lies in the obvious questions raised as to the 'natural' status of shrines such as sacred groves elsewhere. This, for instance, is relevant in interpretation in relation to Iron Age Europe, where, although archaeological testimony for sacred groves might be absent, their use is attested in various Classical sources, and therefore we have to recognize their existence and consider such issues. Cunliffe (1997:198), for example, notes that designated sacred locations were known as *nemeton* (from the Gallo-Brittonic term meaning "sacred clearing in a wood or grove"). Sacred forests, groves, caves, and wells, are often classified as 'natural' and hence deliberately juxtaposed with built places. Instead, it could be posited, based upon the Tallensi case study, that our divisions between human and 'natural' may perhaps often be too simple (Insoll 2007a), certainly with regard to shrines and sacred places, and we might thus need to revisit our concepts and assumptions in this respect (and see Insoll 2007b for others).

A further area of interest in which some more general observations based upon the Tongo Hills shrines can be offered surrounds ethnicity. Lentz (2000:156) has indicated how ethnicity can alter over time in northern Ghana, literally how ethnic identities are "varied, ambiguous and changeable," and there are hints that this might be so in the Tongo Hills as well. As has been described, John Bawa Zuure made the key point that Nyoo should be considered as the great shrine for all the Tallensi, where worship started and spread from, and in the context of the Golib festival it certainly functions as the meeting place of all the Talis. The material indicators of ritual in Nyoo might also offer an insight into the construction of ethnicity as well.

Relevant here are the results of a test excavation completed by one of the authors, Kankpeyeng, at the site of Kusanaab, which according to local tradition (and as is indicated by the name) was linked with the Kusasi ethnic group (see Mather this volume), neighbours of the Tallensi. This thus represents a Kusasi area of settlement in the Tongo Hills, i.e., in what is Tallensi land today, and although now abandoned, shrines located in caves on the hill close to the Kusanaab site are still the focus of periodic rituals completed by Kusasi. Also of interest is the fact that the test excavations were completed at a standing stone similar to those recorded at Nyoo but which also differed from the latter in that a cluster of large potsherds, more reminiscent of the infill at NYOO 06 A was recorded placed around the standing stone (see Fig. 14), rather than the single ritual pots and iron bracelets associated with the standing stones, as has been described, in NYOO 06 (B). Hence, both similarities and differences are evident in ritual practices between Kusanaab and Nyoo, but with a greater emphasis on similarity. Does this also hold implications for tracing the development of ethnicities, of 'proto' Tallensi and 'proto' Kusasi via shrines and the material culture of ritual practices in the future?

Fig. 14. Cluster of pots at base of the standing stone, Kusanaab (Photo: T. Insoll).

CONCLUSIONS

The discussion has deliberately been left open, for this paper is far from being a final statement about the archaeology of shrines among the Tallensi but rather should be considered a preliminary outline. As research proceeds and further data are collected, it is hoped that both the more specific research questions and the broader issues surrounding concept and interpretation will become better understood. What is clear, however, is that the archaeology of shrines potentially offers an insight into many aspects of past lives not directly connected with ritual practice, for shrines seem to serve as a repository of information on social processes of much wider import, be it in relation to land use and resource utilization, materiality, or ethnicity.

ACKNOWLEDGMENTS

Timothy Insoll would like to thank the British Academy for funding the fieldwork, the Ghana Museums and Monuments Board for granting permission for the research to take place, and his co-directors, Dr. Benjamin Kankpeyeng, and Dr. Rachel MacLean for their insights and assistance. He would also like to thank Dr. Bruce Baneong-Yakubo, Dr. Ceri Ashley, Gertrude Abba, Alex Burnard, Simone Davies, Rachel Goodall, Samuel Kizitou, Malik Mahmoud, Richard Plangue Rhule, Abbas Iddrisu, Francis Yin, Eric Yin, Hanson Goldaan, Roger Naatoam for assistance in the field, along with that of all the other local guides, workmen, and informants. Thanks are also extended to the staff of the Upper East Regional Museum, especially Ms Prisca Yenzie, for their co-operation, and to the people of Tongo-Tenzug for their hospitality and patience in allowing the research to proceed.

REFERENCES

Abbiw, Daniel. 2005. *Alphabetical List of Plants on Tongo Hills*. Unpublished Report. Legon: Department of Botany, University of Ghana.

Adams, William. 1996. *Qasr Ibrim: The Late Medieval Period*. London: Egypt Exploration Society.

Allman, Jean, and John Parker. 2005. *Tongnaab: The History of a West African God*. Bloomington: Indiana University Press.

Ashley, Ceri. 2006. *Unpublished Ceramics Field Notes from Tengzug, 2006*. Manchester: Department of Archaeology, University of Manchester.

Awolalu, J. Omosade. 1979. *Yoruba Beliefs and Sacrificial Rites*. London: Longman.

Baneong-Yakubo, Bruce, P.M. Nude, and Y.S. Anku. 2006. *Petrography and Provenance of Rocks in Selected Shrines in the Tengzug Shrine, Upper East Region*. Unpublished Report. Legon: Department of Geology, University of Ghana.

Bellis, J.O. 1982. *The 'Place of the Pots' in Akan Funerary Custom*. Unpublished Report. Bloomington: African Studies Programme, Indiana University.

Bradley, Richard. 2000. *An Archaeology of Natural Places*. London: Routledge.

Cooney, Gabriel. 2000. *Landscapes of Neolithic Ireland*. London: Routledge.

Cunliffe, Barry. 1997. *The Ancient Celts*. London: Penguin.

David, Nicholas. 1992. "The Archaeology of Ideology: Mortuary Practices in the Central Mandara Highlands, Northern Cameroon." In *An African Commitment: Papers in Honour of Peter Lewis Shinnie*, ed. Judith Sterner and Nicholas David, 181–210. Calgary: University of Calgary Press.

De Maret, Pierre. 1994. "Archaeological and Other Prehistoric Evidence of Traditional African Religious Expression." In *Religion in Africa*, ed. Thomas D. Blakely, Walter E. A. Van Beek, and Dennis L. Thomson, 183–95. London: James Currey.

Drucker-Brown, Susan. 1974. *Ritual Aspects of the Mamprusi Kingship*. Cambridge: African Studies Centre.

Finneran, Niall. 2002. *The Archaeology of Christianity in Africa*. Stroud: Tempus.

Fortes, Meyer. 1949. *The Web of Kinship among the Tallensi*. London: Oxford University Press.

———. 1969[1945]. *The Dynamics of Clanship among the Tallensi*. Oosterhout: Anthropological Publications.

———. 1987. *Religion, Morality and the Person: Essays on Tallensi Religion*. Cambridge: Cambridge University Press.

Gabrilopoulos, Nick. 1995. *Ethnoarchaeology of the Tallensi Compound*. Master's thesis. Calgary: University of Calgary.

Garlake, Peter. 1974. "Excavations at Obalara's Land, Ife: An Interim Report." *West African Journal of Archaeology* 4:111–48.

Goody, Jack. 1959. *Death, Property, and the Ancestors*. London: Tavistock.

Horton, Mark. 1996. *Shanga*. London: British Institute in Eastern Africa.

Horton, Mark, and John Middleton. 2000. *The Swahili*. Oxford: Blackwell.
Insoll, Timothy. 1996. *Islam, Archaeology and History*. BAR S647. Oxford: Tempus Reparatum.
———. 1999. *The Archaeology of Islam*. Oxford: Blackwell.
———, ed. 2001. *Archaeology and World Religion*. London: Routledge.
———. 2003. *The Archaeology of Islam in Sub-Saharan Africa*. Cambridge: Cambridge University Press.
———. 2004. *Archaeology, Ritual, Religion*. London: Routledge.
———. 2006. "Shrine Franchising and the Neolithic in the British Isles: Some Observations based upon the Tallensi, Northern Ghana." *Cambridge Archaeological Journal* 16:223–38.
———. 2007a. "'Natural' or 'Human' Spaces? Tallensi Sacred Groves and Shrines and their Potential Implications for Aspects of Northern European Prehistory and Phenomenological Interpretation." *Norwegian Archaeological Review* 40, no. 2:138–58
———. 2007b. *Archaeology: The Conceptual Challenge*. London: Duckworth.
Insoll, Timothy, Benjamin Kankpeyeng, and Rachel MacLean. 2004. "An Archaeological Reconnaissance in the Tong Hills, and Garu Area, Upper East Region, and Nakpanduri, Northern Region, Ghana." *Nyame Akuma* 62:25–33.
———. 2005. "Excavations and Surveys in the Tongo Hills, Upper East Region, Ghana. July 2005. Fieldwork Report." *Nyame Akuma* 64:16–23.
Jacobson-Widding, Anita. 1979. *Red-White-Black as a Mode of Thought*. Uppsala: Almqvist and Wiksell.
Kankpeyeng, Benjamin. 2001. "The Cultural Landscape of Tongo-Tengzuk: Traditional Conservation Practices." In *Traditional Conservation Practices in Africa*, 23–31. Nantes: CRATerre-EAG.
Kense, Frank. 1992. "Settlement and Livelihood in Mamprugu, Northern Ghana." In *An African Commitment: Papers in Honour of Peter Lewis Shinnie*, ed. Judith Sterner and Nicholas David, 143–55. Calgary: University of Calgary Press.
Lentz, Carola. 2000. "Contested Identities: The History of Ethnicity in Northwestern Ghana." In *Ethnicity in Ghana: The Limits of Invention*, ed. Carola Lentz and Paul Nugent, 137–61. London: Macmillan.
MacEachern, Scott. 1994. "'Symbolic reservoirs' and Inter-group Relations: West African Examples" *African Archaeological Review* 12:205–24.
Mather, Charles. 1999. An Ethnoarchaeology of Kusasi Shrines, Upper East Region, Ghana. PhD dissertation. Calgary: University of Calgary.
———. 2003. "Shrines and the Domestication of Landscape." *Journal of Anthropological Research* 59, no. 1:23–45.
Morris, Brian. 2000. *Animals and Ancestors. An Ethnography*. Oxford: Berg.
Mutoro, Henry. 1994. "The Mijikenda Kaya as a Sacred Site." In *Sacred Sites, Sacred Places*, ed. David Carmichael, Jane Hubert, Brian Reeves, and Audhild Schanche, 132–39. London: Routledge.

Phillipson, David. 2000. *Ancient Ethiopia*. London: British Museum Press.

Preston Blier, Susan. 1987. *The Anatomy of Architecture. Ontology and Metaphor in Batammaliba Architectural Expression*. Cambridge: Cambridge University Press.

Prussin, Labelle. 1986. *Hatumere: Islamic Design in West Africa*. Berkeley: University of California Press.

Shaw, Thurstan. 1978. *Nigeria. Its Archaeology and Early History*. London: Thames and Hudson.

Sterner, Judith. 1992. "Sacred Pots and 'Symbolic Reservoirs' in the Mandara Highlands of Northern Cameroon." In *An African Commitment: Papers in Honour of Peter Lewis Shinnie*, ed. Judith Sterner and Nicholas David, 171–79. Calgary: University of Calgary Press.

Turner, Victor W. 1985[1966]. "Colour Classification in Ndembu Ritual." In *Anthropological Approaches to the Study of Religion*, ed. Michael Banton, 47–84. London: Tavistock.

Willett, Frank. 1967. *Ife in the History of West African Sculpture*. London: Thames and Hudson.

Zahan, Dominique. 1974. *The Bambara*. Leiden: Brill.

3

Earth Shrines and Autochthony among the Konkomba of Northern Ghana

ALLAN CHARLES DAWSON (MCGILL UNIVERSITY/STANDD[1])

ABSTRACT

The Konkomba are a people located in the interstices between the larger paramount chiefdoms of northern Ghana. They are a group that has, until quite recently, rejected the institution of hierarchical chieftaincy as a foreign construct imposed upon them by outsiders and colonial rulers. Chiefs, many Konkomba will say, are nothing but thieves – they are out to collect wealth and prestige for themselves and do very little for their own people. The Konkomba's lack of regard for the institution of chieftaincy and the importance they place on the office of earth priest within the village can only be understood in the context of autochthonous origin claims in areas of the Northern Region by many different ethnic groups and in the history of expansion and migration across the Sahel in Burkina Faso, Ghana, Togo, and other West African countries.

Keywords: earth shrines, Ghana, Konkomba, chiefship, Dagomba, kinship, autochthony

INTRODUCTION

The Konkomba people inhabit the eastern half of Ghana's Northern Region and are contiguous across the border into northwestern Togo in the areas known as the Oti flood plain, a region that suffers from both flooding and severe drought. Stretching from the ridges of the Gambaga escarpment down into the northern edge of the Volta region, the Oti plain alternates between swampy fields of red soil during the rains and arid stretches of land covered with patches of hardy shrub grass during the dry season. The earliest anthropological mention of the Konkomba is in Rattray's *Tribes of the Ashanti Hinterland* (1932) – a two-volume work that presents a broad ethnographic survey of Ghana's Northern, Upper East and Upper West Regions – essentially those ethnic groups seen as existing on the periphery of the Asante kingdom. The first long-term ethnographic project to study the lifeways of the Konkomba people was undertaken by David Tait (1961). Tait's work was also supplemented by that of Froelich (1954; 1963), who wrote extensively on the Konkomba living on the Togolese side of the Oti plain.

The Konkomba refer to themselves as *Bekpokpam* and their language as *Lekpokpam*. I use the term *Konkomba* to describe all of the groups subsumed by the term *Bekpokpam* as within Ghana the Konkomba are divided into two groups, the northern Komba and southern Bimotiev – the Konkomba often refer to these groups as two of the 'tribes' of *Bekpokpam*. The Komba reside primarily within territory claimed by the Mamprusi chiefdom around the town of Nalergu, the traditional centre for the Mamprusi and the seat of power for the *Na-Yiri*, the Mamprusi paramount chief. The Komba's traditional centre is at the village of Namong, a settlement, which, although it has the status of a de facto capital or tribal centre, has never witnessed the 'enstoolment'[2] of a paramount chief, the highest form of traditional authority found amongst the Voltaic peoples of West Africa (For more on traditional authority and paramount chiefs in Ghana, see Ray 1996; Skalnik 1987, 1989, 1996).

The same can be said of the southern Bimotiev Konkomba, whose traditional centre has, until recently, been the border town of Saboba. Until quite recently, both groups of Konkomba have resisted investing political authority in a paramount chief. They insist that their experience with the institution of chiefship in their relations with the Dagbani peoples has been one of oppression and extortion and that chiefs in general are not to

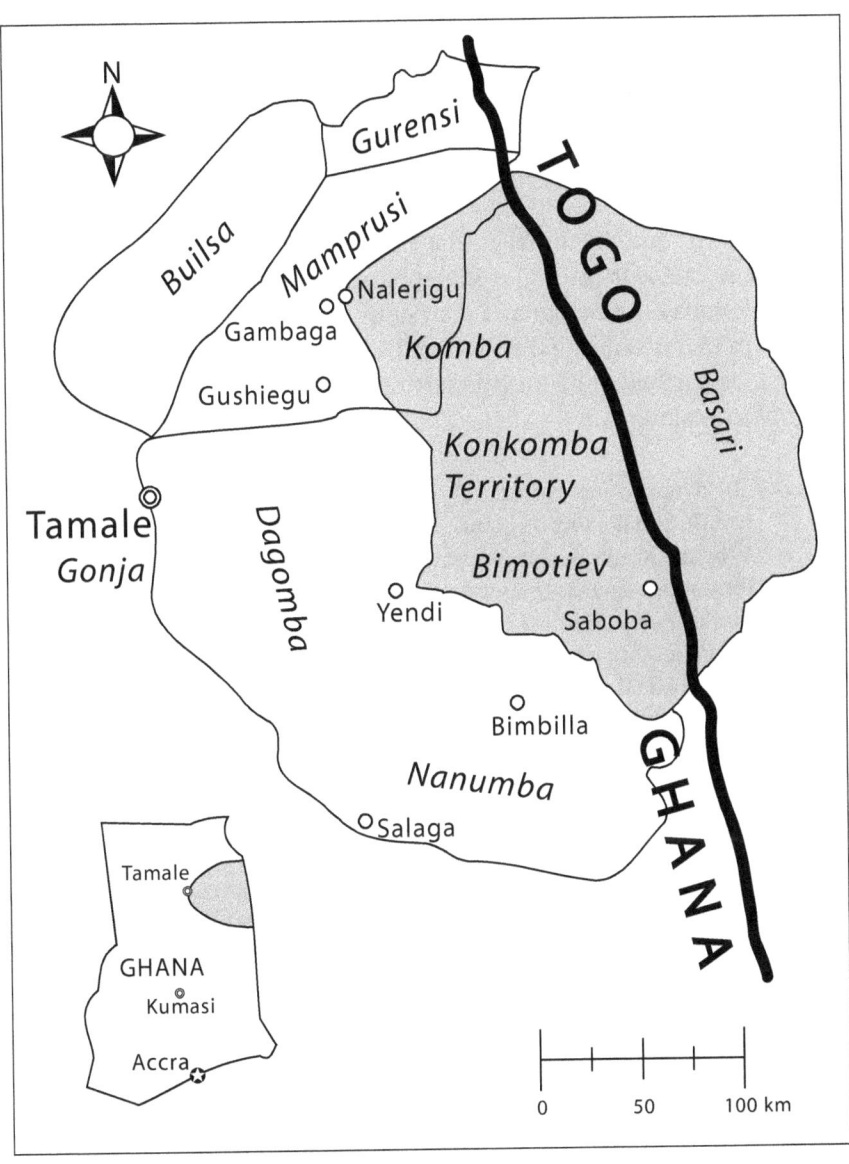

Fig. 1. Detail of eastern section of Ghana's Northern Region and northwestern Togo.

be trusted. To be sure, the Konkomba have had extremely contentious relations with their larger neighbours, the Dagbani chiefdoms of Dagomba, Mamprusi, Nanumba, and the Gonja to the west. They have often been required to pay tribute to the paramount chiefs of these groups and on a number of occasions have engaged in rather bloody conflict with these groups[3] (Barker 1991:2).

The Dagomba are perhaps the most important of these powerful neighbours as it is they, both Konkomba and Dagomba recall,[4] that drove the Konkomba out of town and district of Yendi. This event is vitally important in understanding the Konkomba dislike for paramount chiefs but also serves here as an historical starting point for this paper, which will attempt to explore:

- The dynamic movement and re-arrangement of internal ethnic frontiers in northern Ghana.
- Why the Konkomba revere earth shrines in the form of natural formations such as trees, groves, and ponds as important territorial markers and signifiers of ethnic identity.
- Why the Konkomba have something of a disdain for the office of chief and elevate the position of earth priest or Utindaan above all others in both daily village life and in regional ethnic politics.

YENDI

The Dagomba form the southernmost edge of an expansion of Mole-Dagbani peoples that took place in the early fourteenth century and are part of a network of chiefdoms that span the territory from "the forest bend in the south nearly to Timbuktu in the north; from the Volta bend in the west to northern Nigeria in the east" (Tait 1954:1).

Most northerners agree that it was the Dagomba who expelled the Konkomba from Yendi district, just east of White Volta. After being defeated by the Gonja, a conflict in which their king or Ya-Naa, Muhammad Zangina, was slain, the Dagomba, in the second half of the seventeenth century, were pushed eastwards into the area of the Oti plain (Wilks et al. 1986:122) and occupied a considerable portion of the territory already settled by the Konkomba. Tait places the date of the conquest of Yendi somewhere in the middle of the sixteenth century – he reaches this date by approximating ten years to the reign of each Ya-Naa since the occupation. Wilks' (1986:122) mid-seventeenth century date is recorded in the Gonja Islamic text, the Kitāb Ghanjā, authored in the eighteenth century. Informants with whom I spoke in 1999 and 2003 frequently told me that the Konkomba were expelled from Yendi ten generations ago. Using a baseline of approximately twenty years per generation, these accounts indicate that the Dagomba expansion into Yendi took place approximately two hundred years ago. The date suggested by the Konkomba certainly accords with their overall attitude towards Yendi; that they were only recently removed from this important regional centre and that, to quote a Konkomba elder in the town of Sangur, "everyone knows it." For the Dagomba, their control of Yendi is more of a historical fact and it is of little use for the Konkomba to still be protesting:

> Yes, the Konkomba were here once. But why do they carry on? Everybody used to be somewhere else. We are here and everybody knows that Yendi is a Dagomba town. Also, when the Konkomba were here, hundreds of years ago, this place was so rag-tag. We have made it a proper city![5]

It was also during this period of eastward movement that the Dagomba became instituted as a state under the rule of one man, the new *Ya-Naa* at Yendi. One of the first steps taken by Na Luro, the first Dagomba king at Yendi, was to follow a pattern already set in motion by Zangina and slay a large number of Dagomba earth priests, whom he saw as competitors and rivals for authority, and replace them with royal sub-chiefs (Staniland 1975:4). These royal chiefdoms were to stand guard against possible Konkomba reprisals.

The new Dagomba order was composed of a hierarchy of chiefdoms, known metaphorically as 'skins.' Sub-chiefs would sit on a pile of skins, typically cow hides, each one representing an ancestor through whom the sub-chief's authority has been passed down. Before over-hunting and habitat destruction decimated their population, lion and leopard skins were often draped over a chief's stool. Now however, only the *Ya-Naa* sits on a lion skin – most sub-chiefs sit on a variety of domesticated animal hides. Each royal chiefdom is embedded within another more powerful 'skin,' and each chiefdom is considered a 'gate' to Yendi (Tait 1961:6).

Historically the Konkomba were unable to mount the kind of defence that might put an end to Dagomba raiding, owing to the Konkomba's lack of any regimental system or cavalry. In these raiding incidents, the Dagomba would ride forth out of their fortified encampments on horseback into the Konkomba villages – this marauding tradition they received from the Hausa in the eighteenth century, during a time when some Dagomba paramounts began converting to Islam (Staniland 1975:91–100). Frequently, these raids were to round up slaves for the annual tribute the Dagomba owed to the Asante (Staniland 1975:35). Goody has noted that the Asante acquisition of slaves from the north for the trans-Atlantic trade led to pressure upon the Dagbani states of the north to produce "human booty," which in turn led to cavalry raids upon the horseless groups such as the Konkomba (Goody 1971:57). Groups such as the Konkomba, the LoDagaa and the Tallensi were unable to resist the onslaught of mounted raiders and so were forced into or fled to land that was difficult to access on horseback (Goody 1971:57). For the Konkomba, this meant the riverine land around the Oti River and the mountainous territory around the Gambaga escarpment. Dagomba raiders also attacked for frequent requirements of tribute payment in the form of yams and millet (Staniland 1975:35) and for labour, often women, who were captured and kept in the court of sub-chiefs to cook food.[6]

During the time of German occupation in what is now western Togo and some of eastern Ghana, from 1896 until the end of World War I, independent Konkomba in the Dagomba areas around Yendi were distinguished from conquered Konkomba. However, with the imposition of British rule, Dagomba chiefs began to exert greater degrees of authority over all Konkomba (Tait 1961:9):

> After World War I, the Dagomba got strength from the British. They thought they could do whatever they wanted. But whenever they took one from us, we would take ten from them. We would always thrash them when they tried to battle us.[7]

Under the British, the ultimate authority in Dagomba society, the *Ya-Naa*, delegated territorial control to appointed 'skins' or village sub-chiefs throughout his territory, while individual household heads maintained usufruct rights over the lands in their village (Oppong 1973:17). These sub-chiefs had judiciary power over disputes concerning the boundaries of a family compound's agricultural plot or in boundary disagreements between villages. By contrast, the Konkomba living on the edges of or within Dagomba territory received no such rights of access or arbitration and were forced, with the complicity of the British in an attempt to strengthen the chiefdoms, to pay tribute in return for the right to work the land. Tait records the British District Commissioner's (D.C.) confiscation of two whole truckloads of sorghum in 1950 from the *Ya-Naa* who had required it from the Konkomba settlement at Saboba, with the declaration that "The European says it has got to be paid" (Tait 1961:9). I was informed by elders at Sangur in 1999 that around fifty years ago it was not uncommon for Konkomba carts and the few trucks they owned during this period to be stopped and for all goods on board to be confiscated. Tait's work would seem to confirm this recollection; he writes "Konkomba were stopped by Dagomba on their way into Yendi market and their headloads of new yams taken, on the grounds that they had paid no tribute to the *Ya-Naa*" and of this confiscated lot, "one load went to the District Commissioner, one to the Yendi sergeant of police and the rest to the *Ya-Naa*" (Tait 1961:9-10). In response to acts of Konkomba revenge directed at Dagomba chiefs, District Commissioners would burn compounds and foodstuffs in Konkomba villages. The District Commissioner of Tamale district in 1929 is noted to have said "the only way to stop these fights is to burn all the compounds and food, I hate these fine men to kill each other when I am convinced that by burning their compounds, fights would very soon stop" (Staniland 1975:43).

Despite centuries of displacement, however, the Konkomba still regard the earth shrine at Yendi as theirs, and I was frequently informed that the Dagomba dare not venerate the original earth shrine of Yendi. "They know it is ours, and they won't touch it," one informant in Saboba informed me.

The expulsion from Yendi has become, for both the Konkomba and the Dagomba groups, a pivotal historical event. Konkomba insistence that they are the 'first-comers' on the earth around Yendi follows the pattern of internal frontier expansion outlined by Kopytoff (1987):

> When we came here, the land was rough. We used to call Yendi Charee. The people that had been here were few and not good at farming and you still see some of those people in the bush. They are ragamuffins and can't farm anything, they

spend most time talking to dwarves and taking *akpeteshie* [alcohol]. We planted yams on this land and they grew well, because this is good land for growing. Afterwards our brothers Komba came to the north, you know there are three tribes for Konkomba. We are the Bimotiev, the original Konkomba, and the others are the Komba and also what you call Basari, we say they are Konkomba too. So you know that the earth gods are at Yendi because it is our land and my fathers are there. And the Dagomba when they came they were running from the Gonja and they tried to make us work for them and give them yams and they took some Konkomba women as wives and made some Konkomba be chiefs for them.[8]

This narrative asserts that the Konkomba preceded the Dagomba in the Yendi area but also notes, at one point, that they forced out another, meeker, almost sub-human or 'ragamuffin' population. Indeed, the Konkomba oral history of their connection to Yendi is not dissimilar to the Dagomba story of their westward movement. Staniland (1975:4–5) notes that when the Dagomba arrived in the Yendi district they pushed back the Konkomba to the margins of society where relationships were distant and hostile.

More can be gleaned from this brief narrative of Konkomba occupancy of Yendi. The Konkomba describe the original inhabitants of the Yendi area as humans that have now been relegated to a mythical hinterland in almost quasi-magical terms. The bush, inhabited by so-called dwarves, is a place where powerful magical forces are at play, and that the original inhabitants are connected with this sphere indicates that the Konkomba see themselves as the first truly human residents of the Yendi area. When pressed, many Dagomba in the Yendi area, who still remember the conflicts with the Konkomba in the early 1990s, describe their former adversaries as 'wicked,' as similarly 'not quite human,' or as witches. Murphy and Bledsoe note that the Kpelle of Liberia use a "code of arrivals" to classify inhabitants of Kpelle country based on time of arrival in a certain area and on socioeconomic importance to daily life (1987:131), and we might similarly classify the inhabitants of the Yendi area in this way. The fictive 'original' inhabitants of Yendi are, to the Konkomba, certainly "insignificant previous inhabitants" of little import, socially or economically, and do not play an important role in local history other than to punctuate Konkomba assertions that they were the first 'true' humans to arrive. However, the

Dagomba would likely see the Konkomba as *important previous inhabitants* whose territory has been somewhat subsumed by overall Dagbani advancement eastwards and who have become subordinate labourers and tribute-paying farmers (Murphy and Bledsoe 1987:129–30).

The practice of insisting that 'we are from here,' that we are the autochthonous inhabitants of a particular patch of earth, and that all others are from elsewhere is common amongst competing or historically antagonistic groups in West Africa. In Ghana, ethnic groups regarded as interlopers are often described as hailing from the North or from Mali, anywhere but from 'here.' Among the Tallensi of Ghana's Upper East region, local oral history debates exactly who moved into the Tongo Hills first, why they moved there, and where they are from (see Insoll this volume). Inhabitants of the Nzema village, Nzulezu, a village built on stilts in a lagoon off the western Ghanaian coast, are said to not be true Nzema but rather migrants from Walata, a city of the ancient Ghana Empire in what is now Mali. In the 1990s, distrust and enmity turned into full-scale armed conflict in Ivory Coast as President Gbagbo sought to root out, expel, or kill so-called fake Ivoirians, whom he claimed were really Burkinabé. Geschiere and Jackson explore how these claims of autochthony, a term literally meaning 'of the earth,' have such local resonance, mobilizing power, and what they term apparent "naturalness" in different ethnographic contexts (2006:1). Claims of autochthony, they suggest, serve as a resource for assertions of ethnic identity and unity that transcend the need for a group name, a specific history, or even a common language (Geschiere and Jackson 2006:5). In the context of nation states, global culture, and questions of citizenship, appeals to autochthony possess a great amount of political power and social flexibility when it comes to mobilizing populations. However, Geschiere and Jackson (2006:6) also assert that the frequently redefined categories of who is 'from here' necessarily require a constant reassessment of who is not 'from here' and that such readily adaptable discourse, devoid of culturally relevant particulars, frequently becomes the rhetoric of ideologues and demagogues.

However, for the Konkomba, assertions of autochthony are not merely "empty," to use Geschiere and Jackson's term, rallying points that construct Dagomba as the other, the invader (2006:5). The entire Konkomba worldview revolves around the earth and that which grows from the soil. Konkomba explain that the earth of Yendi is integral to the spirits of their ancestors and so in a very concrete way, denial of access to the earth of

Yendi by the Dagomba is an obstruction to the proper veneration of the ancestors by Konkomba. Moreover, denial of access to an important earth shrine by the Dagomba is, to a certain extent, a negation or refutation of Konkomba ethnic identity.

EARTH SHRINES

In the religious life of the Konkomba, as with many other Voltaic peoples, earth shrines and the cult of the earth play a crucial role. The earth is the essential medium through which the Konkomba, people to whom the spirits of the ancestors play a supremely important role in quotidian life, commune with the past and those who went before. The earth is a vital symbol of fertility in the home and in the fields, and the ancestors are the ultimate source of sanction for social life among the people of the Voltaic region of West Africa.

Manoukian (1951) identifies two important modes in which the earth is considered by the Konkomba, the Dagbani chiefdoms, and other northern peoples. First, a practical, owned, proprietary aspect, in which the land is divided up and allotted for people to work. The second is the mystical, living side of the land, responsible for influencing the activities of daily life and as a source of health or benefactor. The Konkomba do not personify the earth as a deity as the Ibo, Yoruba, or Ashanti do; however, the Konkomba do engender the earth as female (Manoukian 1951:83; Zimoń 2003). This female embodiment of the earth is known as *Ketik*, she who nourishes and cares for the earth through her partner in the sky, *Umbor*, resident in the sun and in the rains (Froelich 1963:150). Ketik is an aspect of *Umbor*, a deity that represents the world and the universe. Through *Ketik, Umbor* is able to exercise influence over the land and the animals that reside upon it (Froelich 1963:150). It is through the earth shrine, the *ntengbe* or *littingbalm*, that the *Utindaan* or earth priest communes with the earth – with *Ketik*. It seems, however, that the animistic aspect of the earth, the 'face' of *Ketik*, is only invoked when the Konkomba wish to contact or appeal for the aid of one of the spirits that inhabit the wild, natural places of Konkombaland. The spirits of the river, the baobab tree, or the crocodile pond are called upon when the earth adjacent to their shrine is in need of assistance through some aspect of *Umbor*, from the warmth of the sun or through the rains. These spirits do not inhabit a material shrine but, rather, are considered to be within the earth.

The earth shrine is central to understanding clanship, territory, and chieftaincy among the Konkomba. The earth shrine is the nexus for ritual that petitions the earth for a good harvest and for proper veneration of the ancestors. The Konkomba view proper worship of the earth and veneration of the ancestors as much the same thing. The earth is often viewed as a powerful supernatural and elemental force, embodied by the feminine *Ketik*, but the spirits of ancestors, who were at one point earthbound human beings, are intimately bound up within this force – to honour one is to honour the other.

Both Manoukian (1951) and Zimoń (2003:421) make the point of distinguishing the economic, material aspect of the earth from the religious dimension and regard them separately. The tendency to make this division is, I think, somewhat reinforced by an assumption that Tait's division of ritual labour in a Konkomba settlement between the lineage that is believed to have been the founders or first-comers in a particular area and the later arrivals also applies to how Konkomba view and talk about the earth. As stated by Tait and others (see Barker 1991; Horton 1971; Tait 1961; Zimoń 2003), Konkomba political structure is based on the dyadic relationship between the *Utindaan* and the elder for the people. Each Konkomba village is typically composed of two contraposed lineages – this refers to a division of religious and secular roles between the so-called 'lineage for the earth' and 'lineage for the people.' The apical ancestor of the earth lineage is the individual who is understood or is claimed to have established a settlement, and the ancestor of the 'people's lineage' is "he who helped the one who first came here" (Tait 1954:214). It is a mistake, even if just for analytical purposes, to attempt to separate the practical from the spiritual side of the earth. In my conversations with Konkomba farmers and with Konkomba earth priests, the cycle of sowing and harvest, drought and flood, good years and bad years is so completely bound up in the religion and ritual of earth and ancestor veneration that it is unproductive, from an ethnographic standpoint, to try and disconnect them:

> When we sow yams or millet, it is also giving libations. When you put anything on the ground, if it is a room [a rondoval hut] or some food or you put yams or millet for eating or selling or

you pour libations it can be the same. Why not? From the earth comes everything.⁹

The earth shrine is the symbolic and ritual centre for each group of related clans and both the Bimotiev and Komba have numerous earth shrines in their territory. Traditionally, both the Komba and the Bimotiev Konkomba use some natural landmark such as a baobab tree, hill or clearing, or crocodile pond as their earth shrine.

The earth shrine at Yendi that the Konkomba claim is theirs and that cannot be venerated by the Dagomba is a large baobab tree on the town's northern edge. To ritually serve a shrine, one needs to provide the appropriate sacrifices and water – libations – to the shrine that ties a particular lineage's ancestors to the earth. Bimotiev Konkomba throughout this region maintain that this shrine still belongs to them and that the Dagomba are unable to "do the gods" of Yendi:

> The Dagomba, you know, they can't touch it! They can't give water to that shrine. The tree, it looks like a crocodile, because it is so old. They can't do the gods of Yendi because it belongs to us. Yendi is for us, the earth from Yendi, from the gods, is for us. Dagomba will say, after the war only, Konkomba get power from this place.¹⁰

> Dagomba have taken our gods only. But we can't go there and look after our land. Yendi is for us but they took it from us. And so we must make our gods somewhere else, but not at Yendi and its not correct, we shouldn't have to go somewhere else when we know that it is our land.¹¹

Indeed, throughout southern Konkomba territory, communities claim to have been forced to move away from what they claim is their 'original' earth shrine – where the ancestors of their village, *Utindaans*, are believed to have founded a settlement. Earth shrines are fixed natural features that serve, for the Konkomba, as implicit markers of Konkomba control over a particular area.

Within the hollow of a sacred baobab tree, in a grove, in a rock overhang near a crocodile pond or in close association with any natural landmark that is considered to be an earth shrine, there is usually placed a collection of small circular stones, pots, and/or calabashes. In the Konkomba village of Tuna in the Northern Region, the earth shrine is a small coppice or grove of trees next to a yam field with a large baobab in the centre. Under the baobab is a small circle of nine red clay pots and one central sacrificial stone. In the Konkomba village of Namong, close to Tuna, the earth shrine is simply a baobab tree with one libation stone in a hollow at the base of the tree. In Katani, the Konkomba earth shrine is again a baobab tree; however, this tree is located next to a stagnant pond claimed by locals to contain a particularly fierce crocodile of which I could find no evidence. Further, I could find no evidence of any object of material culture, pot, stone, or calabash used in association with the Katani shrine.

In the public oratory of village *Utindaans* pertaining to the earth shrines of Yendi and neighbouring towns, there are, as we can see above, continued references to the 'earth' the Konkomba claim they have lost to the Dagomba. Also contained in this speech is the implication that the Konkomba's rivals understand this; they understand that the earth shrine of Yendi is tangible evidence of the Konkomba connection with Yendi. The shrine of Yendi embodies a regionally and cross-culturally shared understanding of religious control over geography. This knowledge of what the Yendi shrine actually means is widely known to Konkomba society.[12]

Dagomba informants often grudgingly admitted that the tree in question in Yendi was a shrine but not one served by their earth priest. When asked about earth shrines in Yendi, most Dagomba informants would emphasize that they, as the people that turned Yendi into a thriving market town and traditional centre, have their own earth shrine. However, few Dagomba argue that Yendi was at one point a Konkomba settlement. When interviewed about the large baobab on the north side of Yendi, on the road towards Tamale, the Northern Region's capital, one Dagomba informant told me:

> Yes. That tree is a place for libations and sometimes some people come through and put things in there. There are witches there in some way. So don't go there or you will go mad. Maybe it is for the Konkomba or also an old Gonja place but it is not for us so we don't touch it. Anyway it is not in Yendi, it is on the perimeter of the town as it is on the road leading to Tamale[13]

ANCESTOR SHRINES

In addition to the important earth shrine in a village or settlement, each compound within the village will venerate an array of protective ancestor shrines. In southern Konkomba or Bimotiev territory, small red clay pots covered with calabashes are brought out to the centre of a family compound and 'served' with the killing of a white fowl and the pouring of *pito* or sun-fermented millet beer. These pots are ancestor shrines and are brought to the compound by the *Gbondaan*, a man who is subordinate to the village's *Utindaan* and the individual responsible for maintaining and storing the *kopanjok*, the ritual paraphernalia of the *Utindaan*, and for serving ancestor shrines within his major lineage.

I was told repeatedly that in Bimotiev territory it is very important that when serving ancestor shrines within a compound, it is of utmost importance to use a white fowl. However, I rarely witnessed a case in which the libations and veneration of a shrine proceeded according to the meticulous play-by-play often related to me by community members, *Gbondaans* or even *Utindaans*.

The photo in Figure 2 is of the sacrifice of a red rooster to the ancestor shrines of a family compound in Bimotiev territory only moments after I had been told that a white fowl must be used. This easy substitution demonstrates the flexibility and dynamic nature of many of the earth shrine rituals of the Voltaic peoples. Frequently an earth priest will improvise a rite, and I never once saw quite the same ritual performed the same way twice. The religious traditions of the Konkomba and indeed many of the Voltaic peoples are very much cosmologies in the making where ideas of ritual purity, codified forms of praxis, and hierarchy do not easily interact with the complex of earth and ancestor veneration. These belief systems are in every way unsystematic and their contained meanings, references, and usages continually change and adapt to new social contexts.

For the Konkomba, land is intimately connected with fertility, and the number of pots used in a land rite is always greater than two. Two of these pots are always supposed to be separated during a land rite and are regarded as the shrine of the twin spirit; twins are seen as symbols of fertile land and of a bountiful harvest to come. Here again, however, I frequently witnessed incidences of earth priests separating three, four, five, or sometimes no pots for the twin spirit. Indeed, one could easily fill an entire volume describing the manifold variations of ancestor veneration found

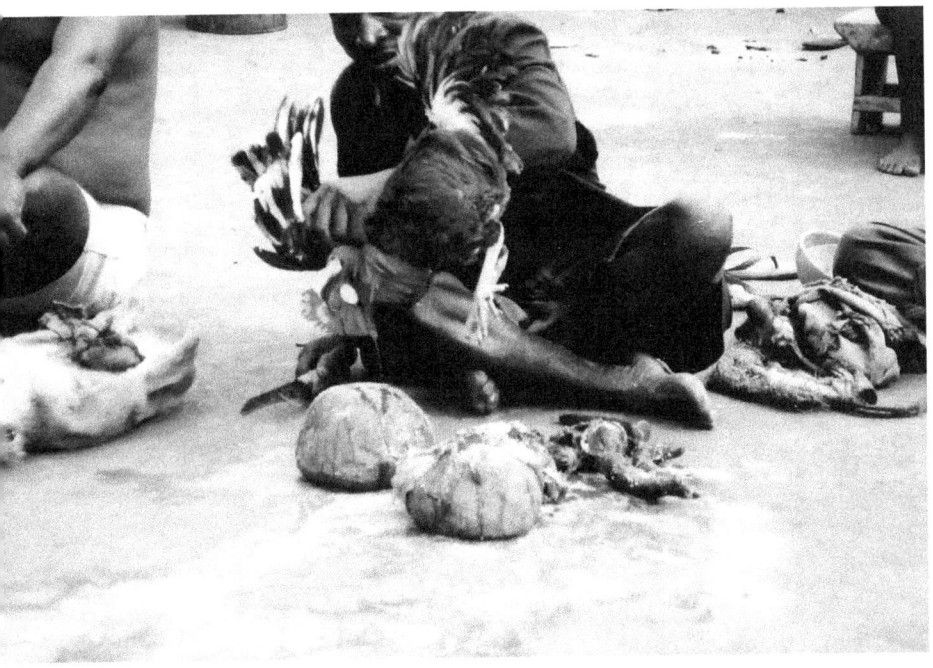

Fig. 2. Gbondaan of Namong.

in Konkomba society. When I asked about this apparent inconsistency, respondents often looked at me quizzically and in the village of Tuna I was informed:

> Yes there should be two pots. But in this case we always use four as that helps us with one harvest for us and for some of the harvest that we are required to give to the *Na-Yiri*. We need fertile land for the Konkomba and also to feed everyone else. You know, the Konkomba feed Ghana. So we need extra libations also to improve our production for the Konkomba yam market. We produce and sell more yams than anybody else and many of our yams get sent to Europe. So we ask for good food for us and good food for others. So then we have to change the libations to the new circumstance. Only in the church do I have to keep things the same all the time.[14]

Fig. 3. Utindaan of Namong.

Indeed, the Konkomba have become extremely important to the agricultural economy of the Northern Region. The large Konkomba yam market in Accra now sells yams not only to the capital region but has also struck an agreement with a European supermarket chain to export yams to Germany and France. This change in agricultural strategy has brought about a small and rather logical change in the practice of land rites.

Another form of protective shrine that is often found in Konkomba yam fields, both in the northern Komba areas and among the southern Bimotiev, are small, square clay posts, approximately twenty centimetres in width and half a metre high. Upon these posts, calabashes filled with medicine, typically the leaves of germinated seed yams, are placed. These shrines are intended to ensure the well-being of village members through therapeutic and curative powers. These shrines are not seen as earth shrines *per se* and neither are they entirely understood to be ancestor shrines. These shrines are served by pouring the blood of two to six fowl or guinea fowl, regardless of colour, over the posts leaving the calabashes untouched. Depending on the status of the individual, goat's blood, and libations of beer are also poured.

CHIEFS

Although often characterized as a so-called acephalous or 'headless' people, the Konkomba do indeed have an office of chief or 'head,' and most villages have a leader in whom political authority is invested – a chief. The typical pattern of first-comer–latecomer relationships that follow Tait's (1961) and others' (Barker 1991; Horton 1971) form of leadership in which two contraposed lineages, one of which is understood to have founded a settlement and maintains a grip on religious authority, typically find elders from the latecomer's lineage occupying a position of only nominal importance in ritual, economic, and indeed political matters. This secondary position, often characterized by informants as 'elder for the people' or 'chief,' is often demeaned by members of a village's primary lineage as a usurper, an also-ran, and not someone that I, as an ethnographer and someone who has come to understand Konkomba society, should bother with:

> All of our villages have chiefs. But they are nobody. They are fools who want to be important. Everyone knows that the *Utindaan* is more important. Those chiefs are puppets put there by Dagomba and they can't do anything for the shrines or to help us fight against people who take money[15]

The Konkomba experience with the institution of chieftaincy has largely been one of tribute and supplication to a Dagbani paramount leader. They perceive the Dagbani expression of this institution as an attempt to control the land upon which they make their living and which they hold sacred. In the towns around Yendi where many Konkomba villages were forced, for a very long time, to pay tribute to the *Ya-Naa*, the elder for the people is often appointed by this external power and is often married to a Dagomba woman. A similar pattern is found in Komba villages near the Mamprusi centres of Gambaga and Nalerigu. "A chief is a thief," I was often told by Konkomba informants:

> These chiefs are nothing but people who want too much power and will be corrupted by outsiders. The Konkomba are becoming very strong in the yam business and everyone knows it so they put these puppet chiefs all-around to try and steal our money and do juju on our fields. But what do they know? They can't do anything! You know, since colonial times they've been trying to do it and even today in the year 2003 we see them still trying to make these chiefs work for them. But soon we will have a paramount chief and all this will stop.[16]

In this comment by a respected leader of the extremely profitable Konkomba yam market in Accra, we see a peculiar irony with respect to the institution of chieftaincy. Although village chiefs appear to be universally reviled throughout Konkombaland, there is a growing movement among wealthy yam-trading families to have two Konkomba paramount chiefs appointed to Ghana's National House of Chiefs. As of 2008, this had not yet occurred, however, the demand for the enstoolment of these chiefs is still strong. In interviews conducted in 2003 and in recent correspondence with leaders of this movement, there is general consensus that the candidates for the positions of Komba paramount and Bimotiev paramount must come from the villages of Namong, considered to be the traditional centre for the Komba, and from Saboba, the traditional centre for the Bimotiev, in lieu of an imagined return to Yendi. Traditional centres are often considered to be the original settlement of a particular ethnic group – the first town or village that was founded, often by a mythical, apical ancestor. With respect to Saboba, the Bimotiev claim that they were forced to make a new traditional centre after the loss of Yendi. In stressing that the new paramounts must come from Konkomba traditional centres, the leaders of this movement are suggesting that the new paramount will be like an *Utindaan* for all Konkomba people:

> You know the Asante have the Asantehene and the Dagomba have the *Ya-Naa* and the Mamprusi have the *Na-Yiri* and we deserve to have a seat in the House of chiefs as the Konkomba are a strong people also. But when a Konkomba paramount comes to the House of Chiefs and sits next to the Asantehene we will help to prevent them from becoming corrupt. Our paramounts will have to come back to Namong and Saboba, and one day Yendi, to venerate the shrine there. Just as I told you Allan, when you came here in 2003, how the paramount must be like the earth priest for the people and watch after the health of village so will the paramount, if we get it, look after the health of the people.[17]

It is interesting here to note that those who strongly support the Konkomba petitions for paramount chieftaincy also speak out vehemently against Dagbani paramounts and against the chiefs in local villages. These individuals, often leaders of the yam market or members of the Konkomba Youth Association (KOYA),[18] invariably claim ancestry from the founders of their respective villages. Throughout my interviews conducted with village members who claimed to be of the lineage of the earth, there existed a general consensus that chieftaincy was, intrinsically, a bad thing. The only real leader of consequence, for these informants, was the *Utindaan*.

Indeed, the *Utindaan*'s primary tasks are to maintain the health and prosperity of the community by soliciting the goodwill of the earth and the ancestors and to direct the rites performed during the planting season. The building of a new village compound also requires the *Utindaan*'s presence, and he receives part of the libations or sacrifices offered to achieve the earth's blessings. The successful establishment of a new compound is a significant event in Konkombaland as it is considered the unit of expansion and movement across the land and is to the Konkomba a powerful signal that the earth has permitted them to flourish.

The *Utindaan*, as the de facto head of the lineage of the first-comers within each village, is the effective head of the biggest ritual unit within Konkomba society – the clan as it is represented within the village. It is the *Utindaan* that presides over and permits earth rites to be performed within Konkombaland and within these rites the *Utindaan* embodies the true authority within Konkomba society. Through sacrificed offerings and libations, the Konkomba establish and maintain contact with supernatural forces whose existence is believed necessary for the prosperity of quotidian life.

The nature of Konkomba political authority in northern Ghana can only be understood in the context of the *Utindaan*'s relationship with the earth shrine and village that his ancestors are believed to have founded, both at the village level and now, with reference to the Konkomba claims to paramount status, at the regional level. This relationship with the land has developed out of a pattern of migration that can be found throughout Voltaic West Africa. In this pattern we see communities pushed out onto the periphery of metropoles by slave raiding, expansion of other ethnic groups, or in search of new cultivable land. In so doing they create new local histories of autochthony and origin. For the Konkomba, the essential historical event that legitimates their claim to a piece of earth is the creation of a new earth shrine – this action, more than anything, brings into existence a new ritual focus for worship of both the earth and ancestor and ultimately a material representation of territorial control. The earth shrine becomes, in effect, the crown jewel of a lineage, the key to power, providing what Lancaster has termed the "spine" of a community, a senior group which holds sway over communal earth and ancestor cults (Lancaster 1987:106).

The essentially territorial nature of group identity in Konkombaland and throughout the Northern Region is made manifest through devotion to the earth shrine – identity, contained and defined by the controlling lineage, becomes intertwined with the concept of the earth. The earth lineage and its connection with the earth shrines come to represent the group against outsiders. Nowhere is this more apparent than in the Konkomba's contentious relationship with the Dagomba over the Yendi shrine. In a region where the daily agricultural and economic activities are similar, where, ethno-linguistically, most groups share a common origin, the earth lineage creates and shapes the image of community (Horton 1971:95) and ultimately of ethnic identity, as it is the earth shrines that truly determine who is not 'from here,' who is the 'other.'

The contested meaning of the tree in Yendi, the actual date of the Dagomba eastward movement, and the legitimacy of the Konkomba claim that they were indeed that first-comers on the earth around Yendi are important components of identity politics and claims of ethnic distinctiveness in northern Ghana. To the outsider, even to the Ghanaian from Accra or Kumasi, there appears, at first glance, to be little to distinguish the lifeways of the Konkomba from those of other northern peoples. Indeed, within the northern Ghanaian ethnoscape, there is considerable similarity between many of the so-called chiefdoms and small acephalous groups. However, these different communities often find themselves at odds on questions of allegiance with representatives of national political parties and in competition over market access for their agricultural produce. Consequently, contested claims of autochthony and territorial access to agricultural land often find expression in the religious idiom.

ACKNOWLEDGMENTS

This research was made possible by a Province of Alberta research fellowship and by a SSHRC doctoral fellowship. Continued research in northern Ghana in 2003 was also made possible by a grant from the STANDD (Society, Technology and Development) research institute of McGill University. I should also like to thank the residents of Namong, Saboba, Yendi, Tamale, and many other small towns and villages in Ghana's Northern Region.

NOTES

1. STANDD: Society, Technology, and Development; A multidisciplinary research institute at McGill University.

2. The term 'enstoolment,' referring to the installation of a new chief or paramount, is taken from the Asante tradition of a new chief being placed 'on the stool' – a carved wooden stool that is essentially a throne for the chief and is representative of the title holder's office. Many northern chiefs are not enstooled *per se*, rather they are 'enskinned'; but the term has come to represent the process of installing or appointing any new chief in Ghana.

3. The tensions in 1994 emerged from petitions made by the Konkomba youth association of Saboba and by the market chief of Saboba himself for the right to own land in the Saboba area. This petition was largely ignored by the northern regional minister as just another incident in the long history of ethnic and chieftaincy conflicts in this region. The Dagomba asserted that the right to farm on land claimed by the Dagomba could only be granted if the Konkomba in the region bought the land from the *Ya-Naa*, the Dagomba paramount. Tensions mounted and eventually erupted into what would be called 'The Guinea Fowl War' – the initial outbreak of violence flared up over a drunken squabble between Konkomba and Nanumba farmers over the sale of a guinea fowl.

4. All interviews and comments by informants were collected during ethnographic fieldwork carried out in Ghana's northern region in 1999 and 2003.

5. Interview with member of *Ya-Naa*'s court, Yendi, Northern Region, Ghana. 28/1/2003.

6. Interview with wife of family earth priest in village of Namong, Northern Region, Ghana. 6/7/1999.

7. Interview with Mr. DB, Saboba, Northern Region, Ghana. 22/8/99.

8. This origin of the Konkomba's claim to Yendi was told to me on 2/7/1999 by a market official of the Konkomba yam market in Accra. Staniland (1975:7) also notes that the Konkomba called Yendi by the name Chare.

9. Interview with Gbondaan of Namong, Northern Region, Ghana. 27/1/2003.

10. Interview with Mr. JB in Wale Wale, Northern Region, Ghana. 19/6/1999. The tree he is referring to is a large Baobab in the north-eastern quarter of Yendi, also in the Northern Region.

11. Interview with Mr. BNB in Tuna, Northern Region, Ghana. 24/6/1999.

12. For more on distinctions between esoteric and exoteric knowledge concerning shrines, see Hatt in this volume.

13. Interview with LD et al. in Yendi, Northen Region, Ghana. 14/17/1999.

14. Interview with Gbondaan in Tuna, Northern Region, Ghana. 5/2/2003.

15. Interview with Mr. TT, Naabule, Northern Region, Ghana. 13/6/1999.

16. Interview with Konkomba yam market official in Accra. 12/02/2003.

17. Personal correspondence with a leader of KOYA, the Konkomba Youth Association, 6/7/2004.

18. KOYA is a sodality formed in the wake of a number of armed conflicts with the Dagbani chiefdoms and with the Gonja. It was responsible for organizing and arming large number of youths in the so-called guinea fowl war; however, it primarily acts as a mutual aid association for Konkomba youth who have moved to major cities, such as Accra. The Dagomba, Dagara, and other ethnic groups in Ghana also have similar youth associations (see Lentz 1995).

REFERENCES

Barker, T. R. 1991. "Small Bands of Strangers: The Contraposed 'Lineage' Reconsidered." *Anthropos* 86:1–18.

Froelich, J. 1954. *C. La Tribu Konkomba du Nord Togo*. Dakar: IFAN.

———. 1963. "Les Konkomba, Les Moba, Les Dyé." In *Les populations du Nord-Togo*, ed. J. C. Froelich, Pierre Alexandre, and Robert Cornevin, 118–57. Paris: Presses Universitaires de France.

Geschiere, Peter, and Stephen Jackson. 2006. "Autochthony and the Crisis of Citizenship: Democratization, Decentralization, and the Politics of Belonging." *African Studies* 49, no. 2:1–7.

Goody, Jack. 1971. *Technology, Tradition and the State in Africa*. Cambridge: Cambridge University Press.

Horton, Robin. 1971. "Stateless Societies in the History of West Africa." In *History of West Africa*, vol. 1, ed. J. F. Ade Ajayi and M. Crowder, 78–119. Bristol: Longman Group.

Kopytoff, Igor. 1987. "The Internal African Frontier: The Making of African Political Culture." In *The African Frontier: The Reproduction of Traditional African Societies*, ed. Igor Kopytoff, 3–84. Bloomington: Indiana University Press.

Lancaster, Chet S. 1987. "The Goba of Zambezi." In *The African Frontier: The Reproduction of Traditional African Societies*, ed. Igor Kopytoff, 102–20. Bloomington: Indiana University Press.

Lentz, Carola. 1995. "'Units for Development': Youth Associations in Northwestern Ghana." *Africa* 65, no. 3:395.

Manoukian, Madeline. 1951. *Tribes of the Northern Territories of the Gold Coast*. London: International African Institute.

Murphy, William P., and Caroline H. Bledsoe.1987. "Kinship and Territory in the History of a Kpelle Chiefdom (Liberia)." In *The African Frontier: The Reproduction of Traditional African Societies*, ed. Igor Kopytoff, 123–47. Bloomington: Indiana University Press.

Oppong, Christine. 1973. *Growing up in Dagbon*. Accra-Tema: Ghana Publishing Corporation.

Rattray, R. S. 1932. *The Tribes of the Ashanti Hinterland*. Oxford: Clarendon.

Ray, Donald I. 1996. "Divided Sovereignty: Traditional Authority and the State in Ghana." *Journal of Legal Pluralism and Unofficial Law* 37–38:181–202.

Skalnik, Peter. 1987. "On the Inadequacy of the Concept of the Traditional State." *Journal of Legal Pluralism and Unofficial Law* 25–26:301–25.

———. 1989. "Outwitting Ghana: Pluralism of Political Culture in Nanun." In *Outwitting the State*, ed. Peter Skalnik, 145–68. London: Transaction Puslishers.

———. 1996. "Authority versus Power: Democracy in Africa Must Include Original African Institutions." *Journal of Legal Pluralism and Unofficial Law* 37–38:110–22.

Staniland, Martin. 1975. *The Lions of Dagbon: Political Change in Northern Ghana*, African Studies Series. Cambridge: Cambridge University Press.

Tait, David. 1954. "Social Change in the Northern Territories of the Gold Coast." (mimeo) Legon: Institute of African Studies, University of Ghana, Legon.

———. 1961. *The Konkomba of Northern Ghana*. London: Published for the International African Institute and the University of Ghana by the Oxford University Press.

Wilks, Ivor, Nehemia Levtzion, and Bruce M. Haight. 1986. *Chronicles from Gonja: A Tradition of West African Muslim Historiography*. Cambridge: Cambridge University Press.

Zimoń, Henryk. 2003. "The Sacredness of the Earth among the Konkomba of Northern Ghana." *Anthropos* 98:421–43.

4

Shrines and compound abandonment: ethnoarchaeological observations in Northern Ghana

CHARLES MATHER (UNIVERSITY OF CALGARY)

ABSTRACT

Amongst the Kusasi, compound abandonment involves curation of usable material culture including shrines. Despite the fact that curation is a normative process, there are instances when compounds are abandoned without the curation of useable material culture. In these instances, shrines stand a good chance of being output into the archaeological record. This paper examines the likelihood of shrines being output into the archaeological record and provides suggestions about the strategies archaeologists can employ to discover shrines at abandoned compound sites.

Keywords: Abandonment, curation, compounds, shrines, ethnoarchaeology, Ghana

SHRINES AND COMPOUND ABANDONMENT

Anthropologists working in northern Ghana have long noted the importance of shrines to the order of society. Fortes (1949:46) remarks that amongst the Tallensi the stages of a compound head's personal destiny, past, present, and future are perpetuated in the many shrines and other ritual objects that are housed within the compound. Other scholars have also touched upon how social relations and patterns of descent are mirrored in the variable placement and size of different shrine types and how shrines commemorate important events, people, and relationships from the past.[1] Most of the objects that anthropologists call shrines are made from durable, common materials such as: stones, ceramic pots, iron rods and bangles, and animal bones and horns. These are materials that stand a good chance of surviving should they get output into the archaeological record. Determining the presence or absence of shrines in the archaeological record could aid in drawing inferences concerning the size, composition, and developmental stages of residential groups. Identifying shrines in the archaeological record requires an understanding of the processes that condition their deposition or discard. The goal of this paper is to examine the sorts of factors that condition shrine deposition among the Kusasi of the Upper East Region, Ghana.

The Kusasi make their shrines from durable materials that stand a good chance of surviving once deposited into archaeological contexts. The frequency that the Kusasi output shrines from systemic contexts is, however, quite low. When a man dies, the younger members of his residential and descent groups inherit his shrines. When people abandon compounds, they take their shrines with them. In short, whether shrines make it into the archaeological record largely depends upon whether they are inherited or curated, and this is ultimately connected to the circumstances surrounding compound abandonment.

All archaeological sites are abandoned and in this sense it is not surprising abandonment has such an important role in shrine deposition. Circumstances of abandonment determine the constitution of de facto refuse at a site. De facto refuse consists of usable or repairable items of material culture left behind when abandonment occurs. The circumstances surrounding abandonment, whether it occurs rapidly or gradually, and with anticipation of return or not, will largely determine the make-up of de facto refuse at a site (Stevenson 1982; Tomka 1993).

Abandonment conditions curate behaviour. Curate behaviour "consists of removing objects from one site and transporting them elsewhere in anticipation of future use" (Schiffer 1976:56). If abandonment occurs gradually, people have the opportunity to plan if, and how, they will curate the objects and features they wish to have at the new location or area. Anticipation of return also affects whether objects or features are curated (Stevenson 1982; Tomka 1993). If they do not anticipate returning to the site, occupants will take away usable materials. If return to a compound is anticipated, and if the new location is close enough to the old, entire "structures may be dismantled and building materials transported" (Cameron 1993:5). Curate behaviour has the potential to deplete de facto refuse, particularly if curation is delayed. If abandonment occurs gradually and people anticipate returning to the abandoned site, curation may be drawn out with items being moved to the new area or locale, as they are needed.

Other processes can affect the make-up of de facto refuse at a site. These include lateral cycling, draw down, scavenging, and collecting and looting (Schiffer 1976; 1985). Lateral cycling "occurs when an object is transferred from one user to another. It includes the many processes by which used, but usable, objects circulate within a sociocultural system and persist in time" (Schiffer 1976:39). Draw down "refers to the tendency for people not to replace worn or broken items when they know they are about to move" (Lightfoot 1993:166). Scavenging refers to the depletion of de facto refuse in the form of neighbours taking away useful items from the abandoned area or site (Schiffer 1985). Collecting and looting refers to the removal of artefacts from de facto refuse by non-residents (Schiffer 1976:35–36). This paper examines compound abandonment and the effect of curation upon the production of de facto refuse, particularly shrines.

The paper begins by providing background information and describing the methods used in the present study. It describes compounds as long-term depositional events and highlights the various transformations of material culture from state to state in systemic contexts over time. Curation and abandonment are the two most important processes governing whether shrines are output from systemic contexts to archaeological contexts. Using observations made in the settlement of Zorse in the Upper East Region of Ghana, the paper will provide information about the preservation of shrines in abandoned compounds. These observations suggest that shrines appear in archaeological contexts as a result of events that are catastrophic from the perspective of the residential group. In conclusion, a methodology for future archaeological research in the area is proposed, paying attention to methods for identifying shrines in the archaeological record.

ETHNOGRAPHIC BACKGROUND

The first anthropologically related research on the Kusasi occurred in the 1930s with a major ethnographic survey of northern Ghana conducted by Rattray (1932), which provides details about Kusasi social organization, history, material culture, religion, and language. During the same decade, administrative reports appeared on Kusasi history and socio-political organization (Syme 1932) and Kusasi agriculture, land use, and management (Lynn 1937). The last seventy years of anthropological study has been dominated by recurrent developmentally oriented research on Kusasi agriculture and the physical environment (Blench 1998; Chilalah 1957; Cleveland 1980, 1986, 1989, 1991; Devereux 1989, 1993; Webber 1996a, 1996b; Whitehead 1988; Wiszniewski 1955).[2]

Observations for this study were made in Zorse, a densely populated rural settlement located near the Northwest outskirts of Bawku, the capital of Bawku East District, Upper East Region (Fig. 1). The area covered by Bawku East District and the neighbouring district of Bawku West is the home territory of the Kusasi. Approximately 3,000 square kilometres, Kusasi home territory is bordered by the Red Volta River, Togo, Burkina Faso, and the Gambaga escarpment. The climate here is arid and semi-tropical. Precipitation is largely limited to the wet season, which lasts from May to September. The dry season is marked by dust storms and Harmattan winds and lasts from November to April.

The Kusasi are politically acephalous sedentary horticulturalists (Blench 1998; Cleveland 1980; Lynn 1937; Webber 1996a). They have a patrilineal segmentary social organization and speak a Gur (Niger-Congo phylum) language (Naden 1988). Polygyny is common in Kusasi society and patrilocal post-marital residence is the norm. The basic unit of settlement is the *yir*, an earthen walled, multi-courtyard compound occupied by a residential group consisting of male agnates, their wives, and children. Traditionally, compounds were subject to abandonment as part of the

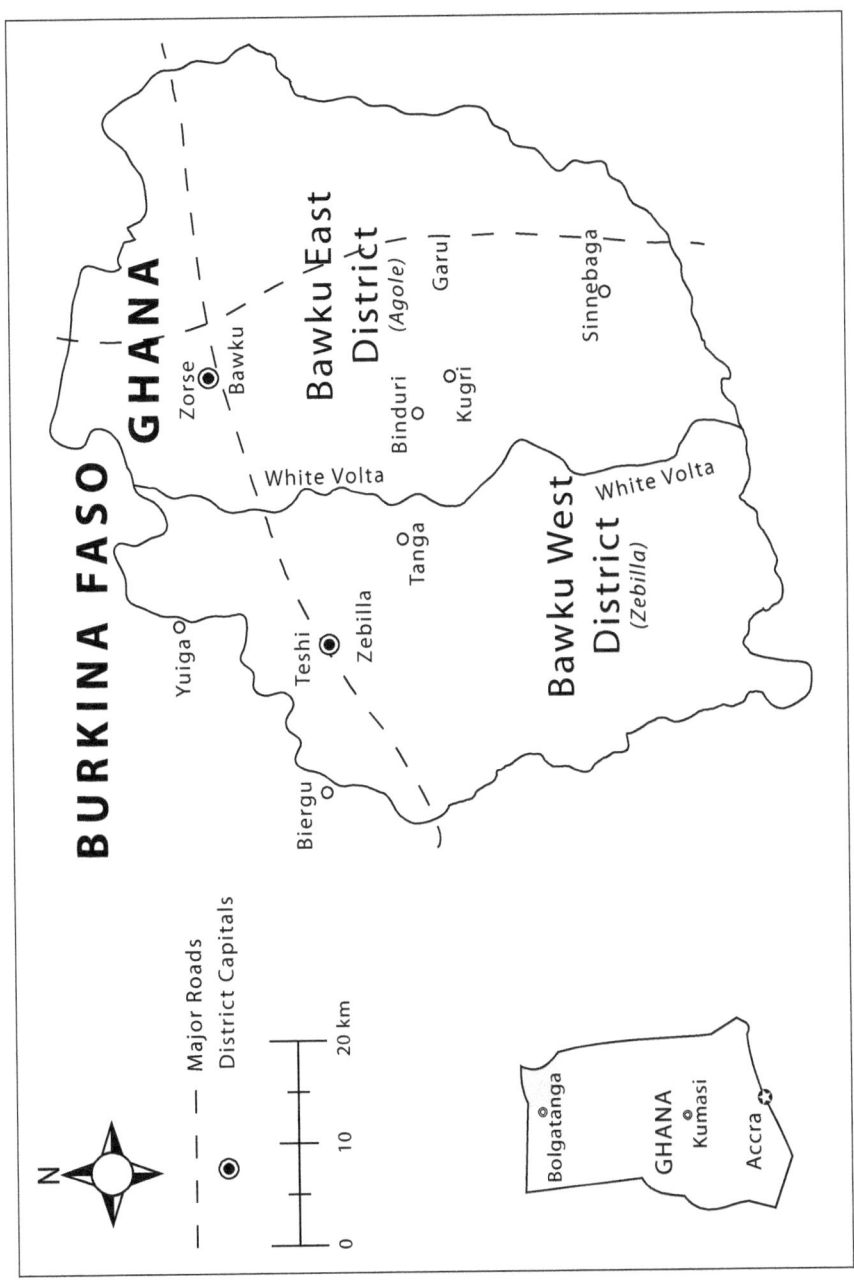

Fig. 1. Location of study area in Ghana, West Africa.

farming cycle. As lands surrounding the compound became less fertile, residents abandoned compounds in favour of locales on more fertile lands. An abandoned compound is a *dabog*, a term that also refers to a lineage and a compound whose founder is deceased.

DATA COLLECTION AND METHODS

Observations used in the present study were made during nine months of fieldwork, from July 1996 to April 1997. The research team included my wife, Rebecca, and our interpreter, Cletus Anobiga. Our study was designed to provide archaeologists with a framework for identifying and interpreting shrines in the material remains of the archaeological record. Research goals included: (1) compiling a shrine typology; (2) deriving a sample of compound plans, including the locations and distributions of shrines; (3) examining abandoned compounds to determine whether shrines get output and survive in the archaeological record.

Information from 237 interviews with 153 compound heads was used to compile a shrine inventory. In total, 1,600 shrines belonging to roughly a hundred types were recorded and classified into five groups, as will be discussed in more detail below. Information was gathered concerning the creation of and patterns of inheritance for shrines, and whether people ever discard shrines. Physical characteristics of shrines such as size and form and raw materials used in construction were recorded. Details on domestic activities and activity areas in and around compounds were recorded along with observations of construction episodes at a half dozen compounds. Scale diagrams were made for twenty-seven compounds from the interview sample and show the locations and distributions of different shrines within compound space. Further interviews were conducted with the heads of these compounds in order to elicit reasons and rationales for the placement of shrines.

Subsequent to collecting data about occupied compounds, research focused on abandoned compounds. In a forest reserve directly to the south of Zorse, three compound sites abandoned during the 1930s were examined. These examinations consisted of pacing out the approximate dimensions of the compounds using elders' memories and surface scatters as guides. Notes on surface materials were also compiled. Similar work was done on three compounds abandoned in the reserve within the last twenty years. Interviews with neighbours and relatives elucidated the reasons for abandonment. Detailed notes and sketch maps were made of compound remains. These examinations revealed whether or not shrines survive immediate abandonment and hence furthered understanding of the depositional processes acting on shrines in the archaeological record.

SHRINES

In the context of this study, a shrine is a physical object at which people make animal sacrifices and pour libations in honour of supernatural otherworldly agents including ancestors, spirits of the land, divining spirits, and nature spirits. Shrines are the foci of ritual practice because they are the dwelling places of the supernatural agents the people pay homage to. A shrine may be made up of a number of objects or it may consist of a single object. The most common objects are animal horns and tails, stones, trees, ceramic vessels, iron rods and bangles, plant roots, and calabashes.

Table 1: Frequency of Different Shrine Types in the Sample of 153 Compounds.

SHRINE TYPE	NUMBER	PER CENT
Personal destiny shrines	454	28
Other	373	23
Paternal ancestor shrines	335	20.2
Maternal ancestor shrines	204	12.6
Spirits of the wild	263	16.2
Total	1,629	100

For analytical purposes, I placed the shrines I recorded into five categories: (1) land gods, (2) personal destiny shrines, (3) ancestor shrines, (4) shrines for spirits of the wild, and (5) other shrines (See Table 1). Analytical categories are based upon function and associated spirit more than physical form. This is largely because the physical form and objects used to make a shrine are not always correlated with the function of and spirits associated with the shrine.

The term *land gods* refers to the spirits of particular places and to the shrines that commemorate human relations with those spirits (see Mather 2003). The Kusal term for land gods is *tengbana*, which literally translates as "skin of the earth." Most land gods are large stones set into the ground of forest groves, hills, ponds, and other natural features. People appeal to the land gods when there is drought, epidemics of disease, or outbreaks of blight on crops. Appeals are also made when witchcraft threatens the larger community or when it faces physical attack. Land gods guard the community much like parents safeguard their children. They hold spiritual and social authority over human communities.

Personal destiny (*win*) is a guiding light that shines upon the individual and provides good fortune, health, well-being, and fertility. Each individual has a *win*, a unique destiny that comes from the high god *Na-Win*. Consequently, personal destiny shrines are the most commonly encountered shrines, accounting for 28 per cent of the shrines recorded in the present study. A personal destiny shrine is a plastered, rounded mound of earth. In most cases an individual's personal destiny shrine is located directly outside that individual's room. Exceptions to this rule are found in the case of the personal destiny shrines of a compound head or of a deceased compound head. In these cases the shrine is generally located either in the public yard, or *saman*, in the front of the compound, or in the main courtyard of the compound. The personal destiny shrine of a deceased compound head is maintained by the dead man's senior son, who refers to the shrine as *ba-win* (father's personal destiny).

Spirits of the wild (*kinkiriis*) are also called "bush spirits" and "fairies." Spirits of the wild are of the "wild" not necessarily because they originated there but because they are without a house; they have no connections to living persons or social groups and hence no source for libations and sacrifices. Many of the spirits in the wild once belonged to houses, but this was so long ago that they have become forgotten and fallen out of the pool of ancestors that receive sacrifices from the living members of the house.

In order to be re-enshrined, the *kinkiriis* take one of two courses. They appear to one of their agnatic or cognatic descendants in the form of natural phenomena or they reincarnate in newborn children. The former situation usually leads to the creation of a chameleon (*dendet*) shrine, while the latter situation requires the erection of a birth shrine.

Spirits of the chameleon shrine come to an individual, or call to an individual by appearing as a pair of chameleons mating in the bush. Chameleon shrines make up 8 per cent of the total number of shrines recorded in the present study. The consequence of seeing the chameleons is blindness. To prevent blindness one has to kill the chameleons, remove their heads and make a protective charm from them, and erect a second shrine at one's personal destiny shrine. The shrines usually consist of a small ceramic vessel, often a water pot, next to a personal destiny shrine. Commonly, people mould a stylized chameleon above the water pot – sometimes in the mound that forms the destiny shrine; other times on a wall. In some cases, people will build and plaster the mound around the water pot, leaving the neck and the mouth of the vessel accessible.

Birth shrines house spirits that cause unusual pregnancies or births. They make up almost the same percentage of the total number of shrines, just under 8 per cent, as chameleon shrines. Women who experience unusual pregnancies or births place the shrines outside their rooms. When the child or children mature and occupy rooms of their own, they relocate the shrines outside their rooms next to their personal destiny shrines. In some cases, individuals locate their birth shrines in the front yard, often at the foot of or built onto the wall of a granary. The most frequently encountered shrine of this type is for breach births (*tula*), and it protects the granary from thieves. There is only one way to enter a granary, through the roof. As a thief enters the granary, legs dangling outside, he or she becomes trapped and caught by the spirit of the shrine. Most birth shrines are undecorated ceramic vessels with a spout on their shoulders that spirits use as an entrance. In the case of twins, the pot has two spouts, one for each spirit.

Ancestor shrines include objects that enshrine maternal and paternal ancestors. Paternal ancestor shrines consist of plum-sized stones set into a mound built onto the outside wall of the compound just north of the front gate. The stones enshrine the spirits of former members of the residential group's patriline, including father, father's wives, grandfathers, grandfather's wives, and great-grandfathers and their wives. Maternal ancestors are enshrined in animal horns (goat, cattle, and wild animals) that are often associated with other objects, including ceramic vessels, stones, animal tails, and paraphernalia used for divining. A third type of ancestor shrine is the chief shrine. Chief shrines house the spirits of maternal or paternal ancestors. They enshrine the latent power within families of chiefly lines and the status of those who fall within the line of succession is reflected by possession of the shrine.

The shrines that belong to the 'other' category are made from a variety of objects, and most of them include more than one object. The seven most frequently encountered objects include animal horns, animal tails, ceramic vessels, stones, calabashes, iron rods and bangles, and trees. The shrines within this category perform one or more of three functions: (1) harnessing or controlling natural forces, (2) launching and protecting against magical attacks, and (3) diagnosing and treating illnesses. The shrines are found throughout the domestic space of the compound, though entranceways are the preferred placements.

Examinations of the spatial distribution of shrines within and around twenty-seven compounds provide some indication of the relative predictability of shrine placement (see Table 2). Several trends are readily seen. Just over half of the shrines within the sample are located in the courtyard while nearly 37 per cent of the shrines in the sample are located in the front yard. Paternal ancestor shrines are only found in the front yard on the exterior wall of the *zong*, the compound entrance hut. Maternal ancestor shrines are the predominant types of shrine found within the *zong*. Personal destiny shrines, paternal ancestor shrines, and chief shrines are never found in personal rooms. Only shrines belonging to the 'other' category are found in animal yards. Drawing upon these observations, it may be possible for archaeologists to determine the type of shrines they find in the archaeological record if they can determine the approximate layout of the abandoned compound from which the shrines were excavated. The rest of this paper will address the likelihood of finding shrines at abandoned compound sites.

Table 2: Distribution of shrines within the sample of twenty-seven compounds.

Shrine	Front yard	Animal yard	Zong	Court yard	Personal Room	Total
Personal destiny	12			91		103
Spirits of the wild	6		1	23	8	38
Paternal ancestor	26					26
Maternal ancestor	10		7	1	10	28
Chief shrine	7			1		8
Other	50	2	1	43	3	99
Total	111	2	9	159	21	302
%	36.7	>1	3	52.6	7	100

COMPOUNDS AND DEPOSITIONAL PROCESSES

One day, while watching a friend fix a roof to a granary in his front yard, I noticed a few pigs grubbing around for food. They found scraps in two large potsherds on the ground near the front gate. A grinding stone with a deeply grooved surface held water from which the pigs drank. My friend stated that his father used the stone to grind tobacco for snuff. Unlike his father, my friend was a smoker and did not need a stone to grind tobacco. The stone had lain in the front yard, where it served as a trough, since his father's death.

The sherds and grinding stone exemplify the recycling and reuse of material culture that takes place within each compound. Tools and objects are modified throughout their life cycle. Broken pots and sherds, for example, are used as lids on other vessels, to give water and food to animals, to support cooking pots, and to make termite traps. When sherds are broken into smaller pieces, people discard them on a heap outside the compound where daily trash burning, walking, and trampling break them down even further. Ground surfaces are littered with tiny pieces of ceramic that have passed through various stages or use-lives. The recycling of objects and tools is a predepositional process, a cultural transformation that affects the condition of objects before they are discarded. Recycling is an example of what Schiffer (1976:37–38) calls "S-S processes," transformations of material culture from state to state within systemic contexts.

Several natural transformations affect Kusasi material culture. Plaster erodes off compound walls under heavy rains, scorching heat, and powerful winds. Without repair, walls decay and rooms become uninhabitable. The same natural phenomena and the recurrent footfall of occupants and visitors wear floors. Many shrines are architectural features built from the same materials and subject to the same erosional forces affecting walls and floors. The mounds built for shrines commemorating paternal ancestors and personal destiny spirits, for example, are slowly worn down by exposure to the elements.

The Kusasi repair their architecture seasonally. Walls and floors are re-plastered at the end of the wet season. Shrines are also repaired. Severely damaged architectural features are destroyed and built anew. New rooms and courtyards are added to existing ones. Remodelling occurs whenever the natural elements have taken their toll or when the residential group grows in size because of the introduction of a new wife or the birth of children. No matter why renovations are needed, rebuilding episodes also exemplify S-S processes; material culture is altered though still used in the same ongoing behavioural system.

A compound is a long-term depositional event. Some compounds in Zorse have been occupied for several generations, experiencing more than a dozen serious episodes of remodelling. Discarded material culture, primarily ceramic sherds, can be found in the front yards of these compounds, mixed and scattered throughout the ground surface. Generally, this detritus forms the bulk of the material assemblage that will ultimately be output from systemic context to archaeological context.

Deposition from systemic to archaeological contexts does not occur until a compound is finally abandoned. Rate and mode of abandonment vary as to circumstances (Cameron 1993:3). Historically, the most common reason for abandoning compounds was the depletion of soil fertility of both compound farms and bush farms. Abandoned compounds remained within the settlement system as sites for farming or as the future locale for a land god shrine for commemorating apical male ancestors and founders. Over the last hundred years, abandonment has become less frequent due to major increases in population density and decreases in available lands for resettlement. In Zorse, because of shortages of unused land for resettlement, compounds are rarely abandoned. Abandonment still occurs, however, in those cases where a compound head dies without having male relatives to inherit his position. This can occur if the compound head has no brothers or sons, or if his brothers have compounds of their own and his sons are too young to assume his role. People call these deaths 'untimely,' or 'coming too early' in the sense that there is no one to continue leading the residential group.

The circumstances surrounding abandonment affect whether and how material culture assemblages will be curated (Kent 1993; Stevenson 1982; Tomka 1993). When a family abandons one compound and founds or moves into another compound, they delay curation until they need their material possessions in their new compound. Constraints upon curation include size and weight of the items involved and the distance to travel between the old and new residential sites (Schiffer 1976:33–34).

People curate shrines along with other useful items. Shrine curation involves libations and sacrifice. Should a compound head have several shrines, curation can be a costly procedure, with the potential that each shrine requires its own sacrifice. Curation also involves divination to learn whether enshrined spirits will allow abandonment without provoking misfortune and whether the spirits are willing to live at the new compound.

People also pass shrines from systemic to systemic contexts by way of 'lateral cycling.' When a compound head dies, the shrines he managed as a senior member of the descent group will be inherited by the man directly after him in the line of succession. The deceased's senior son will inherit the shrines that belong to the man's residential group and those he got on his own volition (e.g., medicine shrines). In the former case, the deceased's successor moves the shrines from the deceased's compound to his own compound. In the latter case, the senior son takes possession of the shrines and, if he no longer lives with his father, he will relocate the shrines to his own compound.

What are the chances of finding shrines in archaeological contexts? Curate behaviour eliminates shrines from material assemblages, making it highly unlikely that shrines will form part of the de facto refuse at an abandoned compound site (Schiffer 1985:26). There are, however, reasons to suspect that shrines will be deposited into archaeological context whenever abandonment occurs because of an untimely death. Observations at three abandoned compound sites support this hypothesis.

THREE ABANDONED COMPOUNDS

The three compounds chosen for analysis differ as to the number of years that have passed since they were abandoned. The first compound was being abandoned during fieldwork for this study, while the second and third compounds were abandoned seven and twenty years ago respectively. Theoretically, each compound represents a different stage of abandonment. They are ordered, by way of presentation, into a sequence. Compound 1 represents the first stages of abandonment, while compound 3 shows us how an abandoned compound site appears following the post-depositional disturbance caused by farming. Compound 2 illustrates an intermediate stage of abandonment – this structure is no longer used as a residence, but it has yet to be knocked down to make way for farming.

Compound 1

Observations of compound 1 were made on March 3, 1997 (Fig. 2). The compound head died in 1992, his final funeral was held in 1994, and the compound was finally abandoned in the middle of December in 1996. The widow and her children continued to live in the compound after the compound head died. They finally abandoned the compound because the widow married one of the compound head's brothers (a man who had the same grandfather).

The wife and her children have curated many of the items of material culture from the compound, including the roofs of buildings. Notwithstanding this, a large quantity of useable items and materials remain in the compound. As she continues to settle into her new home, the widow will take the articles she needs for her new compound. The deceased compound head's brothers, men from the same father, have rights to all of his personal belongings, including the shrines, and they removed most

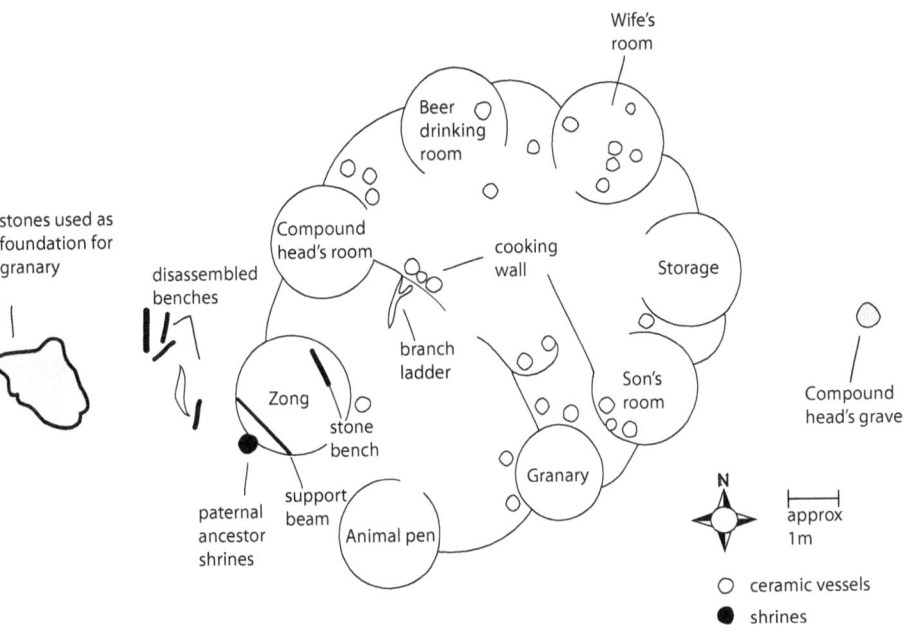

Fig. 2. Sketch plan for abandoned compound 1.

of these items after the final funeral rites for the deceased. Consequently, most of the materials left in the compound are the property of the widow.

The process of abandonment will not be complete until the deceased's relatives perform the appropriate rites to transfer the paternal ancestor shrines that he was responsible for. At this time, the paternal ancestor shrines are still in place on the wall of the *zong*. Once the appropriate rites are conducted, the men in line to inherit the deceased's property (i.e., the senior living descendants of the ancestors in question) will relocate the shrines to their respective compounds. Apart from the paternal ancestor shrines, there is no evidence for shrines in other parts of the compound. The wife has already moved her personal destiny shrine and birth shrines. There is no evidence left of these shrines. This is unexpected because the shrines of this type are frequently built into mounds and the remnants of the mounds would be visible even after the shrines were removed. Likewise, there is no evidence for other shrines in the compound despite the fact that, according to the widow, her husband had controlled other shrines.

Compound 2

Compound 2 was abandoned in 1992 after the sudden death of the compound head (Fig. 3). Apparently, the compound head had no living relatives within the settlement. The deceased's only child, a son, was too young to take control of the house. Since there were no relatives to take responsibility for the child, he moved with his mother to his mother's natal residential group.

Several residents of the sub-settlement wanted to farm where the compound stood, but they could not agree on who could claim the land. The walls of the compound were left standing. Neighbours took roofs from buildings right after the compound was abandoned, while the widow moved her personal belongings to her father's house. Since abandonment, the compound has served as a pig barn.

The compound head's grave is in the front yard about four metres southwest of the compound entrance. A water pot, likely once used as a burial shrine, sits atop the grave. Approximately four metres west of the grave, there is a pile of household refuse. Directly west of the compound entrance, around six metres away, there is a granary. A birth shrine rests at the foot of the granary. Midway between the compound entrance and granary there is a plastered mound, severely eroded, that once served as the compound head's personal destiny shrine. The bathing area between the wife's room and son's room includes the plastered mound and stone that served as the wife's personal destiny shrine. A large potsherd covers the mound. Just south of the personal destiny shrine, there is a small water pot on top of an upside-down metal bowl with a rusted-out bottom. Ethnographic observation suggests that these latter objects once served as a chameleon shrine. In the son's room, partially buried in the floor near the entrance at the north of the room, there is a flat, black, circular stone on top of a medium-sized water pot. The water pot is upside down, placed within a metal ring (most likely the neck of a metal basin), and its bottom is broken. The metal ring was lodged into the top of a circular hole, with the ceramic vessel fit snugly into the ring and resting directly in the hole. Drawing from ethnographic examples, these objects were used as a shrine prior to abandonment.

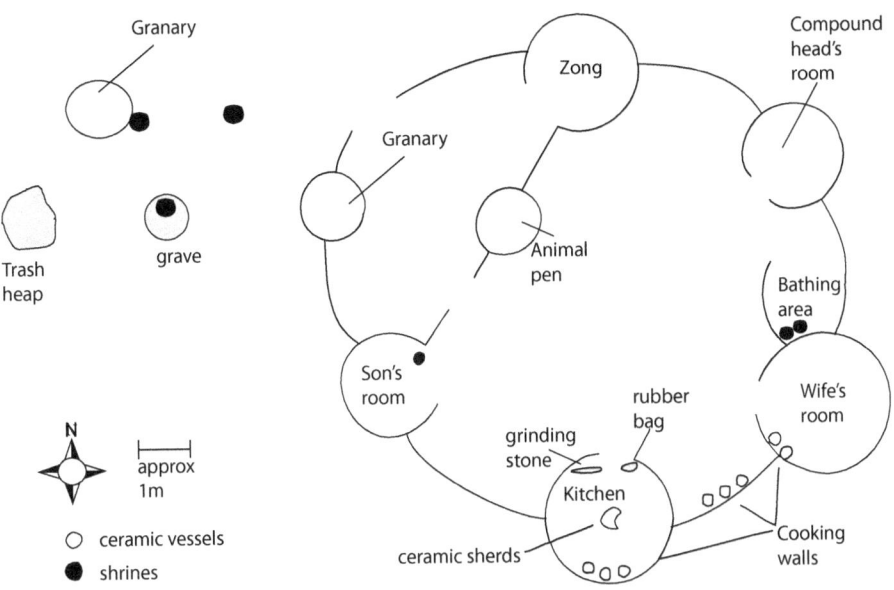

Fig. 3. Sketch plan for abandoned compound 2.

Compound 3

Abandoned compound 3 is located approximately forty metres north of compound 2 (Fig. 4). It was abandoned in 1979 following the death of the compound head and his wife. The couple's only child, a son who worked as a police officer in the south, died shortly after his parents. The son left no descendants.

A few years after abandonment, members of the compound head's descent group knocked down the compound walls and began using the site for farming. Three graves, housing the compound head, his wife, and son, lie in the former front yard (Fig. 4). Near the graves a water pot rests at the foot of a small tree. Little remains of the compound, save for a large roughly rectangular area of lightly coloured soil, about eighteen metres long east to west and nine metres wide north to south. Concentrations of charred ceramic sherds and cement are scattered around this area.

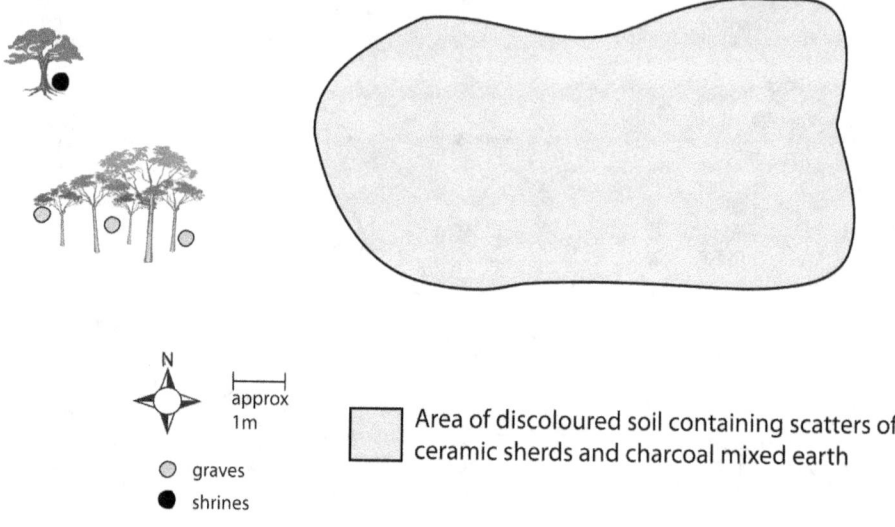

Fig. 4. Sketch plan for abandoned compound 3.

Whatever de facto refuse remained after abandonment is now destroyed and thoroughly mixed with soil and farming detritus. The only indications a compound existed on the site are the shade tree and graves, and a myriad of remnants from household features and activities, seriously disturbed and damaged.

DISCUSSION

The Kusasi use the term *dabog* to refer to an abandoned compound. *Dabog* is also reserved for a descent group whose founder is deceased and to a compound whose founder is deceased. Abandonment is almost synonymous with the death of individuals who hold offices of authority, whether they are compound heads, senior members of descent groups, or chiefs.

In the majority of cases, the death of an office holder does not lead to abandonment of territory or residences. When a compound head dies, for example, the surviving senior member of his residential group, a brother or son, will assume his role. If the deceased was also the compound founder, the compound will thereafter be referred to as a *dabog* (a social and spatial entity whose founder is deceased) and a *yir* (a physical structure occupied by the founder's descendants) (Mather 1999:139).

The three compounds examined above were abandoned under uncommon circumstances; a compound head died and no one in his residential group could assume his role. In each case, a residential group ceased to exist and the physical shelter it occupied was abandoned. These are favourable events from the vantage of archaeology and shrines because, if there is no one to inherit the compound head's office, it is likely there is no one to inherit and curate the compound head's personal shrines. When the compound is abandoned, the shrines are effectively discarded from systemic contexts.

Compound 1 differs from compounds 2 and 3 because the compound head's shrines were or will be curated. His personal shrines are now located in the compound where his children and other relatives live. When his sons are old enough, the senior son will assume control of the shrines as head of the residential group and descent group. The shrines will be held as the common property of all of the deceased founder's sons. The compound founded by the compound head has been abandoned but the residential group he founded still exists. As his sons mature into adulthood and marry, the group will grow and fission, and the founder's personal shrines will be curated down through the generations. The shrines that the compound head controlled as the senior member of the descent group founded by his father are or will be located in his successor's compound. The paternal ancestor shrines, for example, will be relocated once the appropriate rituals are performed at the deceased's successor's compound (Mather 1999:89–90).

Compounds 2 and 3 represent catastrophic abandonments because the residential groups have ceased to exist. The bloodlines started by the compound heads are ended and the shrines the men controlled are now refuse. Compound 2 likely contains six shrines: the compound head's personal destiny shrine, the wife's personal destiny shrine and chameleon shrine, an unknown shrine resting on top of one of the graves in the front yard, a birth shrine, and an unknown shrine in the floor of the son's room. If and when the compound walls and floors are broken down to make way for farming, it is likely that at least three of the shrines, the wife's personal destiny shrine and her chameleon shrine, and the unknown shrine located in the sons' room, will be destroyed. In addition, the compound head's personal destiny shrine will continue to erode away under exposure to the elements. This leaves two shrines that stand a chance of surviving post-abandonment disturbances.

Unlike compound 2, compound 3 has suffered serious post-abandonment disturbance. Nevertheless, an object that could be a shrine, consisting of a water pot at the foot of a tree, survives in what was once the front yard of the compound. There is no guarantee the shrine will be output into archaeological contexts, though it should be noted it has lasted in its present state since 1979.

In summary, abandonment can lead to the discard of shrines if it also involves the demise of a residential group. Despite the fact that shrines can be discarded, post-abandonment processes disturb and further deplete de facto refuse. Given ideal circumstances, such as with compound 2 where post-abandonment farming does not take place, shrines may well remain intact and in situ. It is more likely, however, that post-abandonment farming will destroy discarded shrines along with the rest of the compound. Consequently, to find evidence for shrines one will have to look towards the detritus that forms the bulk of the impoverished material assemblages found in archaeological contexts.

CONCLUSIONS: LOOKING FOR SHRINES

What should one look for to find evidence of human occupations from the recent past? To identify compound sites one can focus on several features. Trees are an excellent sign of human occupation. Compounds occupied for more than a single generation typically have at least one large tree shading the front yard with several graves located nearby. Trees and graves characterize abandoned compound sites, and as the description of compound 2 shows, they are often associated with shrines. Ethnographic observations indicate that shrines are placed in predictable locations in occupied compounds. Archaeologists can expect that shrine remains will be in close proximity to where the shrines they once belonged to were placed in the compound when it was occupied. The front yard and courtyard are the primary areas of interest, while personal rooms and the *zong* are secondary areas of interest.

After an abandoned compound site has been discovered, excavations should focus on covering as much area of the site as possible in order to discover whether shrines were present when the compound was occupied. Archaeologists interested in finding shrines should focus on horizontal rather than vertical excavations. Particular attention should be given to discerning entranceways to the compound, internal courtyards, and rooms. Given that compounds only have one entrance and that this entrance is always located on the western side of the compound, archaeologists can move eastwards to find the inside of the compound and hence the internal courtyards and westwards to locate the front yard.

Once an abandoned compound site is identified and excavated, one is still left with the task of determining whether the materials one uncovers are the remnants of mundane objects and behaviours or whether they are the remains of shrines. Unfortunately, shrines are unlikely to be deposited intact, a somewhat discouraging fact. How is one to discern whether the stone, potsherd, or hoe blade one finds in the archaeological record was a shrine and not just another mundane object?

Various activities and materials create and leave physical traces upon the objects forming shrines. Pots used to prepare medicines are charred black on their bottoms and sides from direct exposure to fire. Sacrifices leave ample amounts of animal blood on the surfaces of shrines and upon the ground surfaces around the shrines. Libations of millet beer and water mixed with millet flour are regularly poured upon shrines. Inside surfaces of the pots that contain medicines absorb residues from the different plants soaking within the pots.

Morphological, histological, and chemical criteria may be used to identify remnants of plants and plant foods on artefact surfaces (Fullagar et al. 1996; Hillman et al. 1993). Blood proteins can be identified in residues using various immunologic techniques including ouchterlony (OCH), radio-immuno-assay (RIA), gold immunoassay (GIA), crossover-immuno-electrophoresis (CIEP), and enzyme-linked-immuno-absorbant-assay (ELISA) (Downs and Lowenstein 1995; Eisle et al. 1995; Fiedel 1996; Kooyman et al. 1992). Lacking target compounds, use of these techniques will require compiling a reference collection by sampling contemporary plants and food plants from the study area and compiling a comprehensive list of animals commonly sacrificed at shrines.

In conclusion, focusing on horizontal excavations and using residue analysis, archaeologists stand a reasonable chance of uncovering shrines in the archaeological record. The likelihood of finding intact shrines is remote. Notwithstanding this, drawing upon ethnographic examples, it might be possible to infer shrine type from spatial context (e.g., personal destiny shrines are generally found near personal rooms). If we can identify and type shrines in the archaeological record, we can extrapolate to the make-up and social dynamic of residential groups represented by material culture assemblages from the past that are comparable to Kusasi material culture.

ACKNOWLEDGMENTS

Research would not have been possible without the encouragement, understanding, and participation of the residents of Zorse, the late Zorsenaba, the Tengindana, and my interpreter, Cletus Anobiga. The Ghana Museums and Monuments Board kindly extended a research permit for the fieldwork. Dr. Nicholas C. David provided funding support through the Social Sciences and Humanities Research Council of Canada (Grant No. 410-92-28). This research was conducted as part of the Mandara Archaeological Project (Ghana Phase) directed by Nicholas C. David.

NOTES

1   Rattray (1932) provides details on shrines amongst northern populations in general, Kirby (1986) amongst the Anufo, Goody (1962) amongst the LoDagaba, and Kroger (1982) amongst the Bulsa.

2   Work has also been carried out on the phonology and syntax of Kusal, the language spoken by the Kusasi (Spratt and Spratt 1968, 1972), on Kusasi vernacular architecture (Bourdier and Min-Ha 1985), Kusasi history (Hilton 1962), and Kusasi marital exchange and prestations (Awedoba 1989a,b, 1990).

REFERENCES

Awedoba, A.K. 1989a. "Notes on Matrimonial Goods Among the Atoende Kusasi, Part 1." *Research Review* 5, no. 1:37-53.

———. 1989b. "Matrimonial Goods among the Atoende Kusasi Contingent Prestations, Part 2." *Research Review* 5, no. 2:1-17.

———. 1990. "Matrimonial Goods among the Atoende Kusasi: Matrimonial Prestations and Exploitation, Part 3." *Research Review* 6, no. 1:49-56.

Blench, R.M. 1998. *Developing Common Property Resource Management: Upper East and Northern Regions, Ghana*. London: Overseas Development Institute.

Bourdier, J-P., and T.T. Min-Ha. 1985. *African Spaces: Designs for Living in Upper Volta*. New York: Africana Publishing.

Cameron, Catherine M. 1993. "Abandonment and Archaeological Interpretation." In *Abandonment of Settlements and Regions: Ethnoarchaeological and Archaeological Approaches*, ed. Catherine M. Cameron and Steve A. Tomka, 3-7. Cambridge: Cambridge University Press.

Chilalah, G.C. 1957. "Advances in Agriculture in Kusasi, Northern Ghana." *Ghana Farmer* 1:198-201.

Cleveland, David A. 1980. *The Population Dynamics of Subsistence Agriculture in the West African Savanna: A Village in Northeast Ghana*. PhD dissertation. Tucson: University of Arizona.

———. 1986. "The Political Economy of Fertility Regulation: The Kusasi of Savanna West Africa (Ghana)." In *Culture and Reproduction: An Anthropological Critique of Demographic Transition Theory*, ed. H. Pennewerker, 263-93. Boulder, CO: Westview Press.

———. 1989. "Developmental Stage Age Groups and African Populations Structure: The Kusasi of the West African Savannah." *American Anthropologist* 91, no. 2:401-13.

———. 1991. "Migration in West Africa: A Savanna Village Perspective." *Africa* 61:222-46.

Devereux, S. 1989. *Food Security, Seasonality and Resource Allocation in Northeastern Ghana (ESCOR R4481)*. London: Overseas Development Institute.

———. 1993. "Observers are Worried: Learning the Language and Counting the People in Northeast Ghana." In *Fieldwork in Developing Countries*, ed. S. Devereux and J. Hoddinott, 43-56. Boulder, CO: Lynne Reiner.

Downs, E.F., and J.M. Lowenstein. 1995. "Identification of Archaeological Blood Proteins: A Cautionary Note." *Journal of Archaeological Science* 22:11-16.

Eisle, J.A., D.D. Fowler, G. Haynes, and R.A. Lewis. 1995. "Survival and Detection of Blood Residues on Stone Tools," *Antiquity* 69:36-46.

Fiedel, S.J. 1996. "Blood from Stones? Some Methodological and Interpretive Problems in Blood Residue Analysis." *Journal of Archaeological Science* 23:139-47.

Fortes, Meyer. 1949. *The Web of Kinship among the Tallensi*. London: Oxford University Press.

Fullagar, R., J. Furby, and Bruce Hardy. 1996. "Residues on Stone Artefact: State of a Scientific Art." *Antiquity* 70:740-45.

Goody, Jack. 1962. *Death, Property and the Ancestors: A Study of the Mortuary Customs of the LoDagaa of West Africa*. Stanford: Stanford University Press.

Hillman, Gordon, Sue Wales, Frances McLaren, John Evans, and Ann Butler. 1993. "Identifying Problematic Remains of Ancient Plant Foods: A Comparison of the Role of Chemical, Histological, and Morphological Criteria." *World Archaeology* 25, no. 1:94-121.

Hilton, T.E. 1962."Notes on the History of Kusasi." *Transactions of the Historical Society of Ghana* 6:79-96.

Kent, Susan. 1993. "Models of Abandonment and Material Culture Frequencies." In *Abandonment of Settlements and Regions: Ethnoarchaeological and Archaeological Approaches*, ed. Catherine M. Cameron and Steve A. Tomka, 54-74. Cambridge: Cambridge University Press.

Kirby, Jon P. 1986. *God, Shrines, and Problem-Solving among the Anufo of Northern Ghana*. Berlin: Dietrich Reimer.

Kooyman, B., M.E. Newman, and H. Cerl. 1992. "Verifying the Reliability of Blood Residue Analysis on Archaeological Tools." *Journal of Archaeological Science* 19:265-69.

Kroger, F. 1982. *Ancestor Worship among the Bulsa of Northern Ghana: Religious, Social and Economic Aspects*. Munich: Klaus Renner.

Lynn, C.W. 1937. "Agriculture in North Mamprusi." *Ghana Department of Agriculture Bulletin* 34.

Mather, Charles M. 1999. An Ethnoarchaeology of Kusasi Shrines, Upper East Region, Ghana. PhD dissertation, Calgary: University of Calgary.

———. 2003. "Shrines and the Domestication of Landscape." *Journal of Anthropological Research* 59, no. 1:23-45.

Naden, T. 1988. "The Gur languages." In *The Languages of Ghana*, ed. M.E.K. Dakubu, 12-49. London: Kegan Paul.

Rattray, R. S. 1932. *The Tribes of the Ashanti Hinterland*. Oxford: Clarendon.

Schiffer, M. 1976. *Behavioural Archaeology*. New York: Academic Press.

———. 1985. "Is there a 'Pompeii Premise' in archaeology?" *Journal of Anthropological Research* 41:18-41.

Spratt, D., and N. Spratt. 1968. *Collected Field Reports on the Phonology of Kusasi*. Legon: University of Ghana Institute of African Studies.

———. 1972. *Kusal Syntax*. Legon: University of Ghana Institute of African Studies.

Stevenson, M. G. 1982. "Towards an Understanding of Site Abandonment Behaviour: Evidence from Historic Mining Camps in the Southwest Yukon." *Journal of Anthropological Archaeology* 1:237-65.

Syme, J.K.G. 1932. *The Kusasis: A Short History* (mimeo).

Tomka, Steve A. 1993. "Site Abandonment Behaviour among Transhumant Agro-Pastoralists: The Effects of Delayed Curation on Assemblage Composition." In *Abandonment of Settlements and Regions: Ethnoarchaeological and Archaeological Approaches*, ed. Catherine M. Cameron and Steve A. Tomka, 11–24. Cambridge: Cambridge University Press.

Webber, Paul. 1996a. "Agrarian change in Kusasi, North-East Ghana." *Africa* 66, no. 3:437–57.

———. 1996b. "News from the Village: Agrarian Change in Ghana." *Geography Review* 9, no. 3:25–30.

Whitehead, A. 1988. *Distributional Effect of Cash Crop Innovation: The Peripherally Commercialised Farmers of North East Ghana*. Sussex: Institute of Development Studies.

Wiszniewski, T. M. 1955. "Dry Season Vegetable Gardening in Kusasi." *Gold Coast Department of Agriculture Quarterly Newsletter* 9, no. 1:3–5.

Constructing Ritual Protection on an Expanding Settlement Frontier: Earth Shrines in the Black Volta Region

CAROLA LENTZ (JOHANNES GUTENBERG UNIVERSITY, MAINZ)

ABSTRACT

While ancestor shrines mark a proper house among the Dagara and other groups in northern Ghana and southern Burkina Faso, the earth shrine signifies a proper village. New settlements are founded through expansion across the landscape and claims of 'who came first' on a particular patch of land become bound up with the creation and jurisdiction of new earth shrines. This paper seeks to explore the dynamics of migration and movement, focusing on the creation of earth shrines, of Dagara-speaking groups in the Black Volta region of West Africa into already thinly settled areas inhabited mainly by Sisala and Phuo-speaking groups.

Keywords: earth shrines, Dagara, Sisala, Ghana, Burkina Faso, frontiers, Black Volta, migration, ritual authority.

INTRODUCTION

Claiming to be the first-comers in an area is the most widespread strategy to legitimate authority in Africa, as Igor Kopytoff (1987) has argued in his seminal article on the internal African frontier. In the West African savannah, and in much of Africa, claims of being the first-comers on a particular piece of land are also intimately intertwined with questions of land rights and ownership. First-comers, be they individuals or, more commonly, groups of frontiersmen, are believed to have established a special relationship with the spirits of the land and thus played a crucial role in 'opening up' the wild bush or forest for human settlement and agriculture. In many places, first-comers established shrines at which regular sacrifices are offered to the earth god in order to ensure the fertility of the land and the well-being of the community (Eyre-Smith 1933; Goody 1957; Zwernemann 1968). The office of the earth priest, the custodian of the shrine, is usually vested in the lineage of the first-comers, at least according to widespread norms, and even where the office was appropriated by a powerful group of late-comers, these late-comers often still present their claims in the idiom of first-comership by re-interpreting the settlement history. First-comers and their descendants distributed land to later immigrants, granted, and still grant, the right to build houses and bury the dead, and often mediate in conflicts over land boundaries and land use. In many areas, first-comer lineages are considered to be the allodial owners of the land, even though it may be highly controversial what this entails in practical terms when, in the course of time, all village lands have been assigned to late-coming families (Kuba et al. 2004; Lund 2006).

If first-comers are believed to be the founders of earth shrines, the reverse is also true: control over an earth shrine supports claims to being first-comers and to allodial property rights. As a consequence, the shrines' origins, trajectories, and jurisdiction were, and continue to be, often subject to intense debate. In this article, I want to explore the dynamics of the historical settlement frontier in the Black Volta region, focusing on the creation of earth shrines.

During the past two hundred years or even longer, the area of what is today north-western Ghana and south-western Burkina Faso has been the site of an impressive agricultural expansion of Dagara-speaking groups.[1] They moved into unpopulated bush, but more often into already thinly settled areas, inhabited mainly by Sisala and Phuo-speaking groups, as

well as Dyan, Bwaba, and Lobi. Unlike the frontiersmen from expansionist centralized polities, the Dagara pioneers were not interested in establishing political control over the previous inhabitants of their new territories, but in gaining control over the land, materially and ritually. Following a first phase of relatively peaceful cohabitation, this aim often involved the displacement of the previous inhabitants. In some cases, the latter were driven away violently, under the threat of being killed; in other cases, they opted to move away 'voluntarily.' In any case, the Dagara's quest for land was more successful than the claims of these earlier inhabitants, at least until the early years of the twentieth century. But even where violence towards previous inhabitants or competing immigrants helped to establish a new settlement, if it was to prosper and attract further settlers, it needed spiritual protection, through peaceful communication with the earth god and the spirits of the bush, and a stable social and ritual order that defined, among other things, the rights of access to and control over the natural resources. In other words, the new settlement needed an earth shrine – either a shrine of its own or close ties to an already existing one.

In what follows, I will compare Sisala and Dagara conceptions of earth shrines and analyze the ways in which the Dagara frontiersmen created shrines or acquired them from the Sisala. These observations are part of a larger research project on the settlement history, the appropriation of land, and the dynamics of ethnic relations in the Black Volta region, in which I have been involved since 1996.[2] Because written sources predating the arrival of the French and the British in 1897 are entirely absent, oral traditions were our most important sources in reconstructing the regional history. Over the years, our team of researchers collected over five hundred stories of 'migration-and-settlement,' including narratives about the construction of earth shrines, in more than 150 villages, covering settlements of all relevant 'ethnic' groups in an area of about 3,500 square kilometres. The interpretation of these oral traditions, however, involved thorny methodological questions. For one, these traditions rarely go back further than four or five generations. Furthermore, in this area there are no indigenous professional historians, like the *griots*, and no official village histories, so that we were confronted with numerous and contradictory accounts related by different patrilineages. Finally and most importantly, these competing traditions play an important role in supporting claims to land and positions of authority and so can obviously not be taken at face value. In order to understand the micro-politics of oral traditions, therefore, we complemented the survey-type interviews in a large number of villages with in-depth case studies in selected localities and compared the 'winner's' and 'loser's' versions of accounts relating struggles over land rights. Furthermore, we looked for non-narrative sources that may confirm or contradict the narrative material. Such sources were trees, and more specifically the composition of agricultural 'parks,' which help to establish relative chronologies of settlement (Lentz and Sturm 2001); village names, which give indications of how a settlement was founded; the spatial distribution of lineage segments, which reveals migration patterns; and, finally, currently existing ritual hierarchies, which often reflect sedimented settlement history. Much of this 'non-narrative' material was accessible because I have been doing fieldwork in the area for more almost twenty years and gained insight through many informal conversations, walking with people through their fields or travelling to neighbouring villages, acquiring a building lot and constructing a house of my own in one of the villages, and assisting at sacrifices at ancestor shrines and earth shrines.

STRATEGIES OF EXPANSION: RITUAL PROTECTION ON THE FRONTIER[3]

Just as ancestor shrines mark a proper house, the earth shrine signifies a proper village. The underlying concept of earth shrines shows some similarities among all societies in the Black Volta region. All land is believed to be under the ritual protection of an earth god with whom first-comers concluded a kind of 'pact' (Dacher 1997; Goody 1957; Kuba et al. 2004; Liberski-Bagnoud 2002; Savonnet 1976; Tengan 1991; Zwernemann 1968). The territory under the protection of a particular earth shrine is called *tengan* (literally the 'crust' or 'skin of the earth') in Dagara and *tebuo* in Sisale. It includes the settlement as well as different categories of uninhabited bush. During the early phases of settlement in the region, when land was not scarce, the earth-shrine 'parish,' to use Goody's (1956) term, was probably understood, not as a flat homogenous territory with separating linear boundaries, but as a field of ritual power, with a well-defined centre (the earth shrine) in the inhabited and regularly cultivated space, and with concentric circles of influence that thinned out towards the uncultivated bush. However, when more and more bush was being cultivated, the boundaries between neighbouring earth-shrine parishes had to be defined more precisely, often in a conflict-ridden process. The custodians of the earth shrine were generally not regarded as the 'owners' of the natural resources in a strictly economic sense. But because of their privileged access to the earth gods, they were the only frontiersmen capable of ritually transforming 'virgin' bush into exploitable resources and surveying the proper order of all earth-related matters (Jacob 2002; 2003), and it is from these indispensable tasks that they derived, and continue to derive, their income (ritual gifts from co-villagers and further immigrants) and special rights to control all hunting, fishing, and gathering activities.

While the Dagara, the Sisala, and most of their neighbours share these basic concepts, each group has developed its own ideas about the installation and handling of an earth shrine and about who should be its custodian. Among the Dagara, the earth shrine itself usually consists of a stone (*tengan kuur*) and a tree (*tengan tie*) under which the stone is buried and where sacrifices are carried out. As mentioned above, the custodian of the shrine, the *tengansob* (the 'owner' or 'master' of the shrine), supposedly a descendant of the first settler, is responsible for sacrifices to the earth, allocates land to new settlers, plays an important role in the ritual opening of new houses, and opens the annual fishing and hunting parties. In cases of suicide or other 'unnatural' deaths, the *tengansob* must intervene to repair the damage done to the earth before the corpse can be buried. The apparent power of the earth-priestly office is restricted by numerous taboos. Although the earth priest benefits from the sacrificial meat and beer and is entitled to lost property and stray domestic animals, the office is generally regarded as dangerous and unrewarding. However, while individuals may be reluctant to become a *tengansob*, the patriclan segment within which the office hereditarily circulates will strongly affirm its right to chose the earth priest from its ranks.

The stone at the centre of the Dagara earth shrine is a surprisingly mobile object; it may be carried in a bag from one location to another. An earth shrine is believed to transfer its powers to any stone lying on the ground surrounding the *tengan*. This is how the 'mother' shrine can produce 'children' (*kubile*, 'small stones'), which may be carried away, by members of the earth-priestly lineage, to be installed elsewhere. All Dagara-Wiile *tengan kube* found in the area of Dano, for instance, are believed to come from the original home, located in what is now Ghana. For the Dagara-Lobr, however, there is a taboo against carrying a *tengan kuur* across the Black Volta, and, although performing sacrifices at the ford can circumvent the taboo, earth shrines with origins that can be traced to the other side of the river are rare.

If a new Dagara settlement is founded on land under the protection of an existing Dagara earth shrine with the consent and help of the shrine's custodian, the ritual dependence of the younger settlement is usually not disputed. Communal sacrifices at the beginning and the end of the farming season were first performed at the older earth shrine, but eventually an elder of the new settlement would be given permission to carry out most of the sacrifices on behalf of the new neighbourhood and to ritually 'open' new houses and supervise the burial of the dead. This could lead to the establishment of an independent earth shrine, whose custodians, in some cases, even denied its past affiliation with the 'mother' shrine. In a number of cases, however, the founding lineages of new settlements refused to ask the neighbouring village for a *kubile*, turning instead to a more distant settlement where a closely related segment of their patriclan held the office of the *tengansob*. On the whole, whatever relationship governs the allegiance between the junior and the senior shrines, be it kinship or territorial ties, an asymmetrical relationship between shrines can be observed in ritual practice. The ritual dependence of a new settlement usually lasts for several generations, but in most cases the new village will strive to gain more autonomy. This is usually a lengthy and tedious process that is generally not well received by the original village. Independence means that serious offences against the earth, even suicide, can be made good through sacrifice at the new village's *tengan* without having to refer to the 'mother' shrine.

Networks and hierarchies between several earth shrines and processes of 'fission' of ritual parishes are much more important among the Dagara than among their neighbours. As I will discuss in more detail in the next section, the Sisala appear to have no concept of ritual dependence between earth shrines, even though alliances between neighbouring villages are in some cases reflected by the identical names that their earth shrines bear. Sisala earth shrines are said to have been founded on the spot or with stones that frontiersmen are claimed to have brought with them, but in no case having been received from earlier inhabitants. For the Phuo, a group closely related to the Sisala, on the other hand, it is completely unthinkable

Fig. 1. The earth priest of Bakoteng at his shrine (a *tengankubile* of Ouessa). (Photo: Carola Lentz, 1999).

that earth-shrine stones are carried along; in their eyes, earth shrines cannot be moved.

Comparing Sisala and Dagara earth-shrine policies, one is left with the strong impression that the Dagara have adopted a somewhat simplified ritual system that allows for more flexibility and, most importantly, more mobility than the systems of their neighbours. The Dagara have few taboos on the admissible origins of the shrine stone and few restrictions concerning the recruitment of the custodians of the shrine. Moreover, the pattern of 'fission' of shrine parishes and of establishing 'daughter shrines' transforms the territorial cult into a surprisingly mobile institution. In addition to the strategic advantages of the patriclan system, this was another factor that supported the territorial expansion of the Dagara.

SISALA EARTH SHRINES AND SHRINE ALLIANCES

Among the Sisala, we encounter an explicit ideology of local stability, cohesion of the 'big house,' and longstanding occupation of one place. The separation of an agnatic kin group from its original home is usually explained in terms of traumatic conflict, and in most cases links with the former settlement are severed. Many of my Sisala interlocutors insisted that still today they could not return to, nor even visit, their ancestors' original village, lest they be afflicted with illness and misfortune or even death. Some Sisala narratives refer to conflicts between brothers as the reason for migration, for instance a struggle over perceived unequal distribution of the spoils of a joint hunting expedition (or one undertaken secretly by one brother alone).[4] Other narratives invoke the 'pregnant-woman-slit-open' motif, i.e., a dispute about the sex of an unborn child, which resulted in the death of the woman (and the embryo) because one party 'operated' her (and subsequently had to migrate) in order to determine who was right.[5] Significantly, and in keeping with their different ethos of mobility, Dagara narratives never resort to these motifs in order to explain migration.[6] Migration-and-settlement stories of Sisala villages, which were established not until the second half of the nineteenth century, explain that the founders of the village fled from the incursions of Muslim warlords or the aggression of neighbouring Dagara settlements, but usually combine such historical 'realism' with the conventional, more metaphorical motifs of the conflict between greedy brothers or the 'pregnant-woman-slit-open' story.[7]

While the Dagara have continued to found new farmsteads and village wards on the settlement frontier up to the present day, Sisala present their migration as an affair of the past: they became mobile, not of their own choice, but because circumstances beyond their control – including conflicts among close kin – forced them to move. Neither the ideal of autonomy nor the ethos of 'go forth young man' is as prominent among the Sisala as among the Dagara. On the contrary, a Sisala who, for whatever reason, decides to leave his original house, will do his best to 'hide' this movement and seek to attach himself as a 'sister's son' (a *tolbie*) to one of the houses in the new settlement, no matter whether he is actually related to this family or not. He will shift his allegiance to the adopted village and even refuse to visit his original house that, in turn, will deny any relationship with the migrant.[8]

One of the oldest Sisala villages in the western parts of 'Sisalaland' is Bangwon, near the Burkina Faso–Ghana border. Leke Siino, a renowned, old diviner and in charge of earth-shrine matters until the new earth priest would be officially installed, insisted that Bangwon's founder did not immigrate from anywhere, but 'came down from God.'

> Our ancestor Bangwon never came from any village.[9] ... From God (*wiise*) he came down and settled here.... As for the name 'Bangwon,' it refers to this beam he and the brother shouldered.... The brother's name was Jaffien. He (Jaffien) went and saw an anthill and dug and opened it [i.e., settled]. Our ancestor went and saw the senior brother (Jaffien) and said: "You came and you were able to put up houses and I still have nothing." So Jaffien said he would come and build for him ... and they went to the bush for a beam. They went, collected and shouldered it. The junior brother complained that his neck was about cutting off. The senior brother said he should throw it down. From there our ancestor vowed that his neck (*benye*) will never carry a log again – *bengmwor*. That is how Bangwon got its name. The house put up by the senior brother was red (*bi fien*), hence the name Jaffien.[10]

Direct descent from the supreme God (*wiise*) is an unusual motif in Sisala narratives, which Leke obviously employed in order to emphasize the seniority of Bangwon. In other parts of his account, he resorted to more common images of migration, relating, for instance, how Bangwon and Jaffien 'walked together.' Leke explained that Jaffien and his people originally settled around the current village of Kolinka but were later driven away by the 'Malians' – probably a reference to slave raiders such as the Karantaos and the Zaberma – as well as the expansionist Dagara, and sought refuge in Bangwon. Whether Jaffien left his original earth shrine behind or took it along and installed it next to Bangwon's shrine was not quite clear, but Leke left no doubt that Jaffien's land was 'added' to the Bangwon territory. In any case, when Jaffien died without leaving male descendants, Bangwon inherited this land. Other informants believed that Bangwon was Jaffien's nephew (*tolbie*) rather than his junior brother, and speculated that Jaffien may have been a Phuo, not a Sisala. Possibly, a group of Phuo were already established in the Ouessa-Kolinka area when Bangwon's group arrived, and the latter eventually married Phuo women.[11]

Be that as it may, all informants agreed that Jaffien and Bangwon belonged to the first Sisala (or Phuo) villages established in the area. If we accept Leke's claim that Bangwon was the grandfather of Bakyolo who, according to early colonial reports, was installed as earth priest in the 1880s and was probably born before 1830, then Bangwon may have been founded around the mid-eighteenth century or even earlier.[12] Two further villages asserted to belong to this first wave of Sisala immigration: Piina, some fifteen kilometres south-east of Bangwon, and Bo, originally established on land later occupied by the Dagara of Tantuo. Informants in these villages reported that Jaffien, Bangwon, and their own ancestors all came from Tokuri (supposedly near Welembele) and jointly ventured northwestwards, into thick, uninhabited bush.[13] Different from Dagara migration-and-settlement narratives, however, such assertions of common origins and/or kinship – joint migration of senior and junior brothers – were not used to claim a superior or dependent status.

A second group of Sisala villages was established in the late eighteenth century – among them Lambussie, Suke, Billaw, Samoa, Kierim, Bouara, and Bourra. In all these settlements, my informants acknowledged that their ancestors 'met' the older villages, but again, this did not imply any obligation of deference. The founders of these younger villages came from diverse origins, some from Kassena or Nuni settlements to the north and northeast of their new habitat, others from places further south, which were later occupied by Dagaba immigrants, such as Sankana, Bo, Han, and Ulo.[14]

Between the 1860s and 1890s, families who fled from the Muslim warlord Karantao, the Zaberma warriors, or the increasingly violent Dagara expansion founded the third and last group of Sisala settlements, comprising Nabaala, Happa, Dahile, Hamile, Nimoro, Hiela, Bozo, and Kyetuu. Apparently, they settled on the extended land reserves of the older Sisala villages and did so with the latter's consent, although my informants were sometimes initially reluctant to admit this and preferred to present the usual narrative about their ancestors' hunting excursions.[15] In any case, even these recently founded settlements enjoyed ritual independence and full property rights over their land from the very beginning.

Different from the negotiable hierarchy of Dagara earth shrines, each Sisala village thus has its own 'major' shrine at which the full range of rituals necessary for protection, fertility, and reparation after the violation of taboos can be carried out without referring to other settlements. However, the origins of the stones or other objects at the centre of the earth shrine seem to be as diverse as among the Dagara, except that the Sisala would never admit to having received – and much less purchased – an earth shrine from any previous non-Sisala inhabitant. In ten of the twenty-one Sisala villages that I visited, I was told that the pioneering ancestor carried a stone from the earth shrine in his original settlement to the new place[16]; in five cases, it was the earth priest of a neighbouring Sisala village who established a shrine stone for the newcomers (apparently by taking some earth or a stone from his village); and only in six cases was the shrine for the new village said to have been created locally – from an 'object' discovered in the bush, from one of the mud bricks used to build the first house, or from a hunting shrine transformed into an earth shrine. No matter where the shrine 'object' came from, in most cases it was placed, together with some local stones, in or near the pit where the first-comer supposedly dug out the earth for the construction of his house.[17]

Sometimes it was not actually being first-comers but ruse and trickery that determined who could impose himself as the legitimate founder of the earth shrine and thus 'owner' of the land. Hiela, for instance, is said to have been founded by a hunter named Kukule and his people. Kukule lived originally in Han but had to flee before the Zaberma warriors. According to Baagyawii Yelgie, a member of the Hiela earth-priestly family, Kukule noticed that nearby Bangwon already existed (people in Bangwon even claim that their ancestors settled Kukule in Hiela) but moved some kilometres further north into an apparently uninhabited area of thick bush. After some time, he met Bokor, another hunter, and a debate over the question of who legitimately owned the place ensued. As one of Bokor's descendants explained:

> Bokor was at Kaa [southeast of Hiela].... He went about hunting, and these people [Kukule and his family] were here [at the site of the Hiela earth shrine]. Bokor did not know they were here. He was going about his hunting activities until the place started opening up. It occurred that one day Kukule and Bokor came across each other. Bokor asked Kukule if he lived here. Kukule said yes, and asked if Bokor also lived here, and Bokor also said yes. As the place opened up, Kukule said that he was the senior [i.e., first-comer]. Bokor said no, that he was senior. What saved Kukule was that there was a pond where they usually went to drink water. Bokor had made a mistake by throwing a broken brick into the water while Kukule had thrown a red stone. Now, when the argument arose between the two, they went down to the pond, and they saw that Bokor's broken brick had dissolved, while Kukule was able to remove his red stone. Thus, it was proven that you [Kukule's descendants] are senior, and I [Bokor's descendant] am next to you.[18]

Similar stories about unsuccessful 'first-comers' were told in Lambussie, Bourra, and Bouara.[19] Tensions with the successful earth-priestly lineages were usually resolved by allowing the 'losers' to control the shrines to the spirits of the bush and/or the water. More generally, in Sisala villages created by immigrants from different places of origin, the offices of *totina* (earth priest), *bakabele* (guardian of the bush), and *fuotina* (guardian of the water) are usually distributed among the different kin groups, while in settlements of more homogenous origins, the *totina* family also officiates as *fuotina* and *bakabele*.[20] In this respect, the Sisala ritual organization seems to be as flexible as the Dagara one, with the important difference, however, that ritual hierarchy exists only within, not between, settlements.

The Sisala villages are connected through ties of 'brotherhood,' expressed in the idiom of shared origins, and alliances created in the new habitat, symbolized by shared earth-shrine names. The earth shrines of Lambussie and Sentuu (as well as the Dagara settlement Nandom) bear the name 'Kabir'; the Dahile, Kierim, and Bo shrines are called 'Bundi'; the Laponé, Pina (Burkina Faso), and Kelendou shrines 'Nigtulo,' and the shrines of Bangwon, Happa, and Hiela 'Niihi.' The explanations that my informants presented for these names differed, ranging from 'resisting all suffering' to 'seeing and becoming envious' for Niihi; 'taking a step backwards' or 'having found good food' for Nigtulo; and 'killing, sacrificing and eating' for Bundi. Jack Goody (1957) – following Lawra District Commissioner John Eyre-Smith's rather speculative history (1933) – saw in common shrine names an indication that an originally very large earth-shrine territory had been gradually sub-divided into minor shrine areas, which retained the original name. Eyre-Smith even believed that all new settlers, be they Dagara or Sisala, continued to recognize the custodian of the oldest shrine as the highest ritual authority in their respective area. However, while these interpretations may partially hold for the Dagara case, they do not apply to Sisala ritual organization. Here, a common shrine name did not necessarily indicate that one village was settled by or had received its shrine from another one. The earth priest of Kierim, for instance, whose shrine name is 'Bundi,' claimed that the shrine stone had been brought along from Han, while Bo, another 'Bundi' village, asserted to have imported the shrine stone from Tokuri; only my informants in Dahile admitted that their 'Bundi' shrine had been installed by someone from Bo. It is likely that, rather than reflecting the settlement history, common shrine names indicate a ritual reinforcement of local alliances against external enemies. My informants in Bangwon, Hiela, and Happa, for instance, explained that all three shrines bore the name 'Niihi' because the villages had sworn a solemn oath at the earth shrine to assist each other against any slave-raiding invader.

Just as in the case of mutual assistance in the settlement process, these defensive alliances did not result in hierarchical relations between the Sisala villages. However, Sisala earth priests often do claim continued ritual authority (and property rights) over the settlements of Dagara latecomers who had once asked the Sisala for a shrine stone. The Sisala insist that their Dagara clients should still consult them in all 'serious' affairs such as suicide or murder – expectations whose legitimacy the Dagara usually vehemently deny. The fact that the Sisala never admitted such claims among themselves may indicate that they constitute more recent

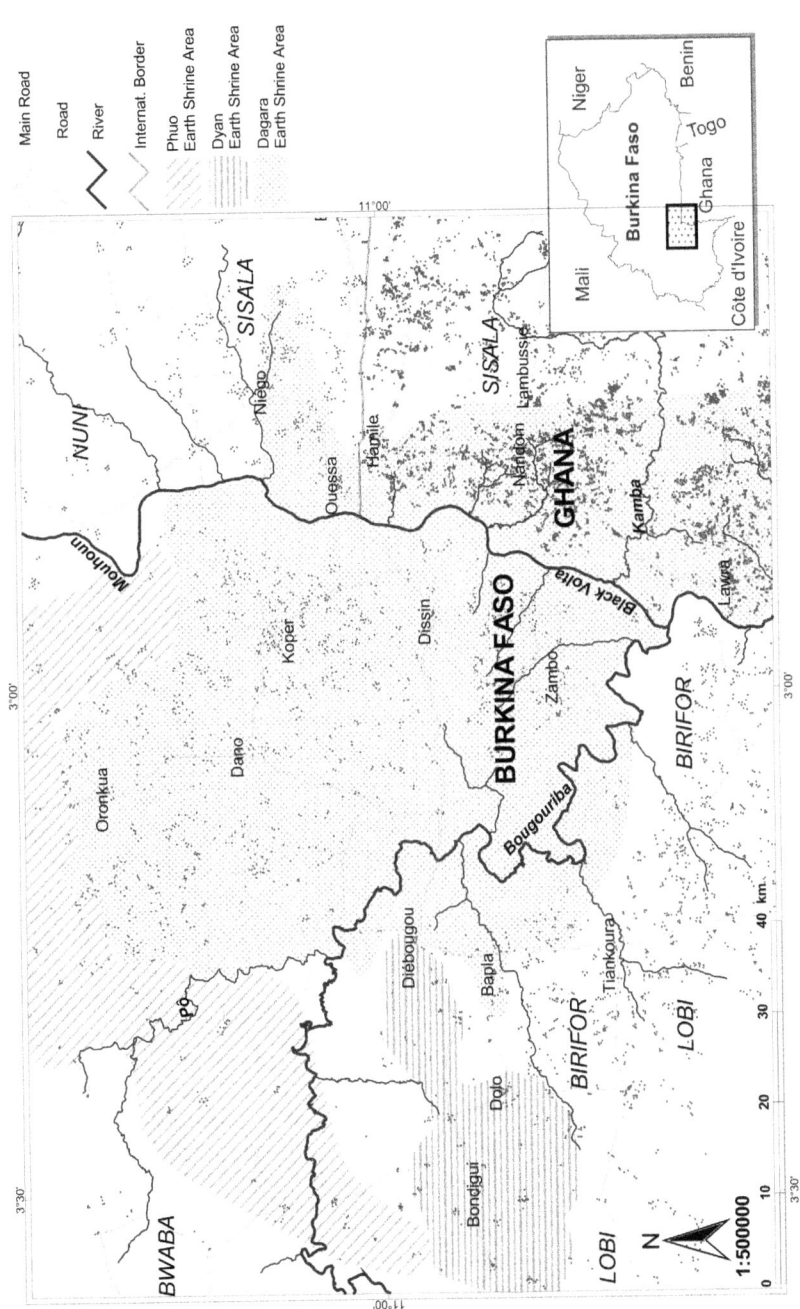

attempts to reinterpret, in the context of diminishing exit options and colonial 'pacification,' originally more egalitarian ritual relations with the Dagara immigrants.

MOBILE STONES AND CONTESTED EARTH-SHRINE HIERARCHIES AMONG THE DAGARA

The multifarious, contradictory migration narratives of the different Dagara patriclans and lineages make it difficult to sketch a general picture of the expansionist movement. Already the British District Commissioner John Guinness noted, with some despair, that the Dagara and Sisala chiefs, earth priests and elders of Lawra-Tumu District, whom he interviewed in the early 1930s on the history of their villages, narrated 'badly beheaded' stories, reaching back only few generations and presenting a 'hopeless tangle of sectional migrations and settlements.'[21] With the exception of Guinness's and his colleague J. A. Armstrong's modest attempts to 'piece together' a 'small collection of family stories'[22] and the compilation of patriclan migration routes by the French White Father and amateur historian Père Hébert and a small team of indigenous priests (Hébert 1976), the history of Dagara mobility and expansion has not received much scholarly attention.[23] The continued movement of Dagara farmers into new territories further diversified the tableau of migratory routes, and the 'telescoping' of genealogies and previous migration stops, typical of oral tradition, partially erased earlier phases of the settlement history from local memory. In short: the difficulties to come up with a comprehensive account of the peopling of the Black Volta region are as discouraging today as they were in Guinness's times.

The 'origins' of the Dagara, or more precisely: the question where a hypothetical proto-Dagara community may have originally lived – beyond the stereotypical *tengkor*, literally 'old country' or 'old village,' to which many local narratives refer – remains speculative and is a matter of heated debate among Dagara intellectuals (Lentz 1994). Some general lines of the subsequent movements, however, may be tentatively discerned. While some patriclans trace their migrations back to what is currently northeastern Côte d'Ivoire and the area around Batié (Nord) in Burkina Faso, others claim to have set out from the present-day Wa district and the environs of Nadawli. Most of the migration narratives that we collected (cf. Kuba et al. 2001) make some reference to the area around Babile, Tugu, Konyuokuo, and Zakpe, where the ancestors are supposed to have settled for a while. This micro-region seems to have served like a kind of turntable from which small groups of Dagara migrated further, some in a northerly direction, some then turning westwards, across the Black Volta, into present-day southwestern Burkina Faso, some remaining east of the Volta and continuing north and north-eastwards, and others, finally, crossing the river more than once.

While it is problematic to speak of Dagara expansion in terms of a self-conscious, planned conquest of new territories for the entire group, the available evidence does suggest that the continuous colonization of new frontiers was more than just the involuntary by-product of the fission of domestic groups and individual mobility. Dagara migration-and-settlement narratives invariably emphasize the pioneer spirit of the ancestors, be they portrayed as hunters, warriors, or great hoe-farmers, and a more or less aggressively asserted feeling of superiority of the Dagara over the earlier inhabitants. There was a strongly developed sense of pushing the 'frontier ... on the margin of the inhabited world,' setting out from the 'hinterland' and moving into 'outlying areas which are both a source of danger and a coveted prize,' as Ladis Kristof characterized frontier processes (1959: 270–71). Furthermore, the Dagara frontiersmen aimed at securing larger territories, not only for themselves and their immediate relatives, but also for their entire patriclan.[24] In this sense, the history of Dagara mobility can indeed be characterized as a history of expansion.

Even today, most Dagara find it neither astonishing nor problematic that many nuclear families move up to three times in the course of an adult life and that in most domestic groups some members have moved out and settled elsewhere. More generally, the ideal of autonomy, i.e., of becoming the head of a house (*yirsob*), is rated highly and may account for the relatively easy and frequent fission of Dagara patrilineages. Tensions and conflicts between siblings are given as one of the reasons for leaving the father's compound, but another is the lack of available land. However, when informants reported that their ancestors migrated because of 'hunger' and 'in search of food,' this usually does not refer to any objectively measurable scarcity of land but culturally defined ideals of sufficient space and decision-making power.

The Dagara continued to extend the area where they settle and farm up until today, but colonial domination had a profound impact on mobility and ethnic relations. The imposition of the *pax colonia* largely removed the opportunities to use violence in the appropriation of new territories, and thus changed the balance of power in favour of the Sisala and halted the advance of Dagara earth-shrine areas. Indeed, since the 1920s, the Dagara no longer created new earth shrines or acquired *tengan kubile* from the Sisala but were forced to establish their new settlements on territory owned and ritually controlled by the Sisala (or Phuo).

For my Dagara interlocutors, an earth shrine created from stones of non-Dagara origin is neither less nor more powerful than one using Dagara-made stones. Indeed, in ten of the thirty-one Dagara villages east of the Black Volta in which I collected details about the origins of the earth shrines, I was told that the shrine stone was given by, or purchased from, the previous inhabitants, namely Sisala, Phuo, or Nuni.[25] In two villages, the Dagara frontiersmen were said to have brought the shrine stone from their original settlements. In five cases, the earth shrine had evolved either out of what was once a *tengankubile*, a small shrine established for the new settlers by one of the older Dagara villages, or out of a *wiekuur*, a 'field' or 'bush shrine,' which the newcomers had installed themselves. The remaining fourteen villages had only *tengankubile* and were still obliged to consult the *tengankpee* in neighbouring Dagara villages for all 'serious' cases.

Dagara earth shrines are territorial cults that communicate with the earth god and regulate a community's appropriation of the natural resources in a circumscribed area. At the same time, however, they can develop into centres of 'de-territorialized' mobile healing cults. The ritual healing power of such earth shrines can extend far beyond the area for which the shrines serve as territorial cults. Some earth shrines have become particularly famous for their extraordinary power to grant fertility, health, and prosperity, and people come from near and far in order to sacrifice at the shrine for the solution of their personal problems. These clients as well as the inhabitants of the shrine's village, if they wish to travel or establish themselves elsewhere, can ask the earth priest for a small stone from the shrine for their personal protection. These travelling shrine stones are kept effective by regularly 'charging their battery,' as my informants put it, through sacrifices at the original shrine in gratitude for the earth god's good services.[26] In the settlement process, these mobile stones could eventually be 're-territorialized,' laying the basis for a personal or lineage protective shrine in a newly founded village or even an earth shrine, if the shrine keepers succeeded in claiming first-comer status vis-à-vis later immigrants. However, the nature of the new shrine – personal healing, lineage protective, or supra-lineage territorial cult – and its obligations towards the original shrine were, and continue to be, often subject to intense debate.

In Eremon, for instance, an old Dagara village in the vicinity of Lawra, the earth-priestly lineage brought a stone (*tengkuur*) from the earth shrine in their original village, Tie. The stone, my informants explained, is called 'Nyoor,' a name derived from the word *nyuvor*, 'breath' or 'life,' and they spoke of Nyoor both as *tengan*, earth god, and as *sigra*, guardian spirit of the Naayire patriclan to which they belonged.[27] Nyoor is thus not only venerated at the Eremon earth shrine but in every Naayire house where small Nyoor stones are put down for protection. My informants also claimed that a number of Dagara villages north of Eremon, namely Varpuo, Piiri, Panyaan, Gegenkpe, Baseble, and parts of Tom, Ko, and Nandom, had been established thanks to their ancestors' assistance. The founders of these settlements 'were strangers, who came looking for food, and our fathers allocated land to them. They were made to understand that the land on which they were settling belongs to Nyoor.' After having 'paid' for the installation of the Nyoor shrine, they were eventually allowed to conduct their own sacrifices but still had to come back to Eremon from time to time. These claims, however, were confirmed only in Varpuo, Panyaan, and some sections of Tom – that is, in villages created by members of patriclans closely related with the Naayire.[28] Informants from other places, which the Eremon earth priest asserted to be under Nyoor's authority, insisted that their ancestors had actually established their earth shrines without any external assistance or received a stone not from the Eremon Nyoor shrine but rather from the 'Kabir' earth shrines of Lambussie or Ko.[29] Indeed, it was in Ko that I first learnt that earth shrines could serve both as territorial and healing cults. My informants in Ko related how their ancestors brought a Kabir earth-shrine stone from their original village Nabing, in what is today Nuni land in Burkina Faso, and later installed Kabir shrines in numerous other Dagara villages – in Guo, a section of Tom, Tankyara, Baseble, Sone, Gegenkpe, Piiri, Panyaan, Domagyie, and even some settlements across the Black Volta, such as Memer and Nakaar.[30] When I expressed my puzzlement about how an earth-shrine stone's jurisdiction – and the property rights that it helps to legitimate – could reach across the river, the Ko earth priest explained that the boundary between territorial and protective cults was not as firm as I had until then believed. He insisted that Ko did hold ultimate property rights over the land of neighbouring villages with Kabir *tenganbile* such as Guo and parts of Tom. But in other cases, Kabir served rather as a powerful healing cult, not an earth shrine:

> It was the *tengan* itself that went across the river, and not us [the Ko *tengandem*] who sent it there. If one is faced with a very serious problem, one will go at every length for solutions – which they [the villagers of Nakaar, Memer, etc.] heard existed here. So we established the Ko Kabir in order to solve the problems these villages faced.... In some respects, the land 'belongs' (*so*) to Ko, since Ko Kabir is there. But that doesn't mean that Ko has any authority over the farmlands of that particular village and can seize them from the owners!

It is precisely this ambiguity between ritual and economic 'ownership' that the earth priests in Eremon exploited in order to convince me that they 'controlled' a very large area. Similarly, it seems to be the long-standing competition between the two powerful earth-cum-healing cults, Nyoor and Kabir, which accounts for shifting ritual allegiances of some villages in the Lawra and Nandom area – allegiances which some interested parties have attempted to interpret as connected with an allodial title in land.

As I went on interviewing Dagara earth priests and other informants about the history of their particular shrines and earth shrines in general, I learnt about a puzzling variety of medicinal, hunting, and field shrines and listened to competing views about permissible transformations of these shrines into *tenganbile* or even *tengankpee*. Neither did my interlocutors agree on the terminology, nor were they in accord about the question who was authorized to establish which shrines and who benefited from their protection. Some insisted that *wiekuur* ('bush stones') were exclusively hunting shrines and, although ultimately under the control of the earth priest, could never be transformed into earth shrines because the latter only accept domestic animals as sacrificial gifts while hunting shrines have to be 'fed' with wild animals. Others explained that only particular patriclans, namely the Kpagnyaane and the Gane, could establish

Fig. 2. The Zegnii ancestor shrine at the 'Jeffian hill,' near Hamile. Many earth shrines look similar, but I was never allowed to photograph them. (Photo: Carola Lentz, 1999).

proper hunting shrines, and that members of these clans always took some *wiekube* along on their migrations and could, when they founded a new settlement, create an earth shrine from these stones. Still others used the terms *wiekuur* and *puotiib* (field medicine) interchangeably and held dissenting views on the question whether non–earth-priestly lineages were allowed to establish such shrines autonomously, only with the consent of the earth priest, or not at all. And they disagreed whether a field shrine protected only the fields of a particular lineage or of an entire village section, thus functioning as a *tengankubile*, and whether it could eventually be transformed into a *tengankpee*.

These contradictory statements about the nature and potential trajectories of hunting, field, and earth shrines reflect the fact that creating new villages on the frontier was a gradual process. When the frontiersmen 'discovered' a suitable site and constructed their first provisional huts, they often did not see an immediate need to establish an earth shrine, because they felt sufficiently protected by their mobile personal and clan 'medicines' (*tii*) and various hunting and field shrines. An earth shrine only became necessary when the women and further settlers from different patriclans arrived. The earth cult regulated the social relations between the first-comers and these late-comers by instituting taboos against violence, bloodshed, and illicit sexual encounters ('in the bush') and by ritually sanctioning the leading role of the earth-priestly lineage. The continued fertility of the land, the women and the domestic animals, so the Dagara and their neighbours believed, could not be ensured without internally peaceful relations and the good offices of an earth priest. However, just as the settlement history, clan composition, and interaction between first-comers and late-comers varied from village to village, so did the specific circumstances of the creation of an earth shrine and its relation to existing protective and medicinal shrines.

Furthermore, the negotiable rapport between the various shrines and cults allowed ritual hierarchies to adapt to changing constellations of power. In principle, the *tengansob* had to, and still has to, be informed about, and give his consent to, the installation of any other shrine or cult, be they part of a patriclan's ancestral traditions or newly imported 'foreign' medicines against witchcraft or theft. However, the authority of the *tengan* was, and still is, usually imposed only *post facto*: the illicit introduction of a new protective cult or the arrogation of *tengankpee* powers by a *tenganbile* is only 'discovered' (and punished) when a diviner attributes specific incidences of death, infertility, illness, or other misfortunes to this transgression. However, depending on their influence and power, the transgressor and his followers may either make reparations at the *tengankpee* or decide to ignore the diviner's dictum and, if they already live at some distance from the major earth shrine, opt for ritual secession. If misfortune continues to trouble the new ritual community, they may eventually reorient themselves towards the original shrine. Thus, instead of seeking to condense the welter of shrines names and attributes into a well-ordered taxonomy, we should understand that the contradictory terminology and explanations that my interlocutors put forward are part and parcel of the ongoing negotiation of ritual hierarchies.

Negotiation as well as conflict also characterized the relations between the Dagara pioneers and the earth priests of older Sisala and Phuo villages. While the incoming Dagara were usually aware of their existence and sometimes sought their consent before settling, there was always an alternative, though confrontational strategy, namely to establish an earth shrine through filiation with an existing Dagara shrine. The latter became symbols around which local identities could crystallize and helped to transcend the latent antagonism between individual houses or patriclan segments. Some villages, such as Ouessa, thus ritually controlled over a dozen villages and hamlets where they had established branches of their earth shrines (*tengankubile*), and although earth priests were never themselves military leaders, they may have played a considerable role in mobilizing military alliances – for instance, against Sisala or Phuo resistance. The system of hierarchical earth shrines may thus be seen as a cultural strategy capable of creating solidarity and military support beyond the immediate local community.

However, ritual dependency on senior Dagara villages did not exclude the possibility that the new Dagara settlers eventually also came to terms with their Sisala or Phuo neighbours. Indeed, they often did so, following initial conflict, by acquiring an additional earth shrine, which could then be used to gain independence from the older Dagara settlements. Indeed, this may have been the major motive for the new Dagara frontiersmen to negotiate with the Sisala or Phuo for an earth-shrine stone.

My informants sometimes compared the transfer of an earth shrine (and the allodial title to the land) between different groups, and particularly across ethnic boundaries, to a 'marriage.' Because of its intimate association with fertility, land is regarded as a woman, and the Dagara often interpret the cowries and cows that they claim to have exchanged with the Sisala for the allodial title as the 'bride price' that they have paid to the bride's family, that is, the landowners. In Ouessa, for instance, some informants claimed that the earth shrine was given by the Phuo, or Sisala, in recompensation for saving the life of one of the original earth priest's women or sparing the earth priest's wife when attacking the previous landowners. In other cases, the Dagara claim to have received the earth shrine in exchange, not for cowries and cows, but directly for a marriageable woman. Although the Sisala and Nuni nowadays usually deny having ever received such a 'bride price,' 'wife,' or any other payment, for the land, they often do concur with the land–woman equation. There is disagreement, however, about the practical consequences of this metaphorical equation, particularly concerning the land/woman's relationship with her original family/owner. In Bayagra, for instance, east of Niégo, the Sisala of Kelendou insisted that when the Dagara family had temporarily abandoned the land that their grandfathers had once transferred to them, the wife/land returned to its original house, and if the Dagara family wanted her/it back, they needed to plead with the Sisala owners once again.[31] Thus in the eyes of the land-givers, the land transfer established a relationship that implies the retention of a strong bond of the 'gift' to the original owners, or, in other words: even after marriage, the woman always remains a full member of her paternal house. The Dagara land receivers, on the other hand, usually argue that the separation of the woman from her family is complete, to all intents and purposes, once the bride price has been paid. As my Dagara informants in Niégo explained, after acquiring an earth-shrine stone from Hiela, they never called any Sisala names during sacrifices but only those of their own ancestors because it was 'like in marriage, and when we marry, the woman no longer belongs to her family; from time to time she may write letters to them or visit them, but we [the husband's house] would have nothing to do with them.'[32]

In any case, an earth shrine is not an ethnically bounded resource. In the eyes of the Phuo and Sisala, the already-established Dagara settlers were just as much 'late-comers' as the more recent Dagara arrivals. For the latter, the hierarchical relationship with an older Dagara settlement may have implied heavier burdens than the ritual dependency from another ethnic group. Moreover, the Sisala and Phuo were not merely passive victims of the Dagara expansion but often seem to have actively asserted their rights. What kind of ritual protection the new Dagara settlement finally chose, whether from a senior Dagara village or the Phuo or Sisala neighbours, depended on the specific local power relations.

CONCLUSION

In the Black Volta region, earth shrines stand at the centre of territorial as well as mobile healing cults. At the same time, they constitute economic, social and political institutions. This article has explored how frontiersmen and late-comers established, expanded, or transmitted earth shrines and how these practices arose in response to the challenges of securing ritual protection and property rights in a socio-historical context of mobility. Focusing on the relations between Sisala 'first-comers' and Dagara 'late-comers,' that is: a frontier situation characterized by ethnic heterogeneity, we can distinguish three phases of earth-shrine related politics. The first covered the time until the beginning of the colonial regime and was characterized by the 'autochthonization' of the newcomers who managed to acquire full property rights and ritual authority over their new habitat – even though sometimes the previous inhabitants later attempted to reclaim their original property. There were several ways how an allodial title could be established. In some cases, the Dagara frontiersmen moved indeed into 'uninhabited' territory, or successfully drove the previous inhabitants away, and established their own earth shrine, often around a stone that they had carried along from their original village. In many cases, however, the Dagara pioneers had to come to terms with previous inhabitants. Sometimes, they received the allodial title to the land together with an earth-shrine stone from the Sisala, usually in exchange for some substantial gifts (although the previous owners sometimes later denied that this exchange ever took place). In other cases, they acquired only the land and placed it under the protection of an existing Dagara earth shrine. In a few cases, however, mounting tensions with the custodians of this older earth shrine or unexpected problems such as inexplicable deaths, lack of drinking water or drought could motivate the new settlers to acquire from their Sisala neighbours an additional shrine stone, replacing – or complementing – the Dagara earth shrine.

These strategies of extending existing earth-shrine areas and, when confronted with competing property claims, negotiating with the Sisala for an allodial title, continued into the second, intermediate phase, lasting approximately until the 1920s. However, although the Sisala sometimes seem to have ritually validated the expansion of Dagara property claims by accepting substantial gifts in exchange for the additional land put under Dagara authority, they more or less stopped giving earth-shrine stones to their Dagara neighbours. The narratives concerning these transfers are usually hotly contested and subject to current re-interpretations, which makes it difficult to assess the extent to which full property rights still passed from Sisala into Dagara hands. In any case, it is highly probable that after the 1920s, during the third phase, the transfer of ritual authority – and shrine stones – to the Dagara ceased altogether, and the Dagara thus no longer became fully fledged land owners, although they continued to found new settlements. The *pax colonia*, which only really became effective in the Black Volta region from the 1910s onwards, definitely changed the balance of power in favour of the Sisala, by removing the opportunities to use violence in the appropriation of new territories. The Sisala refusal to cede earth shrines to the expanding Dagara suggests that the previous transfer of earth shrines had perhaps not been quite as 'voluntary' as some narratives claim. On the other hand, in the 1930s and 1940s, a good number of Dagara opted deliberately to settle outside Dagara earth-shrine parishes, on territory controlled ritually and politically by the Sisala, because they wanted to escape the particularly harsh rule of some Dagara paramount chiefs. Thus much of the current landscape of allodial titles is due to the colonial 'freezing' of a previously more dynamic situation, but only because some local actors were only too happy to support colonial officials' ideas about the impossibility of 'alienating' ancestral land, and others thought it better to live on 'foreign' land. This 'freezing' of property transfers, however, did not put an end to the contestation and re-interpretation of claims to ownership and of the history of the earth shrines, on the contrary. Up until today, particularly those allodial titles that were acquired in the turbulent last decades before colonial rule are closely scrutinized and, when changing power constellations provide room for manoeuvre, questioned.

NOTES

1   Considerable controversy has surrounded the 'Dagara' ethnic names. British colonial administrators introduced the terms 'Dagarti' and 'Lobi,' which some Ghanaians continue to use. French district commissioners often referred to the term 'Dagari,' which is still used by many Burkinabè. Jack Goody (1956: 16–26) introduced the term LoDagaa, which he subdivided further into the LoDagaba and the LoWiili. Most of those so labelled reject all of these names as incorrect or even pejorative, but there is much discussion of what to use instead. Some believe that the people living around Wa, Nadawli, and Jirapa (in Ghana) form a distinct group, the 'Dagaba,' speaking their own dialect, 'Dagaare'; that most of the settlements around Diébougou and Dano (in Burkina Faso) are inhabited by the 'Wiile,' speaking yet another dialect; and that the term 'Dagara' finally, should be reserved for the speakers of the 'Lobr' dialect, that is, the population of Lawra, Nandom, and parts of southwestern Burkina Faso. Others hold that 'Dagara' is the only correct unitary term for both the language and the ethnic group. For more details on the controversies on ethnic names, see Lentz (2000a):120–24, and Bemile (2000). For simplicity's sake and because most of my discussion indeed refers to the speakers of the 'Lobr' dialect, I use the term 'Dagara' throughout this article.

2   This project was part of the interdisciplinary Special Research Project 268 (*Sonderforschungsbereich*) on the West African savannah, at the University of Frankfurt/Main. Field work was carried out mostly between 1997 and 2002, with the financial support of the *Deutsche Forschungsgemeinschaft*. For some results of our project, see Kuba (2006), Kuba et al. (2001), Kuba and Lentz (2002; 2006), Lentz (2005), and Werthmann (2006) and Oberhofer (2008). I am particularly grateful to my co-researcher Richard Kuba for our many inspiring discussions, and to the Netherlands Institute for Advanced Study, which provided a congenial environment for the first analysis of my interview material and for the conception of the basic outline of my book, *Land, Mobility and Belonging* (that unfortunately, due to many administrative commitments, is still a 'work in progress').

3   Some of the material in this section has already been published in Lentz and Kuba (2002).

4   Interviews with Laponé Kuoro (chief) Kumasi et al., 22 Feb. 2000; Mahama Baanuomake et al., Bo, 10 Dec. 1997; Zankor Bahiise et al., Dahile, 10 Dec. 1997; Happa Kuoro Hilleh Babrimatoh et al., 30 Nov. 1994.

5   Interviews with Bozo Kuoro (chief) Banuosin Kel-le et al., 17 Dec. 1997; Bourra Kuoro Issa Nadie et al., 27 Nov. 2001; Bouara Kuoro Nawie Zogyir et al., 19 Dec. 1997. On the 'pregnant-woman-slit-open' motif, see also Schott (1990).

6   The only exception seems to be a legend reported by Edward Tengan (1994: 15), which explains the separation of the Kuwere patriclan from the original Kpiele house with a 'pregnant-woman-slit-open' story.

7   Interviews with Topulwy Bukari et al., Piina (Burkina Faso), 26 Jan. 1998; Hiela Kuoro Emoho Yelgie, Baagyawii Yelgie et al., Hiela, 18 Dec. 1997, 22 Feb. 1999; Hamile Kuoro Puli Nagie, Bewaar Bei et al., Hamile, 29 Dec. 1996; Tigwii S. Amoah, Hamile, 13 Dec. 1997; Kierim Kuoro Bombie Naagyie, Buuyor Naagie et al., Kierim, 19 Dec. 1997; Mahama Baanuomake et al., Bo, 10 Dec. 1997.

8   Interviews with Tigwii S. Amoah, Hamile, 12 Dec. 1997, 20 Jan. 1998, 10 Feb. 1999, and 26 Feb. 2000. On the static ideal model of the lineage among the Sisala, see also Mendonsa (1979); on the spiritual power of Sisala elders and the role of divination and the ancestor cult in controlling the migration of dependent juniors, Mendonsa (1982): 50–53, 149–210; (2001): 185–218.

9   As in many Sisala settlement narratives, Leke merged the names of the village and of its founding ancestor.

10 Interview with Leke Siino, Bangwon Kuoro Yinaroh Wiyor et al., 11 Dec. 1997.

11 Interview with Piina Kuoro Bakuoro Yesibie et al., 12 Dec. 1997. John Guinness and J. A. Armstrong, two colonial administrators collecting information on the regional settlement history in the 1930s, reported that the Bangwon earth priest stated that his ancestors originally came from 'Jaffiung' [Jaffien] (John Guinness, Interim Report on the Peoples of Nandom and Lambussie, 1932; J. A. Armstrong, Report on the Peoples of the Lambussie and Nandom Divisions, 1931/1934; National Archives of Ghana (Accra) (NAG), ADM 11/1/824).

12 Entry in the Lawra District Record Book by Captain Taylor, 21 April 1906, NAG, ADM 61/5/2: 34.

13 Interviews with Piina Kuoro Bakuoro Yesibie et al., 12 Dec. 1997; and Mahama Baanuomake et al., Bo, 10 Dec. 1997.

14 Interviews with the Lambussie earth priest Nasie Isifu Tomo et al., 29 Nov. 1994; Darte Bason Boyuo et al., Lambussie, 2 Dec. 1994; Billaw Kuoro Forkoh Manoh, the Billaw earth priest Kager Banuosin et al., 3 Dec. 1994; Samoa Kuoro Shaku Tigwii et al., 28 Nov. 2001; Suke Kuoro George Yiriminor Mawiise et al., 28 Nov. 2000; Kierim Kuoro Bombie Naagyie et al., 19 Dec. 1997; Bouara Kuoro Nawie Zongyir et al., 19 Dec. 1997; Bourra Kuoro Issa Nadie, Naoulé Siyil et al., 27 Nov. 2001.

15 Interviews with Happa Kuoro Hilleh Babrimatoh et al., 30 Nov. 1994; Zanko Bahiise et al., Dahile, 10 Dec. 1997; Nabaala Kuoro Kanii Kambang, 4 Dec. 1994; Suleiman Balesemule et al., Nimoro, 14 Dec. 1997; Baagyawii Yelgie et al., Hiela, 18 Dec. 1997; Hiela Kuoro Emoho Yelgie et al., 22 Feb. 1999; Kyetuu Kuoro Niepor Kombui et al., 16 Dec. 1997, 22 Feb. 1999; Bozo Kuoro Banuosin Kel-le, 17 Dec. 1997.

16 These places of origin included Ulo, Han, and Tokuri, as well as Bon, Millo (?), and Setii, currently inhabited by Nuni and Kassena. It was not quite clear whether the frontiersmen were believed to have actually carried a physical object or rather the spiritual power enabling them to become earth priests in their new home. The Phuo and Winye, who are closely related to the Sisala, distinguish between two sources of earth-priestly power: membership in a specific 'noble' lineage and first-comership (see Jacob 2003; Kuba 2006). Among the Sisala, however, no one originating from an earth-priestly family would automatically have the right to establish a new earth shrine unless he could also successfully claim first-comer status.

17 On this, see also Tengan (1991): 84–88. However, Tengan's informants apparently only claimed a 'local' origin for their earth-shrine stones and made no mention of ancestors carrying stones along on their journey. Unfortunately, Tengan does not specify his analysis according to the different villages where he gathered information, but in Piina (Ghana), where one of his main informants lived, the earth priest told me that the shrine stone was imported from Tokuri. It would be interesting to compare these different versions.

18 Interview with Baagyawie Yelgie, Balitor Naagie et al., Hiela, 18 Dec. 1997. Interestingly, in a second interview with members of the earth-priestly lineage, where none of Bokor's descendants were present, the contest between Kukule and Bokor was not mentioned; interview with Hiela Kuoro Emoho Yelgie et al., 22 Feb. 1999.

19 See Tengan (1991): 81–84 and Schott (1993) for further examples.

20 Interviews with Tigwii S. Amoah, Hamile, 9 Dec. 1997, 20 Jan. 1998, and 10 Feb. 1999.

21 Lawra-Tumu District Commissioner John Guinness, Interim Report on the Peoples of Nandom and Lambussie, 1932, NAG, ADM 11/1/824, § 1, 11, 41. For more details on Guinness's report and the harsh criticism it provoked among other colonial officers, see Lentz (1999): 146–58. It is interesting to note, however, that in many of my own interviews, Guinness's findings on migration routes were corroborated.

22 Guinness, ibid., § 1; J. A. Armstrong, Report on the Peoples of the Lambussie and Nandom Divisions in the Lawra-Tumu District, 1931/1934, NAG, ADM 11/1/824.

23 The few more comprehensive accounts of Dagara expansion – Der (1989), Goody (1993), Hien (2001), and Somda (1989) – are based on a rather limited corpus of interviews and, like the micro-studies (in the form of B.A. dissertations), tend to take oral traditions at face value without systematically comparing contradictory versions (if they ever collected more than one version).

24 On the territorial strategies of patriclans and lineages, see also the case studies in Perrot (2000).

25 These villages were Lawra, Goziir, Nandom, Burutu, Ko, Kokoligu, Ouessa, Niégo, Dadoune, and Kondon. However, in Lawra, Burutu, Ko, Ouessa, and Kondon, there were competing versions that denied such a 'foreign' origin of the earth shrine.

26 For an instructive analysis of the nation-wide ritual networks around such a mobile-medicinal-cum-territorial cult, namely the Tongnaab in the Bolgatanga area, see Allman and Parker (2005).

27 Interview with Kporkar, Dome Tang et al., Eremon, 22 Dec. 1994. On the concept of the personal and clan guardian spirit (*sigra*), see Goody (1962): 410–11; on Nyoor, Goody (1957): 70–83. Taking Nyoor only for a territorial cult, Goody interprets the spatial distribution of Nyoor stones as an indication of the original boundaries of the earth-shrine parish, which is highly problematic.

28 Interviews with Panyaan Naa Edward Yirbekyaa et al., 23 Dec. 1996; Tom Naa Severio Termaghre, Nandom, 26 Dec. 1996; and the earth priest of Varpuo, Damian Bognye et al., 22 Nov. 1989 (interview by Barbara Habig). On Tom, see also Goody (1957).

29 Interviews with Gegenkpe Naa Yebpone Babai Tuolong III et al., 26 Dec. 1996; Gaamuo Mwinpuo Le-ib et al., Nandomkpe, 11 Dec. 1989; Dibaar, Nandomkpe, 29 Dec. 1994; and Soglikuu-Saakum et al., Nandom-Bilegang, 17 Dec. 1994.

30 Interview with Ko Naa James Bayuo, *tengansob* Gabriel Tangsege et al., Ko, 18 Dec. 1994.

31 Interview with Mwiensang Somda Kondon, Bayagra, 4 Mar. 1999.

32 Interview with Somda Beyaa et al, Niégo, 23 Feb. 1999.

REFERENCES

Allman, Jean, and John Parker. 2005. *Tongnaab: The History of a West African God.* Bloomington: Indiana University Press.

Bemile, Sebastian. 2000. "Promotion of Ghanaian languages and its Impact on National Unity: The Dagara Language Case." In *Ethnicity in Ghana: The Limits of Invention*, ed. Carola Lentz and Paul Nugent, 204–25. London: Macmillan.

Dacher, Michèle. 1997. "Organisation politique d'une sociéte acéphale : Les Gouin du Burkina Faso." *L'Homme* 144:7–29.

Der, Benedict. 1989. "The origins of the Dagara-Dagaba," *Papers in Dagara Studies* 1:1-25.

Eyre-Smith, R. St. John. 1933. *A Brief Review of the History and Social Organisation of the Peoples of the Northern Territories of the Gold Coast.* Accra: Government Printer.

Goody, Jack. 1956. *The Social Organisation of the LoWiili.* London: H.M. Stationery Office.

———. 1957. "Fields of Social Control among the LoDagaba." *Journal of the Royal Anthropological Institute of Great Britain and Ireland* 87:75–104.

———. 1962. *Death, Property and the Ancestors: A Study of the Mortuary Customs of the LoDagaa of West Africa.* Stanford: Stanford University Press.

———. 1993. "Peuplement. Études comparatives, Nord-Ghana et Burkina Faso." In *Images d'Afrique et sciences sociales : Les pays lobi, birifor et dagara*, ed. Michèle Fiéloux and Jacques Lombard, with Jeanne-Marie Kambour-Ferrand, 51–55. Paris: Karthala.

Hébert, Père Jean. 1976. *Esquisse d'une monographie historique du pays Dagara : Par un groupe de Dagara en collaboration avec le père Hébert.* Diébougou: Diocèse de Diébougou.

Hien, Pierre Claver. 2001. "Frontières et conflits chez les Dagara et leurs voisins au sud-ouest du Burkina Faso (XVIIIème–XIXème siécle)." *Berichte des Sonderforschungsbereichs 268* (Frankfurt) 14:427–40.

Jacob, Jean-Pierre. 2002. *La tradition du pluralisme institutionnel dans les conflits fonciers entre autochtones : Le cas du Gwendégué (Centre Burkina Faso).* Document de travail de l'Unité de Recherche 095, 3, Montpellier: IRD/GRET.

———. 2003. "Imposer son tutorat foncier : Usages autochthones de l'immigration et tradition pluraliste dans le Gwendégué (centre-ouest Burkina Faso)." In *Histoire du peuplement et relations interethniques au Burkina Faso*, ed. Richard Kuba, Carola Lentz, and Claude N. Somda, 75–96. Paris: Karthala.

Kopytoff, Igor. 1987. "The Internal African Frontier: The Making of African Political Culture." In *The African Frontier: The Reproduction of Traditional African Societies*, ed. Igor Kopytoff, 3–84. Bloomington: Indiana University Press.

Kristof, Ladis K. J. 1959. "The Nature of Frontiers and Boundaries." *Annals of the Association of American Geographers* 49:269–82.

Kuba, Richard. 2006. "Spiritual Hierarchies and Unholy Alliances: Competing Earth Priests in a Context of Migration in Southwestern Burkina Faso." In *Land and the Politics of Belonging in West Africa*, ed. Richard Kuba and Carola Lentz, 57–75. Leiden: Brill.

Kuba, Richard, and Carola Lentz. 2002. "Arrows and Earth Shrines: Towards a History of Dagara Expansion in Southern Burkina Faso." *Journal of African History* 43:377–406.

Kuba, Richard, Carola Lentz, and Katja Werthmann. 2001. *Les Dagara et leurs voisins : Histoire de peuplement et relations interethniques au sud-ouest du Burkina Faso*. Frankfurt: Sonderforschungsbereich 268.

Kuba, Richard, Andrea Reikat, Andrea Wenzek, and Katja Werthmann. 2004. "Erdherren und Einwanderer. Bodenrecht in Burkina Faso." In *Mensch und Natur in Westafrika: Ergebnisse aus dem Sonderforschungsbereich 268*, ed. Klaus-Dieter Albert, Doris Löhr, and Katharina Neumann, 373–99. Weinheim: Wiley-VCH.

Lentz, Carola. 1994. "'A Dagara Rebellion against Dagomba Rule?' Contested Stories of Origin in North-Western Ghana." *Journal of African History* 35:457–92.

———. 1999. "Colonial Ethnography and Political Reform: The Works of A.C. Duncan-Johnstone, R.S. Rattray, J. Eyre-Smith and J. Guinness on northern Ghana." *Ghana Studies* 2:119–69.

———. 2000. "Contested Identities: The History of Ethnicity in Northwestern Ghana." In *Ethnicity in Ghana: The Limits of Invention*, ed. Carola Lentz and Paul Nugent, 137–61. London: Macmillan.

———. 2003. "This is Ghanaian Territory: Land Conflicts on a West African Border." *American Ethnologist* 30:273–89.

———. 2006. "First-Comers and Late-Comers: The Role of Narratives in Land Claims." In *Competing Jurisdictions: Settling Land Claims in Africa*, ed. Sandra Evers, Marja Spierenburg, and Harry Wels, 157–80. Leiden: Brill.

Lentz, Carola, and Hans-Jürgen Sturm. 2001. "Of Trees and Earth Shrines: An Interdisciplinary Approach to Settlement Histories in the West African Savannah." *History in Africa* 28:139–68.

Liberski-Bagnoud, Danouta. 2002. *Les dieux du territoire : Penser autrement la généalogie*. Paris: CNRS Éditions.

Lund, Christian. 2006. "Who Owns Bolgatanga? A Story of Inconclusive Encounters." In *Land and the Politics of Belonging in West Africa*, ed. Richard Kuba and Carola Lentz, 77–98. Leiden: Brill.

Mendonsa, Eugene. 1979. "Economic, Residential and Ritual Fission of Sisala Domestic Groups." *Africa* 49:388–407.

———. 1982. *The Politics of Divination: A Processual View of Reactions to Illness and Deviance among the Sisala of Northern Ghana*. Berkeley: University of California Press.

Oberhofer, Michaela. 2008. Fremde Nachbarn: Ethnizität im bäuerlichen Alltag in Burkina Faso. Köln: Rüdiger Köppe Verlag (Mainzer Beiträge zur Afrikaforschung 18).

Perrot, Claude-Hélène (ed.). 2000. *Lignages et territoire en Afrique aux XVIIIe et XIXe siécles : Stratégies, compétition, intégration*. Paris: Karthala.

Savonnet, Georges. 1976. *Les Birifor de Diépla et sa région insulaire du rameau Lobi (Haut-Volta)*. Paris: Mouton.

Schott, Rüdiger. 1990. "'La femme enceinte éventrée.' Variabilité et contexte socio-culturel d'un type de conte ouest-africain." In *D'un conte à l'autre : La variabilité dans la littérature orale*, ed. V. Görög-Karady, 327–39. Paris: Éditions CNRS.

———. 1993. "Le caillou et la boue : Les traditions orales en tant que légitimation des autorités traditionelles chez les Bulsa (Ghana) et les Lyéla (Burkina Faso)." *Paideuma* 39:145–62.

Somda, Nurukyor Claude. 1989. "Les origines des Dagara." *Papers in Dagara Studies* I.

Tengan, Edward B. 1991. *The Land as Being and Cosmos: The Institution of the Earth Cult among the Sisala of Northwestern Ghana*. Frankfurt: Peter Lang.

Werthmann, Katja. 2006. "Gold Diggers, Earth Priests, and District Heads: Land Rights and Gold Mining in Southwestern Burkina Faso." In *Land and the Politics of Belonging in West Africa*, ed. Richard Kuba and Carola Lentz, 119–36. Leiden: Brill.

Zwernemann, Jürgen. 1968. *Die Erde in Vorstellungswelt und Kulturpraktiken der sudanischen Völker*. Berlin: Reimer.

6

Moroccan Saints' Shrines as Systems of Distributed Knowledge

DOYLE HATT (UNIVERSITY OF CALGARY)

ABSTRACT

The white dome of a saint's shrine is a ubiquitous sight in the Moroccan landscape, and this paper contends that such shrines form a country-wide network of signifiers that symbolically and structurally mediate ideas of the local and the national, the rural and the urban, the heterodox and the orthodox in a manner that projects the identity of places and peoples over great distances and that reconfirms the Islamic identity of the country. This system of knowledge and meanings, though on the decline over the past fifty years as a consequence of the spread of literacy, technological changes, and policies of the Moroccan government, still persists with considerable force in many areas and may find new ways to regenerate itself in a postmodern world.

Keywords: Morocco, saint shrines, knowledge, geography, maraboutism, Islam.

INTRODUCTION

This paper is concerned with the meaning of shrines, specifically Moroccan popular saints' shrines. It is not, however, a paper primarily concerned with the 'deep' or esoteric meaning of shrines in the consciousness of the community in which the shrine is located, or of those who visit it on pilgrimage. Rather, the focus of this paper is on a level of more 'external' meanings that relate to these shrines as a general category of phenomena situated within the wider culture in which these meanings are native, and upon their place in the overall system of knowledge of landscape and space. My choice to focus here on these externals should not be taken to imply that I think that the inner meanings of religious phenomena are not important. I quite agree that the highest vocation of anthropology is the sensitive documentation of the ways in which people infuse and co-create meaning in their immediate lives (Geertz 1973:126ff.). However, that does not preclude the investigation of wider spheres of meaning that may become institutionalized in domains of which people are not always conscious but which are equally important 'webs of signification' in which humans remain suspended.

My argument, briefly put, is that in the past, before the rise of general literacy and modern forms of transportation, Moroccan saints' shrines constituted a country-wide system of signifiers that both symbolically and structurally (that is, culturally and socially) mediated the local and the national[1] in a distinctively Moroccan way, projecting, among other things, the identity of places and peoples over great distances, allowing the particular and the general to be articulated to one another in an Islamic idiom. Through these mediations, I suggest, what might otherwise be regarded as heterodox religious beliefs and practices – the rural cult of saints – received a degree of indirect legitimization, and a de facto situation of religious heterogeneity was able to be synthesized into a unity of practice. Though this system of knowledge and meanings has been on the decline over the past half century or more as a consequence of the spread of literacy, changes in the country-wide transportation system, and policies of the Moroccan Ministry of Religious Affairs that promote more orthodox alternatives to the saint cults, it still persists with considerable force, and in a postmodern world it might renew itself in unexpected ways.

It is not the mission of this paper to expatiate on the nature of sainthood in Morocco, a subject that has been treated extensively elsewhere

(Bel 1938; Gellner 1969; Hatt 1981b). I will here only summarize a few key points as background to the following discussion. Suffice it to say that, in Muslim religious belief, the existence of saints (ṣāliḥīn, awlīya) is accepted.[2] A saint is a person, elect in the eyes of God, whose life is an example unto his or her people. In Morocco, a large proportion of those who come to be regarded as saintly were those involved in the original islamization of various lands, or key members of various religious orders that have grown up from time to time to renew the faith and defend the land from invaders. During the lifetime or following the death of saints, miracles (xaraqāt l-il ʿāda) may occur that come to be cited as proof of their extraordinary status. Elevation to sainthood is purely a matter of popular consensus; there is no central body that examines the lives of saints or that certifies their saintly status. The most characteristic marker of saintly status is the erection over the grave of a particular type of tomb (qubba), often with a domed roof. Popular sainthood of this sort is differently elaborated from one Muslim country to another but is particularly developed in the Maghrib, where, among the Berber-speaking peoples in particular, a secondary phenomenon has developed, namely 'maraboutism,' in which the agnatic descendants of saints, called 'marabouts,' have special relationships with local populations in the tribal sector of the society, based on a sort of mutual protection compact. In return for the lay tribesmen providing ongoing material support to the saint's descendants, these latter are credited with interceding with their saintly forebear to provide supernatural protection from harm, judicial services, and the dispensing of generalized good luck and prosperity (baraka). Sometimes, particularly in remote Berber-speaking regions in the mountainous or desert areas, these marabouts have come to define little quasi-independent societies, dispensing a range of quasi-governmental and quasi-clerical services (Gellner 1969; Hatt 1992a), to the detriment of the central government and the orthodox national religious institutions. Often illiterate and sometimes deeply involved with magical or divinatory practices incompatible with Islam, the 'cult of saints' is generally regarded by urban theological scholars as completely unorthodox or at best marginally heterodox and has been opposed by them for centuries. On the other hand, maraboutism has been a key force in the history of Morocco. As an institutional complex, it shades into the orthodox belief in saints, on the one hand, and into veneration of the šurfā (descendants of the Prophet, the focus of another distinctively Moroccan institution), on the other, in manifold and subtle ways, so that opposition needs to be couched in muted terms. On sainthood in Islam, particularly in its more popular forms, see also Alfred Bel (1938); on the emics of *baraka*, see Westermarck (1926:35–260).

THE MOROCCAN SAINT'S SHRINE

In one sense, a Moroccan saint's shrine is simply the grave of a person who has come to be venerated as a saint. Typically the graves of such persons are architecturally elaborated in certain locally distinctive ways, in particular by the erection of a distinctive structure (*qubba*) over the grave. Most shrines are found in cemeteries, but sometimes they are found outside of cemeteries, and sometimes it is the case that cemeteries grow up around shrines.

Architecturally, Moroccan saints' tombs are usually four-sided stone or rammed-earth buildings, which are plastered, whitewashed, and surmounted by a dome. Sometimes they are further decorated with architectural features and bright-coloured paints. Except in the most sparsely populated parts of Morocco – and sometimes even there – a traveller is rarely out of sight of one or more saints' tombs gleaming in whitewashed splendour in the distance, in contrast to the prevailing dun-coloured landscape (later in this paper we shall see that not all shrines are also tombs, but most are). Whatever else one might say about them, we can say that Moroccan saints' shrines tend to stand out visually from their surroundings. In almost any landscape and weather, they attract the eye and can often be discerned from many kilometres' distance. Take for example the shrine of Sdī Ḥmad Lfāsī, shown in Photo 1. This photo of a village named Timəkṭṭi was taken with a telephoto lens from a mountain pass (Tizi-u-Šaṭr), almost exactly one kilometre in distance from the tomb. In other words, it zeroes in on a very small rectangle of the panorama visible from the pass. It shows a fairly typical montagnard Shilha[3] village, with two localized descent groups settled in their respective hamlets that have grown over the years on either side of a ravine, both hamlets overlooking the irrigated fields that are planted with a light cover of date palms. In surveying the scene from the pass in question, one can with some difficulty discern a number of villages and hamlets, all built of mud, and so blending into the predominant colour of the earth. However, one's eye is immediately

Photo 1. Village of Timekṭṭi (Idaw Tanan) and shrine of Sdī Ḥmad Lfāsī

attracted to the bright, whitewashed saint's tomb, contrasting with the dark green patch of the palm grove.[4]

Saints' tombs are built over the burial place of a person venerated as a saint. Some saints' graves consist of a grave marker alone, exposed to the elements, but the majority have some sort of tomb erected over them. Inside, in the case of smaller shrines, there may be barely enough space between the tomb and the wall for a person to pass. Such shrines are typically quite dark inside, the only light being whatever enters through the doorway. Larger and more elegant shrines in urban areas may have more spacious interiors, with multiple tombs of saint family members. These shrines may also have walls hung with rugs or killams, the tombs may be draped with brocades, and the interior lit by candelabras or electricity.

A few definitions: in this paper I refer to the building enclosing a saint's grave as the 'tomb' ('*qubba*' in Arabic, '*lqubt*' in Tashelhait), and the marble or other stone marker that is enclosed within the tomb as the 'grave marker.' A saint's tomb becomes a 'shrine' (*maqām*) by reason of certain distinctive human actions, specifically, rituals, that take place in reference to, and in proximity to, it. Some of these ritual actions, such as the *maʿrūf*, or periodic commemoration of the dead, involving the recitation of standard prayers, are part of standard Moroccan Islamic mortuary ritual that might be observed at the gravesite of any deceased person on the anniversary of his or her death. In respect of an important saint, however, the scale of the *maʿrūf* is much larger and takes on the quality of a pilgrimage, with people coming relatively long distances for it. In addition to the *maʿrūf* there are other types of rites performed at saints' tombs that are distinctive of saints' shrines only, viz.:

- The sacrifice of hoofed animals in front of the tomb as a token of adhesion to the saint's cult,
- The circumambulation of the tomb in processions, three, five, or seven times,
- The swearing of oaths, using the tomb as a kind of 'witness' or guarantor of the oath's truth,
- The transmission of requests to God via the saint buried within, while touching the tomb.

Other social institutions connected with saints' tombs are the growth of maraboutic communities (lineal corporations of the saint's descendants) in the vicinity of the tomb, the development of pilgrimage systems, and the holding of fairs (*mwāsim, inəmugg^{w}arən*) in the spring or fall (or sometimes both) at the site of the tomb that sometimes attract thousands of faithful who live in temporary tent cities for the duration of the fair, and who often come and depart by chartered bus.

THE DOME AND THE MINARET

Over the past half century, the Moroccan Ministry of Religious Affairs has made long-term loans available to mosque-congregations – loans to enable the erection of square minarets, in the style of that ultimate icon of Moroccan civilization, the minaret of the Kutūbīyya in Marrakesh. In Moroccan religious culture, the minaret, proclaiming at a distance the presence of a mosque, is the symbol, par excellence, of a congregation – a local community of Muslims who worship together and who are a minimal social unit of the Dār al Islām. The minaret of a mosque is in this sense analogous to the church steeple of Christian countries – a marker of a local community of coreligionists. In Europe, rural villages, often obscured by trees, can so often be discerned at a distance by the church steeple rising up above the trees. Similarly, looking over a townscape from a high place, one can easily spot the large cathedral churches and form a sense of the various quarters or parishes of a town by the spires of smaller churches scattered throughout the town. Nowadays in Morocco the minarets of mosques have an analogous signalling effect – they proclaim, "Here is a community of pious Muslims."

However, prior to the late twentieth century in Morocco, minarets were uncommon outside of cities and towns, and mosques in the *blad* (rural districts) tended to be architecturally indistinguishable from ordinary houses. In the villages of the berberphone south, for example, absent a minaret, the surest external indicator that a building might be a mosque and not a large house is that it is a large building facing onto the *asais* or village dance floor, the analogue in the Berber world of the town square or plaza of a town. If the building is plastered on the outside, there may be some attempt to mark the *qibla*, but if it is a stone building, even this is usually absent on the exterior.

In these earlier times, it was the whitewashed saint's shrine, and not the minaret, that called attention to the inconspicuous clusters of earth-toned houses that constitute hamlets and villages in the countryside. The gradual proliferation of minarets attests to the imposition of an orthodoxy and a kind of uniformity over a land whose history has notoriously been one of the most intense religious fervour and spiritual motivation, though not necessarily of religious unity (Montagne 1930). The saints' shrines are, in the eyes of the orthodox urban theologians, emblematic of fissiparous and heterodox tendencies that have played out over more than a millennium of Moroccan Islamic history, and – though the saints are so deeply embedded in the fibre and sinew of Moroccan society that there is no way they could be displaced entirely – the emphasis on the construction of cookie-cutter-Kutūbīyyas is part of the Ministry's mission to centralize and homogenize the religious landscape. Thus the minarets proliferate, but the saints' shrines – much more diverse in their forms – have not concomitantly disappeared. In the true spirit of the postmodern, the two coexist. Indeed, in the *blәd*, religious institutions of various types – mosques, saint's shrines, *madrasas*, maraboutic *zāwiyas*, and ṣūfī *zāwiyas* – tend to reinforce one another as social and economic enterprises, and hence tend to be found in one another's proximity (Hatt 1981a).

THE 'SAINTS OF THE LAND'

When a tradition-minded Moroccan man travels about the land and comes up over a rise that provides him with a view onto a river valley or an expanse of landscape before him – in other words, when he enters a topographically new district – he will often utter a salutation (*tslīm*) to the saints whose shrines lay ahead of him on his route, whether they are visible or not from his vantage point. The typical explanation for this practice is that it is a good thing to acknowledge the powers-that-be of the country into which one is entering. If pressed on the matter, the word '*ḥimāya*' (protection) may crop up; however, it is not a question of a formal relationship of saintly protection (such relationships do indeed exist in other contexts), but merely a way of letting the saints – other peoples' saints it must be added – know that one is there, and that one has arrived in peace, and not with malicious intent. This same pattern of verbal acknowledgment can be replicated at any of a number of increasingly smaller levels. For example, if one crosses the great pass of the Tizi-n-Test, headed northward, one would at the pass *tsәllәm* (verbally acknowledge by uttering the word *tslīm*) Sdī Bәl ʿAbbās, the patron saint of Marrakesh, and the regional saint of the Ḥāwz region. If one crossed the Tizi-n-Test (a famous pass of the High Atlas) headed southward, one would *tsәllәm* Sdī u Sdī, the patron saint of the town of Tarudant and of the Sūs Valley. And as one entered various tribal or sub-tribal territories along the way, or passed particular villages, one would *tsәllәm* their patron saints, once again uttering a *tslīm* as one entered Marrakesh or Tarudant, depending on which direction one was travelling.

Most often, the names of the saints of the land are known, and pronounced, because men tend to travel in places they know. But today, just as Edmond Doutté (1905) reported almost a century ago, if one is travelling to an unfamiliar region, and the names of the saints of the land are unknown, as one approaches a mountain pass or other natural divide between landscapes, one can utter, simply, "*tslīm i-rrjāl lbləd*" – "greetings to the saints of the land (whoever they may be)!"

This custom of proclaiming a salutation to the 'saints of the land' provides us with our point of entry into the analytical substance of this paper. It points to a nexus of elements that are conjoined in Moroccan culture: the land, the saint, and the people of the land (Berque 1955). For in the Moroccan cult of saints, a saint is a dead man or woman who has a continuing relationship with a populace of living people situated in space and on the land. Local accounts of this continuing relationship can be somewhat variable but seems nearly always to contain some variant or aspect of the notion of protection. When the traveller enters a new region or district, he or she is entering into the zone of a covenant of protection, and the prudent and pious individual takes the precaution of acknowledging this relationship.

As Westermarck was the first to point out, in Moroccan popular religion, this aura of protection appears almost always to be geographically centred and limited. Unlike the mercy of God, it is not a universal phenomenon that follows a protected individual wherever on earth he or she goes. God is universal and saints are particular, and their spheres of protection are localized. Protection is strongest in the immediate vicinity of the saint's tomb and is null when the protected individual is in Europe, for example. But exactly how far the protection radiates around the shrine remains vague.

In the case of tribes or tribal confederations that have special collective ritual relationships with well-known 'patron saints,' such as the Idaw Ltit of the Anti-Atlas mountains have with Sdī Ḥmad u Musa of Tazərwalt, or the relationship that the Idaw Tanan of the western High Atlas have with the saint of their confederation, Sdī Brahim u 'Ali of Tiyanimin – two saints who will be discussed further on – saintly protection extends to the land of the tribe or confederation and to the people of the tribal units (the nested segmentary sub-tribes that compose the confederations in question). In these cases, people contend that the saint's protection follows the tribal member when he or she travels outside of the tribe, but within the Sūs (the region of southern Morocco roughly coterminous with the Shilḥa Berber language); and there is uncertainty and dispute whether and how long saintly protection might follow a person who went to live in the north, e.g., Tangier. Also there is fair certitude that saintly protection is not operative in Christian countries, e.g., France or Belgium, where Moroccans go to work on labour contracts.

THE GAMUT OF SHRINES IN THE SHILḤA WORLD

Natural phenomena

Saints' shrines are only one of a range of types of objects, natural and materially constructed, that fall broadly within the range of phenomena anthropologists have called 'shrines' in world ethnography. I shall discuss 'constructed' shrines in the following sections. Here, I propose to discuss briefly 'natural' shrines. In the Berber world, there is a variety of phenomena that are regarded as being endowed with some sort of sacred significance and toward which people orient themselves in prescriptive ways, normally either avoidance (bogs, fens, and other locations where water seeps or oozes, as opposed to gushes, which are the typical habitat of *jnūn*, as well as certain caves and caverns) or minor verbal acknowledgment when they are passed by (strange geological formations, narrow gorges, hanging valleys). The verbal acknowledgment may involve a slight bowing of the head and the pronunciation of a *tslīm* or other formula when they are approached. There may be beliefs that failure thus to acknowledge their spiritual presence may result in misfortune – a tumble or a snakebite in the vicinity, for example. In addition to the presence of *jnūn*, such localities are richly endowed with legend, the most common of which relate to the Birtqīz, the mythic 'Portuguese' who figure in so much southern Moroccan folklore. These are seen either as previous inhabitants of the land who were chased away when the first Shilha people move northward from their original homeland in the Bānī Mountains, or the historical

Portuguese who, in the sixteenth and seventeenth centuries, occupied coastal Morocco and had spheres of influence as far inland as the Tafilālt. One way or another, the legendary Birtqīz are usually associated with buried treasure. Rumours and tales abound of hidden Birtqīz chests – full of gold coins – that remain nestled undisturbed in caverns and canyons of the foothills and mountains.

Very old trees, especially if they are very gnarled or twisted, or if they are found in unexpected locations, as in a mountain pass, are in my experience almost always claimed locally to be endowed with some sort of *baraka*, which, following the 'laws' of its transmission (Westermarck 1926), require physical contact, usually in the form of placing the palms of the hand upon the tree to absorb the power. Almost every Berber village has its ancient olive tree, usually a blasted old snag with only a few scraggly branches remaining. Its enormous trunk possesses bark worn smooth where people have rubbed it for luck over the decades. It is not unknown for such ancient trees to have human and, particularly, saint-like characteristics attributed to them, or to bear the name of actual or putative persons, or, indeed, to have periodic rites conducted in association with them, exactly in the same fashion as with 'constructed' saints' shrines.

As an example, I will discuss a lonely thuya tree that stands like a sentinel near the top of a long, steep, climb to a mountain pass in Ait Waʻzzun country (Idaw Tanan), appropriately named the Tizi-n-Tagurramt, literally, "the pass of the female agurram (hereditary saint)." This pass separates two major drainage systems, and the tree in question – obviously of great antiquity and, when I last saw it, apparently dead, but claimed to have put out a few leaves a couple of years previously – is asserted to 'be' (*tga*) a *tagurramt*, 'saint.' My efforts to ascertain precisely in what sense a tree can 'be' a saint yielded only a series of incomplete and contradictory answers. The most common account is that a venerated *tagurramt* was either killed (martyred, in the Muslim sense) there or buried there, and that the tree sprang up as a sign. There is a difference of opinion over whether she was or was not the same person as Lalla Tašaixt, another female saint buried atop a nearby ridge, and who is also asserted to be a *tagurramt* of the family of Sdī Brahim u ʻAli. The names Lalla Tagurramt and Lalla Tašaixt both mean, connotatively, 'Saint Saint, (feminine)' a common indication in Moroccan hagiography of a figure whose sanctity is established but whose personal name has been lost. One particular account of the legend of Lalla Tagurramt is that – true to the prototypical vocation of an *agurram* – her father was working to avoid a battle in a protracted war between Tazəntut-Ix^wərḍiḍən, a group of villages to the east of the pass, and the people of Inɣarən-Ankəluṭ, to the west of the pass. In this legend, one day, while out together with his young daughter, the *agurram* in question physically interposed himself between two feuding factions, with the result that, in the ensuing melée, the young girl was somehow killed. How and by which side is unclear – people on both sides of the pass, however, say that the killer came from the opposite side of the pass. Now, in Shilha culture, there is no other sin so dreadful than the slaying of a holy person, and the fact of her being a young virgin only adds to the poignancy of the legend. Yet this legend, which I have collected both in respect of Lalla Tagurramt and Lalla Tašaixt – who, as we have seen, may or may not be the same person – is dismissed by many others, including high officials of the Ait Sdī Brahim u ʿAli, the saintly family of which the female-saint-of-the-mountain-pass is supposed to have been a member, and who, as *šurfā*, have more than a casual interest in their own genealogy. Thus, even though the legend seems almost tailor-made to further the reputation of the Ait Sdī Brahim u ʿAli as peacemakers whose services might be resisted only at the utmost peril, they curiously disavow it. One official of the saintly corporation speculated to me that the pass with its lonely sentinel-tree had probably been a venerated place "even before the Islamic period" (*ur ta illa lislam*), i.e., a time when, "it is known" (*iṭṭiusan*) people attributed extraordinary powers to certain trees, and that the connection with the *tagurramt* may be nothing more than the way the people in later periods expressed themselves, that is, in terms of marabouts. I have been told (though I have not personally witnessed this) that "some people" hold a small *maʿrūf* at the thuya tree in question, thus making it indubitably a 'shrine' in the sense I use in this paper.

Often, indeed, such natural phenomena have names like Sdī Miskīn ("Saint Poor Fellow") or Sdī Flān ("Saint Whoever"), which play on the use of the verbal category of the saints in the religious system, but which are also obviously arch or nonsensical usages. Faced with such usages, it is difficult to resist the thought, following the reconstruction techniques of writers like Alfred Bel (1938:53–82) and Westermarck (1935), that we are dealing with syncretism between the Moroccan cult of saints and more ancient Berber ways of thinking about life and the sacred. Waterfalls, where falling water crashes onto rocks and releases ozone, and springs from which water actively spurts or gushes are prime sources of *baraka* and may be anthropomorphized as 'holy men', but without any whiff of the *jnūn* about them.

For an extensive survey of natural phenomena that have supernatural powers and/or saintly identity invested in them (albeit mainly oriented toward the Central Maghrib), see Émile Dermengham's *Culte des saints dans l'Islam maghrébin* (1954), which contains a number of photographs of these phenomena.

Constructed shrines and their elaboration

By the term 'constructed' shrines, I refer to man-made structures that stand in contrast to their environment by reason of the architectural design and human labour that has been invested in them. On a scale from the least elaborated to most elaborated graves that can also be called shrines, the structures that best exemplify the lower end of the scale are the rock assemblages or piles – they are not nearly well enough organized to merit being called cairns – that tend to be found in the more southerly regions of Morocco, on the southern slopes of the Anti-Atlas range and beyond. Viewing them, it is hard to resist the thought that one is looking at a construction site containing the materials necessary to build a saint's tomb, but that, for some unexplained reason, construction has been stopped. However, in the architectural grammar of the desert peoples, these rock piles are finished constructions. Indeed, when one looks around and realizes from how far the rocks have been transported, one understands that they are, in their way, impressive structures – testimony, certainly, to the purposiveness that caused so much labour to be expended on their assemblage. Commonly seen in the desert regions, amongst both Arabic- and Berber-speakers, they can occasionally be found in northern Morocco on vacant lots or on the outskirts of cities – wherever black-turbaned Ṣaḥrāwīs gather. One shrine of this sort that I know in Agadir does not have a saint buried beneath it. Rather it is a sort of proxy for another shrine in Rgībāt country. The Bedouin truck-drivers living in Agadir built this shrine so they could continue devotions in their new home-away-from-home.[5]

Leaving aside the rock-assemblages of the desert, Moroccan saint shrines can range from the very simple to the most elaborate. The simplest may be one-room sheds built out of dry rock, sometimes not even tall enough to enable a grown man to stand up inside – assuming the roof has not collapsed (which it most often has done). These simple shrines may

Photo 2. Shrine of itinerant Saharans, Agadir.

be without any architectural distinction or elaboration that might signal their significance. Conversely, the most elaborate shrines may be as the shrine of Mulāy Idrīs I, which consist of an entire 'holy town' populated by the saint's descendants dwelling in the vicinity of the tomb, and called (appropriately enough) Mulāy Idrīs. Examples of these two extremes are discussed below and appear in Photos 3 and 8.

In between these two extremes, most Moroccan saints' shrines consist of elaborations of two basic structural designs:

Figure 1A represents the basic domed *qubba* – a simple cube surmounted by a dome, either smooth or ribbed. Figure 1B represents a variant with a pyramidal green-tiled roof, usually reserved for shrines of *šurfā*

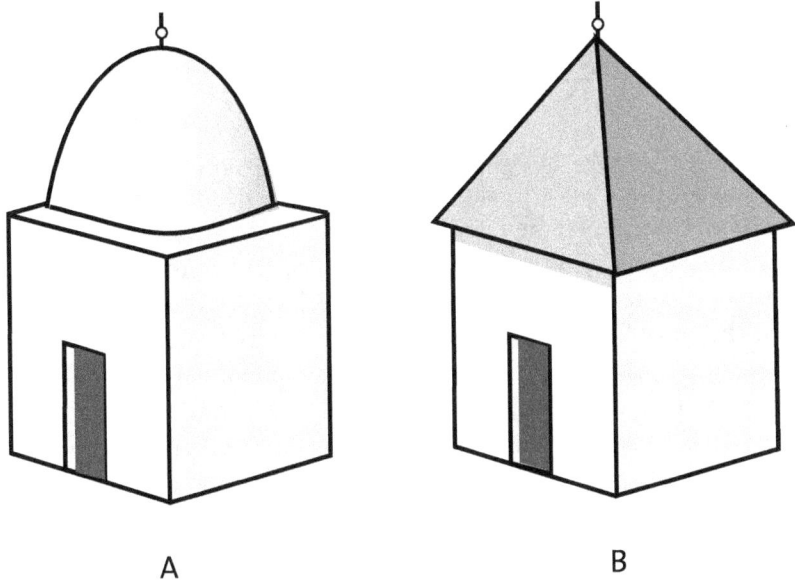

Figure 1. Basic tomb designs.

(descendants of the Prophet), although not all sharīfian shrines use this design.[6] By adding these basic elements together, a variety of designs can be derived.

In size, they range from modest and cramped structures barely able to accommodate a dozen or so persons standing inside to structures that have much the same form and proportions (cube surmounted by a dome) but are many times the scale. Seen at a distance, very large shrines sometimes fool the eye and lead one to imagine they are much nearer than they are, and this trompe d'œil causes them to appear to recede as one approaches them.

SHRINE AND COMMUNITY: TERRITORIAL COMMUNITIES

Most Moroccan saints' shrines define communities of persons who have special relationships with the saint whose grave is the focus of the shrine. These communities may be territorial communities (a village, a tribe, a tribal section, a quarter of a town, or a town itself), pilgrimage communities (persons gathered together by a personal bond to the saint in question) or they may be communities of elective affinity (e.g., sick or injured persons falling within certain categories of affliction, hoping for a cure, or persons attracted by some symbol or detail of the saint's biography and finding signs of a mystical affinity in their visits to the shrine).

The range of territorial communities that may be associated with Moroccan saints' shrines is extremely broad, ranging from localized patrilineages to the whole nation itself. In this section, I shall attempt to demonstrate the range of territorial communities that may be symbolically associated with a saint's shrine by providing examples at various levels of inclusiveness. Figure 2 is a schematic diagram that illustrates some of the magnitudes of social grouping that are typically identified with saints' shrines, and which serve as pilgrimage centres for those groupings.

In my survey, I shall attempt to classify these territorial shrine communities using a pair of binary oppositions referring to the distribution of knowledge relating to the saint in question: endosemiotic versus exosemiotic, and esoteric versus exoteric.

The terms endo- and exosemiotic are borrowed from the 'ecological semiotics' of Thomas A. Sebeok (1974) and are used here to indicate whether the communicative signal emitted by a shrine-cum-icon is, so to speak, 'recognized' primarily internally, within a particular territorial community (endosemiotic) or externally, in a wider outside community (exosemiotic). 'Recognition' in this context refers to whether people in general have heard of, and know about, the shrine in question such that they could identify or contextualize it briefly – whether, as we might say, the name of the shrine 'resonates' with them. For example, a shrine would be classed as endosemiotic if only its particular cultic community recognized it, whereas outsiders would not. Most of the 'natural shrines' discussed above would, of course, by their nature, be endosemiotic. A stranger could see them, but in the absence of local knowledge, would not even recognize them as shrines, i.e. be able to fit them into a category of phenomena that the stranger and the local person shared. This would be a case where there is no substitute for local knowledge. This would be in contrast to most other 'constructed' shrines, in the cases of which the stranger would perhaps not know whose shrine it was but would certainly recognize that the structure is meant to be a shrine because it falls within the Moroccan architectural vocabulary of shrines. For purposes of classification in this discussion, the term 'stranger' should be understood to mean another Moroccan, i.e., someone familiar with Moroccan Islam and the architectural conventions of that country but who is not familiar with the particular history of regions distant from his or her own locality.

The reader who has followed the argument thus far will now perhaps realize that it is the exosemiotic aspect of Moroccan saints' shrines that constitutes the focus of this paper. However, it is important not to lose sight of the fact that a shrine may be suspended in a double semiotic: in addition to whatever meaning it may connote to strangers, it may also be endosemiotic with respect to its particular shrine community. This inner meaningfulness may range from the superficial to the profound, and each shrine constitutes a universe of its own when it comes to documenting it.

The esoteric–exoteric distinction is of course familiar from sociological studies of religion in the Weberian tradition and is used here to refer to relative patterns of distribution of cultic knowledge, with respect to a saint's shrine. At the two extremes, knowledge may be either widely known (or at any rate accessible) to the public at large, or it can be restricted to a subset of that public who gain access to it by the following: birth into a privileged group, initiation and training, and education. Most religious institutions are neither exclusively esoteric nor exoteric in their pattern of knowledge distribution. Highly institutionalized cults and world religions typically have differential spheres of knowledge, some of which are exoteric and others esoteric. The Roman Catholic Church, for example, has a formal system of doctrinal and practical education of young Catholics, and in countries with significant Catholic populations, even non-Catholics have a pretty fair idea of Catholic beliefs, dogmas, and liturgical practices. This is the domain of exoteric knowledge, available and accessible to all. At the same time there are large bodies of esoteric religious knowledge which are restricted to church professionals and members of particular religious orders. The majority of esoteric knowledge in any religion consists of the minutiae of ritual practices: their details and sequences, their texts and

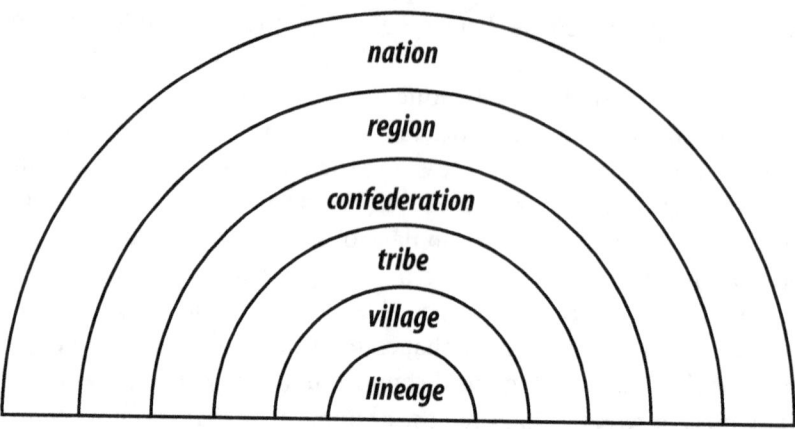

Figure 2. Schematic of shrine communities based on territory or descent.

formulae, their origins and efficacies. It is publicly known that this esoteric knowledge exists (and, in 'open societies' in the Popperian sense, much of it is in fact relatively accessible), but most cult members do not find this knowledge relevant to their lives and "leave it to the experts" to immerse themselves in this domain of knowledge.

To the eso- and exoteric distinction, I find it necessary to add a third term, asoteric – a term which I realize has sometimes been used to refer to knowledge that is 'hidden' (e.g., in the Ṣūfī sense of occultation) – but which I stipulate here to denote knowledge that is so sparse or unsystematic that it cannot be determined whether it is eso- or exoteric. This usually occurs when no one claims authority over knowledge about a saint.

The domain of the asoteric is not an uncommon property of folk belief systems generally (Borhek and Curtis 1975: 115–20), where large parts of the cultural landscape consist of particularized bits of knowledge that are not incorporated within larger frameworks of meaning. Although the overall argument of this chapter is that saints' shrines form part of a broader system of distributed knowledge, it is important to recognize the large number of shrines that exist and are at least minimally maintained, but for which virtually no hagiographic or cultic details can be obtained. Such shrines are often in a state of visible, though not utter, dilapidation both physically and historically. Few details of the saint's life, attributes, and miracles (*xairāt*) survive – this lack of specificity being explained by the fact that he or she lived "very long ago" (*zik, zik, bəkri*) or that "all his (or her) people are gone." But this fact in no way diminishes the sacredness of the shrine. Passers-by will utter their *tslīms* and the occasional person will stop and pass a contemplative moment in its shade, absorbing its *baraka*. Before the shrine collapses entirely into a heap of rubble, someone, it seems, will arrive and invest the time and energy and money to refurbish it to the point at least where imminent structural collapse is avoided – one of the random acts of generosity and piety so common in the quotidian life of Muslims. To borrow the terminology of Mary Douglas on the degree of organization of belief systems, asoteric cults are simply 'low grid' (Douglas 1966). As intellectual structures, they may be little systematized, but their social importance and their significance in the praxis of sainthood should not be underestimated.

In order to provide some specificity for the points I have made, in the following section I list a series of examples of shrines and discuss them in terms of the inner-versus-outward orientation of the knowledge systems associated with them. We have already seen an example of a shrine at the local level – that of Sdī Ḥmad Lfāsī who is at once the lineage-ancestor of one of the major groups settled in the village, a point of identification for the village as a whole, and focus of a small annual commemoration that brings together the people of a half dozen villages in the area. The subsequent examples presented here are intended to illustrate something of the range of territorial shrine communities and of magnitudes of saints and shrines that is indicated in Figure 2. The particular examples selected reflect cases familiar to me by firsthand knowledge and because there are some interesting interconnections between several of them which bear on my larger argument about saints' shrines as systems of distributed knowledge. Although it might be more convenient to begin at one end of the range and move systematically in one direction to the other end, I in fact begin with a case at the middle of the range of magnitude and move outward in both directions. I do this so that the interconnections alluded to may be followed.

Sdī Brahim u 'Ali: Exosemiotic and esoteric

My first example will illustrate an almost ideal-typical case of a tribal patron saint. I should make it clear here that 'patron saint' is not an emic concept in Shilḥa culture but rather an analyst's concept. Nonetheless, as a category, it denotes a neatly demarcated range of phenomena on the ground whose attributes are the strong identification, both internal and external, of a tribally organized people with the persona of a saint who is believed, through the flow of his *baraka*, to provide supernatural protection. It is believed that this protection carries out the following actions: it increases the food supply as the population grows (thus speaking to the primordial anxiety that results from as people with a fixed land supply adopting the Islamic rule of equal partable inheritance); it fends off animals, pests, and plagues that have so often devastated Moroccan cities; and it diverts attempts on the part of the central government and its *qā'ids* to take away the cherished autonomy of tribal peoples and to impose taxation.

Sdī Brahim u 'Ali is the patron saint of the Idaw Tanan, which is a confederation of three[7] major tribes of varying size found in the extreme western High Atlas Mountains, north of Agadir, with a total population of around 55,000. The three tribes differ markedly in elevation, topography, vegetation, soil types, and relative remoteness from the historical loci of state power in the Sūs (namely the towns of Marrakesh, Essaouira, Agadir, and Tarudant). Although all Idaw Tanan can be described as agro-pastoralists, different parts of the confederation vary in the proportion of pastoral to agricultural production in their annual output. Those with a high proportion of agricultural production differ in the proportions of irrigated to un-irrigated land they sow, and among those who are primarily irrigated farmers, there are differences in the proportion of orchard crops to market vegetables to grains. Some Idaw Tanan, who live on the seacoast, combine farming with offshore fishing, which is done in small boats. In December, it is not unknown for the inhabitants of the hamlets of Ait ʷAnzig, near the highest elevation, to be waiting for the snow cover to melt off their fields, while inhabitants of certain villages of Ait ʷAnukrim, near the seacoast, are tending the finger bananas they sell in small shops along the coastal highway. From the point of view of marketing, people in different sectors of the confederation orient their economic endeavours in all directions. In other words, the Idaw Tanan are a quite diverse people, and although their historical unity is obviously rooted in the contiguity of the six tribes to one another, it cannot, however, be reduced to any obvious geographic, topographic, economic, or (indeed) ethnic homogeneity.[8] What makes them one people is in fact their common adherence to their patron saint, Sdī Brahim u 'Ali, who is buried in a small neutral enclave where a number of tribes come together near the centre of the confederation. This location and enclave is considered to belong to all Idaw Tanan – not to any one tribe in particular.

Islam was implanted into the western High Atlas by a generation of eleventh- and twelfth-century CE missionaries known as the Irəgragən,[9] a number of whom later came to be regarded as saints in their own right, with shrines of their own. The generation of saints to whom Sdī Brahim u 'Ali belongs dates from a later period of religious activity, the sixteenth century, a time of political upheaval and concomitant religious revival. The upheaval was due in part to the colonial expansion of the Spaniards and Portuguese along the Mediterranean and Atlantic coasts of Morocco, and the inability of the old Marīnid-Ḥāfsid state to recapture the lands seized by the Christian powers. In the general chaos, a variety of charismatic leaders arose in the interior, all vying with one another and with the decadent remnants of the old state to lead the *jihād* against the European colonialists. These movements were of two main sorts: 'maraboutic' leaders, consisting of magically inspired firebrands who appealed to the berberphone population, and Arabic-speaking *šurfa* ('Sharīfians' or descendants of the Prophet) who gained following among the nomadic populations of the desert fringes of Morocco. These various forces fought it out for over a century, with the Sharīfians, in the form of the Saʿādian dynasty, triumphing in the end, and ushering in the Sharīfian model of the Moroccan monarchy that continues down to the present day. But, their triumph was tempered by the number of maraboutic principalities that had arisen in the interior and had done much of the work in driving out the Christians. These little 'maraboutic states' had become firmly established and rooted into the local populaces among whom they lived, and they were in effect autonomous political entities within Morocco, which the central Sharīfian government was unable to uproot.

Sdī Brahim u ʿAli belonged to the missionary 'order' (if it can be called that) of Sdī Muḥammad bin Slīmān al Jazūlī, a prolific theologian and revivalist. Other followers of al Jazūlī who became important regional saints include: Sdī Ḥmad u Musa of Tazərwalt, arguably *the* patron saint of southern Morocco; Sdī Saʿīd u ʿAbd al Naʿīm of Ait Dāwd (Iḥaḥan); and

Sdī u Sdī of Tarudant. Sdī Brahim u ʿAli and Sdī Ḥmad u Musa are held to be legitimate *šurfā*, and not simply 'marabouts.'

One of the few really solid facts known of the life of Sdī Brahim u ʿAli is his death date: 1583. Much of his life was probably spent organizing the Berber-speaking peoples of the interior to deal with the Portuguese, who had established themselves in and around what is today the town of Agadir and who sought allies and trading partners as far inland as the oases of the Tafilālt.

What comes down to us in text and legend of his life portrays him as an almost ideal typical saint of his time: he was a *šrīf* or descendant of the Prophet who associated himself with a Berber-speaking population, and he propagated Islam among them. Through his moral example and inspirational leadership, he welded the inhabitants of the southern slopes of the western High Atlas – who had no distinctive identity up to that time – into a cohesive mass. This collective effort would become known in history as the Idaw Tanan – a confederation renowned far and wide throughout the Sūs for their determined spirit of independence and commitment to self-government.

The great saint is credited with many of the amenities of the Idaw Tanan landscape, in particular the discovery of many of the springs that water the land. For this reason, his descendants number among them several water-diviners renowned throughout the Sūs. Much of the corpus of legend surrounding Sdī Brahim u ʿAli relates to various customs and structural arrangements peculiar to the Idaw Tanan confederation that are related to their having maintained de facto autonomy for three centuries following the death of the saint. The 'three-thirds' system of internal balance is credited for staving off any major internal bloodletting since the time of the saint. Also, a variety of particular arrangements, such as the partitioning of the Idaw Mṭat sub-tribe between the two rival tribes of Ait Tankərt and Ait Waʿzzūn, might be regarded as the archetype of the saint's political leadership: achieving a balance of interests and populace through innovative thinking.

Of greater importance in the minds of Idaw Tanan than the political arrangements Sdī Brahim effected within the confederation, however, was his action on behalf of the confederation vis-à-vis the state. In a protracted contest with the great Saʿādian *sulṭān*, Mulāy Aḥmad al Manṣūr al Ḏāhabī, who reigned from 1578 to 1603, Sdī Brahim is believed to have secured state recognition that the Idaw Tanan, under their sharīfian marabouts, were 'justly governed' and hence absolved from paying taxes to the government. For the Idaw Tanan this is the charter of their righteous autonomy. However, no official of the state seems ever to have heard of this charter, and the Idaw Tanan were largely treated as rebels and brigands in dealings with the state.

In addition to this disparity between the indigenous and state accounts, there is a curious disjuncture between the indigenous legend and what we know of the history of the period as well. The oral accounts of the Idaw Tanan make no mention of the fact that, during the lifetime of Sdī Brahim u 'Ali, the Portuguese had colonies along the Atlantic coast of Morocco, with a bastion on the tiny island of Tamaraxt, where Idaw Tanan territory abuts the ocean, and that the Portuguese had several times conducted raids into the mountains of 'Dautanente' (Cenival 1934:17). When added to the standard explanation in Moroccan historiography of the rise of the 'maraboutic challenge' in the late sixteenth and early seventeenth centuries – namely the inability of the state to drive out the Christian colonists – with the concomitant rise in the interior of various marabouts who promised a successful jihād against the Europeans, it is hard to believe that the ascendancy of Sdī Brahim u 'Ali, too, was not somehow related to the Portuguese challenge. Yet there is no hint of this in the folk legend.

Suffice it to say, the Idaw Tanan and the *igurramən* who lived near the saint's shrine at Tiyanimin prospered in their relationship with one another. The *igurramən* grew numerous and many moved out from Tiyanimin to live amongst the people who supported them, situating themselves in small *zāwīyas* (holy villages) mainly located on inter-tribal borders, the better to safeguard peaceable relations and to bring their baraka closer to the people.

So prosperous did the Ait Sdī Brahim u 'Ali become through their association with the Idaw Tanan that, in the nineteenth century, they were able to construct a magnificent five-domed shrine over their ancestor's grave (Photo 3), and the spring and fall fairs that were held there, not only were celebrations of Idaw Tanan identity and solidarity (Photo 4), but also were famed afar and attracted visitors from throughout the Tashelhait-speaking area of Morocco. Although the shrine itself is highly exosemiotic, the cult remains esoteric since the protection of Sdī Brahim u 'Ali is fundamentally linked to the people and the land of Idaw Tanan. If a stranger comes to live amongst the Idaw Tanan, he or she must "take Sdī Brahim u 'Ali as his wālī." A stranger temporarily visiting Idaw Tanan

Photo 3. Village of Tiyanimin (Idaw Tanan). The shrine of Sdī Brahim u ʿAli is the domed, whitewashed complex, centre-left.

Photo 4. Head of the maraboutic community pronouncing a blessing on the Idaw Tanan people at the shrine of Sdī Brahim u ʿAli, Spring *anəmuggʷar*, 1969.

may, by the mere proclamation of a tslīm, put him or herself under the saint's temporary protection. The question of whether the saint's powers go with Idaw Tanan people when they leave the country is slightly more vexed, but on the whole it is agreed that they do not.

Sdī Ḥmad u Musa: Exosemiotic and esoteric

If Sdī Brahim u ʿAli presents an ideal-typical case of a tribal or confederational saint cult, our next case presents a similarly ideal-typical case of a regional saint cult. What we have here is a similar phenomenon, except at a higher level of organization. The shrine is located high in the Anti-Atlas Mountains in what is today the sleepy little village of Illiɣ, a location which was, up through the nineteenth century, a caravan town of the first importance and the capital of a powerful state that maintained diplomatic relations with several European powers.

Sdī Ḥmad u Musa is the most renowned and most powerful saint of the Sūs. This vast region of southern Morocco includes the High and Central Atlas ranges and the area to the south, including the *ḥammādas* and steppes, up to the edge of the sandy desert itself. His saintly persona is hagiographically rich and his legend and exploits well-known and oft-told throughout the Sūs.

Like Sdī Brahim u ʿAli, he is one of the so-called 'Tenth-Century Saints' – a radiation of charismatic missionary saints of the tenth Muslim century (roughly the sixteenth century CE), who reinforced Islam in a land that has been nominally Muslim since the era of ʿAbdullah bən Dris – the son of Mulāy Idrīs II, who established Muslim rule in southern Morocco, which he governed from his provincial capital at Aɣmāt. But by all accounts, up through the sixteenth century CE, the religious life of remote rural areas was a syncretistic mélange of Christian and Jewish beliefs and practices that were continued on from Romano-Berber antiquity with an admixture of indigenous pre-Islamic beliefs and practices, including allegedly mummery, thaumaturgy, and orgiastic nocturnal revelries by the light of gigantic bonfires. Whatever their doctrinal tenets – which tended toward Mālikī rigorism and Sunnī orthodoxy – the Tenth-Century Saints established a distinctively Moroccan social form: the 'maraboutic state.' This state existed as a regional theocratic political form that was able to send down deep Islamic roots in the local society. It did so by de-emphasizing the abstract, universal, and remote elements of Islam, and

Photo 5a. Tazərwalt, in the Anti-Atlas, general view of Illiy on the opening day of the *musəm* of Sdī Ḥmad u Musa, Fall 1969. Various groups of visitors and adepts are gathered in groups and in tents on the hill above the mosque, performing rites and reciting prayers. The bottom half of the picture shows the market associated with the *musəm*.

by creating local foci of religious devotion and local politico-religious elites in the form of maraboutic *zāwīyas*. Much of the long-term success of the maraboutic states that sprang up all over Morocco rested upon their ability to muster mass support for *jihād* movements that eventually led to the expulsion of the Spanish and Portuguese from Morocco. The central government, using its standing army, had proved unequal to the task of expelling the Christians, and for two centuries, as we have seen, the Moroccan government was plagued with small, dissident theocratic states in its midst, governed by the maraboutic descendants of the Tenth-Century Saints. One of the longest-lasting of these was the 'kingdom' (as it came to be called) of Tazərwalt, with its capital at Illiy, in the Anti-Atlas, governed by the descendants of Sdī Ḥmad u Musa (Justinard 1954). Several times in the course of its history, this southern state nearly overcame the 'kingdom of Fez' (Julien 1985:493), and it maintained its own separate diplomatic relations with European powers and dominated much of the trans-Saharan trade between Morocco and West Africa.

Photo 5b. The green-tiled shrine of Sdī Ḥmad u Musa at Illiy. On the first day of their visit, pilgrims queue to enter the tomb and utter their respects to the saint and his descendants.

As a saint of extraordinary powers (*izmawən*), Sdī Ḥmad u Musa impressed himself deeply on the socio-political life of the Anti-Atlas Mountains. Although there is little direct evidence to prove it, there is some reason to believe that much of the success of the saint himself and his descendants related to their role in managing the feud-like relations that were endemic in these mountains between two ethnic blocs (*ləffs*) who inhabited the Anti-Atlas, the Ahuggwa, and the Igəzzulən. At the risk of over-simplifying, we may speculate that the marabouts used their sacred status to symbolize a wider whole and were thus able both to dampen the internecine violence of the *ləff* wars and to turn the energy they involved outward, against the Europeans and the Moroccan state.

Today the peoples of the Anti-Atlas participate in the semi-annual fairs and markets held at the saint's shrine at Illiy, and indeed many dozens of busses and trucks bring pilgrims from the entire Sūs. Most adult Berber speakers I know have attended the fair at Illiy several times and acknowledge Sdī Ḥmad u Musa as "a saint of saints."

As a major regional shrine, Sdī Ḥmad u Musa is obviously exosemiotic. I think it is the case that every man in the Sūs knows of this great shrine and, if he has not done so already, aspires one day to visit the *anəmugg^war* at Illiy. But it is not a question of a proselytizing religious order. Sdī Ḥmad u Musa 'means' something special to all the people of the Sūs, and non-Sūsī Moroccans may honour him. But they do not aspire to 'take him' as their saint or to be initiated into the rites of the shrine. Thus, although his cult has a much broader constituency than that of Sdī Brahim u ʿAli – and includes that of Sdī Brahim u ʿAli – it is still fundamentally particularistic and esoteric.

ʿAli u Ləḥsən: Endosemiotic and asoteric

About forty kilometres east of Agadir and some six kilometres from the small town of Aməskruḍ, in a wilderness location far from any human habitation, a dirt track passes a simple rammed-earth shed that once had a flat roof, which is now collapsed. This humble structure turns out to be a saint's tomb. Indeed, it is said to be the tomb of a *šrīf* (descendant in the agnatic line of the Prophet), none other than ʿAli u Ləḥsən, father of Sdī Brahim u ʿAli and (presumably), uncle of Sdī Ḥmad u Musa. Inside the building, there is no visible sign of there being a grave, and the site is without elaboration.

Photo 6. Shrine of ʿAli u Ləḥsən, Idaw Tanan.

On genealogical grounds – following the logic of maraboutism – one would have guessed that this would be a very important site in the confederation, and yet so far as I have been able to ascertain there is no *maʿrūf*, no *musəm*, and no *anəmugg^war* connected with this tomb. In fact, I have driven past it a number of times in the company of tribesmen who failed to pronounce a *tslīm*. It is not even clear to me whether it can even be considered a 'shrine.' When asked if it is a *maqām*, some say "yes," some say "no," and others shrug their shoulders. If it is a shrine, it is obviously near the lower threshold of that semantic category. All this, despite the fact that there is complete agreement that it is the actual grave of the actual biological father of Sdī Brahim u ʿAli of Tiyanimin. In contrast to the richly elaborated corpus of legends that pertain to Sdī Brahim, his father's life is strikingly devoid of incident and detail. Other than his name and burial place, there are no biographical details. According to legend, Sdī Brahim u ʿAli arrived into Idaw Tanan by accidentally straying into the country while on a lion hunting expedition (lions being the iconic signatures of Tenth-Century Saints). The question then naturally arises: where was Sdī ʿAli's original home? Unknown. Did he have an uncle named Sdī Musa – as the claim that Sdī Brahim u ʿAli and Sdī Ḥmad u Musa were first cousins would seem to imply? Unknown. How and where did he die and how did he come to be buried out in this wilderness? Unknown.

Was 'Ali u Ləḥsən even a saint? Here again, a range of answers. If one asks the question using the term '*ṣsaliḥ*,' some say yes and some say no. If one asks the question using the term '*wālī*,' the answer is, "no, but his son was a wālī."

The tomb is endosemiotic – most strangers passing by would, I think, guess that it was a shelter for goatherds or, if they were familiar with the local economy, possibly a storage shed for people out collecting dwarf palm (the fibre of a plant, *Sereona repens*, that grows wild over the Idaw Tanan highlands, and which can be processed for use as mattress stuffing). The complete absence of ritual and of a shrine community and nil elaboration of the usual hagiographic details and legends makes it, in my terms, 'asoteric.' Indeed, for a 'constructed' shrine, I think it must come close to defining the lower possible limit of institutionalization. Tumbledown and ramshackle as the structure might be, someone has at some point invested energy in the effort, however incomplete, of refurbishment and maintenance.

Lālla Maryam G^{w}ugadir: Endosemiotic and asoteric

Here we have another shrine of a putative relative of Sdī Brahim u'Ali, this time his daughter, Maryam. The shrine of Lālla [Saint, feminine] Maryam G^{w}ugadir is located inside the perimeter wall of the Qaṣba, the old Portuguese bastion later turned into an urban quarter of Agadir. The shrine is not visible at all from any vantage point within the Qaṣba, and, indeed, might well be the most endosemiotic shrine in all of Morocco, for it is literally underground, buried under several metres of earth and rubble that covers the quarter.

In the first half of the twentieth century, the Qaṣba was a thriving urban quarter of Agadir, a port town that had grown steadily from the end of World War I onwards. On February 29, 1960, a devastating earthquake struck Agadir, killing a third of its inhabitants, injuring another third, and utterly flattening the Qaṣba and the adjacent quarters of Iḥšaš and Talburjt, in all three of which the death toll approached 90 per cent. These three neighbourhoods were eventually deemed beyond repair and were covered over with huge mounds of earth that were smoothed over and preserved as memorials to the victims of the earthquake, and eventually the centre of gravity of the town of Agadir shifted southward along the seacoast. The perimeter walls of the Qaṣba were reconstructed, but nothing was ever rebuilt in the interior. It is today an historic site and viewpoint from which one can, on a clear day, look far down the Atlantic coast, as far as the Wādī Māssa.

However, in the 1960s and 1970s, if one had a guide, it was possible to locate, amid a rubble of large boulders in a certain precinct of the Qaṣba, an opening that led down into a dark, cave-like space that had been surreptitiously excavated, and from the far end of which one could, with some difficulty, by laying prone on the ground, reach one's hand down through a fissure and touch a corner of what was claimed to be a remnant of the dome of the shrine of a female saint, Lālla Maryam. In 1970 I paid a visit to this shrine.

Being a *tagurramt* or marabout, and being of the flesh and blood of one of the most venerated saints of the region, Lālla Maryam would ipso facto have been a personage of considerable sanctity and venerability during her lifetime (first half of the seventeenth century CE), but hardly anything is known of her biography, including the circumstances whereby she came to be buried in the bastion of Agadir.

So far as I have been able to ascertain, her *qubba* in the pre-earthquake period was a modest, neighbourhood shrine that was an object of visitation mainly by Idaw Tanan tribesmen who had moved to Agadir, and it was adjacent to a small *zāwīya* in which living descendants of Sdi Brahim u 'Ali through Lālla Maryam subsisted on donations from the visitors. Living, as they did, away from the *igurramən* of their homeland, Idaw Tanan tribesmen working as labourers in the Port of Agadir, or in the citrus- and sardine-packing houses of the region, appear to have behaved in respect of this shrine in much the same way they did and still do the various 'daughter-*zāwīyas*' scattered throughout the Idaw Tanan confederation – that is, treating it as a source of *baraka*. Or perhaps it was functionally similar to the proxy stone shrine that the Rgībāt had erected a couple of kilometres away – a token in a strange land of a highly local religion that does not travel well. There is some suggestion also that the marabouts who tended the shrine provided rudimentary inn facilities for Idaw Tanan tribesmen who had business in town – that is, in return for a small donation, one could find a place to sleep, some tea to drink, and water for ablutions.

By the 1980s, the civic authorities had closed down this shrine, declaring it to be illegal, and a threat to public safety and sanitation. The telltale boulders were removed and road graders smoothed over the surface, so that absolutely no trace remained of the entrance. Even in pre-earthquake times, the shrine of Lālla Maryam appears to have been endosemiotic; it does not show up at all on aerial photos taken from several angles of the old Qaṣba, and its cultic significance appears to have been esoteric in the sense that its appeal was limited to extraterritorial members of a tribal community through the indirect connection to its patron saint. In the 1960 to 1980 period following the earthquake, when the shrine was made accessible via the illegal excavations, it was an 'underground' cult in more than one sense. It was known only by word of mouth and access to it required negotiations with and payments to the half-blind custodian. Now it is no more, although I have been told that a dwindling number of devotees gather annually on what they reckon to be the site for a maʿrūf.

Sdī Bū Qnādil: Exosemiotic and exoteric

Not more than a hundred metres downhill from Lālla Maryam is another saint's shrine: that of Sdī Bū Qnādil, who is, so far as is known, no relation of the saints previously discussed here. This shrine is aboveground and consists of the classic square whitewashed qubba with a high dome that glistens in the sunlight, visible for many kilometres up and down the Atlantic seacoast.

Amongst people of learning and piety in Morocco there is a form of locution whereby, when a man is intending to visit a particular town, he does not state his intention by mentioning the name of the town, but rather he states the name of an important saint associated with that town. For example, if I were intending to go to Salé, I might say, "I am going to visit Sdī Abdallah bin Ḥasūn." In this way, the names of the important saints of the land are remembered and propagated. Used in this way, the locution is not taken literally, the term 'visit' also being used to mean 'make a pilgrimage to.' It is merely a convention of expression.

Thus, if I were going to Agadir, I would say "I am going to visit Sdī Bū Qnādil" (ra-n-nftu nzur sdi bu qnadil). Sdī Bū Qnādil is the shrine of a saint on the slopes of the great promontory that overlooks the Bay of Agadir and the saint's name doubles as a synonym for the typonym Agadir. Even more than the great old Portuguese qaṣba (bastion) of Santa Cruz that is situated high above the shrine on the top of the promontory, the whitewashed saint's shrine dominates the natural harbour and port of Agadir, a key strategic locality of Atlantic Morocco for centuries.

By any measure, Sdī Bū Qnādil is a rather marginal saint, as saints go, to occupy the august role of 'patron saint' of a town as large as Agadir. But, Agadir, being an essentially modern town, which did not exist in its present form before the twentieth century, can be said to be somewhat short of indigenous saints and has to do with Sdī Bū Qnādil, whose tomb can at least claim some iconic merit (see Photo 7). Like the Old North Church of Boston, it is a beacon from land and from sea, visible from afar in a wide range of light and weather conditions.

The cult of Sdī Bū Qnādil is quite minor indeed. Many residents of Agadir are unable to say anything definite about the saint himself and most have never visited his shrine in the sense of having stopped there, removed their shoes, and entered the qubba, despite having passed it hundreds of times on coastal highway that leads north to Essaouira.

What Sdī Bū Qnādil shows us is that a saint's shrine can be a significant symbol on a regional level without being an important focus of religious devotion within the community it has become an icon of. Certainly few people ever come to Agadir for the sole purpose of visiting the shrine of Sdī Bū Qnādil. Perhaps a certain number visit it because they happen to be going to Agadir and pass by it on the road. Moreover, few residents of Agadir would say that Sdī Bū Qnādil is in any way 'their' patron saint, though if they are traditionalists they would certainly pronounce a *tslīm* as they pass by.

Therefore in terms of our contrasts, Sdī Bū Qnādil is highly exosemiotic. That it, it has a high level of iconographic recognition over a broad area – few adults in the Sūs (including Agadir) would fail to comprehend what I mean when I say I am going to visit Sdī Bū Qnādil, and of those that had been to Agadir, few would fail to pick it out of a set of photographs of saints' shrines that I showed them. But while this is true, it also has a low degree of meaningfulness, qua religious symbol, and a low degree of elaboration as a religious cult. For the citizens of the town of which it is emblematic, Agadir, it is a landmark that projects local meaning and identity to the outside world, in a fashion similar to the Coit Tower in San Francisco, the CN Tower in Toronto, or the Eiffel Tower in Paris. To be sure, the shrine even has its cultic adherents, who appear to be residents of the nearby industrial suburb of Anfa, and who constitute, so far as I can ascertain, a community of elective affinity of persons who have made it their shrine, and who attend a small *musəm* (annual gathering) in connection with it, and who obviously contribute to its maintenance and annual

Photo 7.   Sdī Bū Qnādil and the Port of Agadir, circa 1950.

whitewashing. But, as a cult, it ranks low on doctrine and legitimization – and, in this sense, is typical of a very large number of small shrine cults throughout Morocco. I class it as 'exoteric' since the knowledge system of the adherents of the cult community is in no way specialized or restrictive. The sum total of the cult's doctrine is small and, unless I am quite mistaken, little systematized: perhaps it is a degree more systematic than the shrine of ʿAli u Ləḥsən, but probably less even than the cult of Lālla Maryam, located nearby.

Mulāy Idrīs I, Al Kāmil: Exosemiotic and exoteric

I conclude this little survey with two examples that relate to shrine communities at the national level. Without question, Mulāy Idrīs I (ca. 740–791) is the national saint of Morocco, the founder of the nation in its Muslim identity. A direct descendant of the Prophet (šrīf) and great-great-grandson of ʿAli, last of the four 'rightly-guided' caliphs revered by both Sunnīs

Photo 8.
Town of Mulāy Idrīs
of Jbel Zarhūn. Center:
tomb of Mulāy Idrīs I,
al Kāmil

and Šī'īs (Shi'ites). Idrīs ibn 'Abduḷḷah al-Kāmil found refuge in Morocco from persecution by the 'Abbāsids in Iraq. He was accepted as a spiritual leader by a group of tribal chiefs in Walīlī (the old Romano-Berber capital of Volubulis), given a Berber wife, and invited to convert the Berbers to Islam. As it happens, he died before he had much of an opportunity to govern, but at the time of his death, his wife, Kanza, was pregnant with a male child who would become Mulāy Idrīs II. Mulāy Idrīs was buried in a *zāwīya* on a hill (Jbel Zarhūn) near Walīlī, the site of the present-day shrine erected to revere him.

Idrīs I essentially determined the direction of Moroccan Islam. Given the fact of his descent from 'Ali, together with the fact of his enmity toward the 'Abbāsids, he might well have been expected to have Šī'ī leanings. The regime he established in Morocco was, indeed, separatist: it proclaimed itself a 'caliphate' in opposition to the 'Abbāsid caliphate in Baghdad – a challenge of considerable magnitude. But his regime was a Sunnī regime.

The son (Idrīs II) was literally the embodiment of Morocco itself. He bore the double legitimacy of a sharifian spirit *(ruḥ)*, which he acquired through his father, and a Berber body, which he acquired through his mother, and an even larger corpus of legend has grown up around him than around his father, for he lived much longer and accomplished much more, both politically and culturally. Under his leadership,[10] a new national state was created, centred on the new town he built some forty kilometres away: the city of Fez. This city is the spiritual and intellectual capital of Morocco and was built congruent with a new style of statecraft that emanated from it over much of the present-day territory of Morocco. Idrīs II died in 824 and he was buried in Fez.

The shrine of Mulāy Idrīs I (Photo 8) consists of a green-tiled shrine structure, which houses a *madrāsa*. Just as with the village of Tiyanimin (Photo 3) – though on a far grander scale – the saint's shrine is surrounded by the houses of his descendants. Indeed, the whole of the hill now consists of a 'holy town' that is the great pilgrimage centre of all Morocco, residence in which is restricted to blood descendants of Idrīs I. The great pilgrimage in Morocco consists of a trip to Fez to visit this shrine, followed by a day-trip out to Jbel Zarhūn. This pilgrimage is at once a celebration of religious and national identity. In this sense, it exemplifies on a broad scale what smaller and more localized shrine communities achieve on a more modest scale. Only the *ḥajj* to Mecca is a greater pilgrimage.

Clearly, the shrine is exosemiotic, as every Moroccan knows of it. And, although there is an additional corpus of esoteric knowledge available to pilgrims who can prove they are *šurfā*, for most of its visitors, the knowledge connected with the shrine is exoteric – open to all.

Sdī Muḥammad Laxamīs: Exosemiotic and exoteric

Sdī Muḥammad V was the sultan of Morocco from 1927 until his death in 1961, a period that included the last years of the French Protectorate and the early years of independence (during which period, to be technically correct, his title was changed from *sulṭān* to *mālik* [king]). In 1953, he was forcibly taken into exile and a puppet king appointed in his place. Popular resistance to this move constituted the beginnings of active resistance to French colonialism and combined with other currents in post-war international politics led to the ending of the protectorate in 1956 and the restoration of the Sharīfian throne in Morocco. The firm and astute leadership provided by Muḥammad V during his exile contributed to the respect in which he is held, even to those Moroccans who might have preferred to see an end to the monarchy. Following his death, he was buried in a mausoleum on the grounds of the Ḥasan Mosque in Rabat (Photo 9), a modern

Photo 9. Mausoleum of King Muḥammad V, Rabat

building that is a de facto shrine of Moroccan independence, reinforcing the thread of continuity between past and present, and the centrality of the monarchy to national identity.

One needs only watch a group of schoolchildren, bussed to Rabat from some remote location in the country, gathered on the steps of the mausoleum, listening to a lecture on the independence struggle, and then follow them inside as they gaze in hushed silence at the grave markers of the king-saint who is presented as the founder of modern Morocco, just as Mulāy Idrīs I was the founder of ancient Morocco, to realize the illocutionary power of place and space when they are set within an interpretive schema.

The building is officially dubbed a mausoleum and not a 'shrine,' and the official texts that accompany it are understated and diplomatic (after all, a large proportion of the visitors are French nationals). But the artful use of vast space, and the distinctive lighting and acoustic effects provided by marble, and the reverential piety that overtakes the noisy schoolchildren as they ascend the steps and enter into the tomb, leave no doubt that this is the very essence of a Moroccan shrine.

Unlike the other shrines in our survey, entrance into this shrine is not restricted to Muslims. Indeed, it is one of the three or four key tourist sites of Rabat, the national capital, and it is daily filled with visitors from abroad, and its meaning explained by numerous tourist guides who inhabit the place and explain it to whoever pays their fee.

SUMMARY

Table 1. Summary of attributes of territorial shrine communities.

	Endosemiotic	Exosemiotic	Esoteric	Exoteric
Sdī Brahim u 'Ali		✓	✓	
Sdī Ḥmad u Musa		✓	✓	
'Ali u Ləhsən	✓		[asoteric]	
Lālla Maryam Gʷugadir	✓		[asoteric]	
Sdī Bū Qnādil		✓		✓
Mulāy Idrīs I Al Kāmil		✓		✓
Sdī Muḥammad V		✓		✓

If we look at Table 1, which summarizes the attributes of the knowledge systems of the territorial shrine communities surveyed in this section, we can see that they seem to fall into three broad categories. First, there are the very minor shrines known only to small constituencies in a locality ('Ali u Ləhsən and Lālla Maryam Gʷugadir). They are endosemiotic and their ideologies are esoteric, or, perhaps (as I have suggested), so diffuse and fragmentary as to merit another term, sub-esoteric or 'asoteric.' The shrine of Sdī Ḥmad Lfāsī, discussed earlier, would probably also fit into this category.

Then (second), at the opposite extreme, there are the shrines of 'patron saints' of identifiable territorial communities at the tribal, confederational, urban, regional, and national levels (Mulāy Idrīs I Al Kāmil, Sdī Muḥammad V, and – despite appearing out-of-place in such august company – Sdī Bū Qnādil. The knowledge systems of the shrines at the higher (or wider) levels are exoteric and accessible to all.

Finally (and third), there are the regional and tribal "patron saints". These are the shrines that are most obviously at the nexus of a double semiotic. Their "inner" and "outer" meanings are different, but equally important. In the table, I have classed the knowledge and ritual systems of the patron saints of smaller communities as 'esoteric' simply because there are so many of them throughout Morocco that one needs to tap into local knowledge to access them, and their inner meanings are not likely to be of interest except to the communities they serve.

SHRINE AND COMMUNITY: PILGRIMAGE COMMUNITIES

A pilgrimage is, in Arabic, a *ziyāra*, from the root √zwr, "to visit." The pilgrim arrives at the shrine bearing a gift or donation called, in Tashelhait, '*əzziyart*.' One does not go empty-handed on a pilgrimage. The donations, ideally including at least one animal for slaughter, are presented upon arrival to the descendants of the saints or other persons who tend the shrine. If the visit is in an off-peak period for visitors, or if one is visiting an *agurram* (hereditary saint or marabout) with whom one has an established tithing relationship, the *əzziyart* would certainly entitle one to lodging and meals in the *agurram*'s guest room. However, most pilgrimages occur on fixed dates and in connection with a fair called '*anəmuggwar*' (plural '*inəmuggʷarən*'). Large fairs attract thousands of people at a time, so that there is no possible way the hosts could accommodate them all in their houses and guest-rooms, and thus the pilgrims have to live in vast tent communities on the outskirts of the fair grounds.

The Moroccan *anəmuggʷar* is in many respects similar to the medieval European fall fair. On a fixed date, the visitors converge from all directions, speaking diverse languages (Tashelhait, Tamazight, Arabic) and dialects. They come by horse, by mule, by donkey, by auto, by trucks, and, nowadays, most often by chartered busses, and spend two or three days, alternately visiting the shrine itself and engaging in a variety of ancillary religious activities surrounding it. Also they are participating as buyers and sellers in the temporary market – a vast suq of tents, temporary stalls, and merchants operating in a space no bigger than a carpet or reed mat that has been rolled out on the ground.

For most Moroccans nowadays, a pilgrimage to a distant *anəmugg^war* is an organized affair, usually promoted by a local entrepreneur who arranges the hire of a bus or a truck and collects money in advance to transport tribesmen to a shrine they have likely heard about all their lives and now, having the disposable cash, the free time, and the opportunity, they resolve to visit. The voyage involves a mixture of sacred and secular motives and thoughts. To visit a famous saint's shrine is a good thing (*xir*) – a meritorious accomplishment in and of itself – and will also garner *baraka* for the pilgrim. When it is all over, he (for it is usually a he) will return home with tales of faraway lands and peoples and also a range of goods purchased at the fair that will be redistributed widely to kith and kin.

The pilgrimage community gathered at an *anəmugg^war* is not a temporary gathering of a far-flung community composed exclusively of devotees of the saint's cult. Rather it is a short-lived and adventitious social grouping of people who have come out of diverse motives, ranging from those who have come primarily for marketing purposes (the merchants and wholesalers) at one end of the spectrum, through those first-time visitors who go on pilgrimages as a type of destination-tourism combining travel, marketing, and religious learning, to many-time repeat-attendees who actually are, in the strict sense of the term, devotees of the particular saint, at the opposite end of the spectrum.

In the case of well-established saint cults associated with maraboutic corporations, one can say, with no disrespect implied, that the *anəmugg^war* is an important part of the "saint business." The associated market and fair bring in significant revenue from required fees that merchants have to pay before setting up their tents or rolling out their mats. The association of markets with pilgrimages is obviously synergistic, and in the fall, when farmers and tribesmen have paid off their debts and have a bit of disposable cash on them, the busses make their return journeys to the tribal homelands from whence they came, their luggage compartments and roofs heavily laden with goods and gifts.

By definition, a shrine that has the renown and reputation to attract pilgrims by the thousands from a wide catchment area is exosemiotic. The very desire that drives many ordinary people to visit a particular shrine someday is planted in the telling and retelling of the pilgrimage accounts of kinsmen and neighbours who have returned from earlier pilgrimages. And it follows from this that such communities are enmeshed in an exoteric corpus of knowledge – the legend of the saint and his or her powers and miracles needs to be encoded in an accessible and memorable narrative that sparks the imagination of listeners.

For most ordinary Berber tribesmen, a pilgrimage to Mecca – the gold standard of all life experiences – is understood to be on the far outer edge of what is economically possible. But a pilgrimage to a shrine a day's bus ride away from home is within the realm of possibility, and every autumn the highways of the Sūs are crowded with traffic moving to and from saints' shrines on the *anəmugg^war* circuit.

The pilgrimage community is thus primarily an ad hoc community, consisting of a variety of people who have foregathered for a variety of motives – all having something to do with the shrine, but, in most cases, a fairly heterogeneous lot. Some are no more than tourists, their pockets brimming with cash from the sale of fall produce and off to have a bit of fun. Next year, many of these visitors will go off in a different direction to attend the fair of another saint. Casual visitors of this sort will visit the saint's shrine to pay their respects but otherwise may spend their day or two at the site in mainly secular pursuits. Others are simply itinerant merchants, there to engage in commerce. Others may be members of local communities that have a special relationship with the saint. These may come bearing prestations – bulls or sheep to be sacrificed at the shrine, mules laden with bags of grain or carpets and teapots, all to be presented as tokens of membership in tribal or regional communities. Yet others may be cult devotees who have deeply personal connections with the saint and who have never missed an *anəmugg^war* for years. These spend hours together praying and chanting and demonstrating their devotion.

SHRINES AND SOCIETIES: COMMUNITIES OF ELECTIVE AFFINITY

Over time, some shrines become oriented to specialized communities that are neither territorial publics in the vicinity of the shrine nor communities of devotees who gather periodically, but rather categories of persons sharing afflictions or aspirations in common.

In northern Morocco there is a tradition of health shrines that are associated with mineral springs and baths that goes back to Roman times and probably before. In the Muslim period, these have become associated with the personæ of Muslim saints. Further south, the tradition of curative baths and springs is only weakly developed.

Health shrines can be roughly divided into two categories. The first type is the shrine of a female saint, which attracts only women and is concerned with fertility and other gynaecological issues. The women who visit these shrines tend to be brought there by their fathers, and not their husbands, because it is their fathers who are anxious about the possibility that their married daughters might be returned to them if they fail to conceive after a year or so of marriage. Visitors to these 'fertility shrines' return home with an assortment of medicinal herbs, ointments, and amulets purchased at the shrine.

The second category of shrine caters to both men and women of all ages and is a place where persons suffering from any of a broad range of afflictions, physical and mental, come, or, if they are moribund, are brought, hoping to find a cure. The ritual action at these shrines consists quite simply of prayers to God, but transmitted through the intercession of the saint at whose tomb the prayers are uttered. I am unaware of any 'magical' actions or rites practiced at or in connection with these latter shrines, or of any curative substances sold at them, but it would not be surprising if such were found. Some shrines in this category are highly specialized as intercessory venues and may have up to a dozen recumbent persons, propped up against doorways, staring into space, or lying in the shade for most of the day, while others may have only one or two visitors coming for health purposes per week. Most of the 'patients' at such shrines are brought by relatives and left in the care of shrine custodians, who care for the patients for a week or more, having received a gift of *əzziyart* at the beginning of the visit.

Unlike the territorial communities and pilgrimage communities discussed above, this latter category of 'health' shrine creates a community that is discontinuous both in space and time and whose 'members' have no substantial degree of interaction with one another. Also, those who tend specialized shrines of this sort generally claim no genealogical connection with the saint in question, and it would not be amiss, I think, to think of these shrines essentially as businesses in which hope and a certain amount of compassionate care are offered in return for a few alms.

One last type of shrine that attracts visitors on the basis of elective affinity is what might be called the 'talent' shrine to which individuals aspiring to various sorts of creative careers come in order to augment their natural-born talents. There are shrines for drummers and flautists and I know of one shrine where aspiring singers may come "to find their voice."

CULTURAL KNOWLEDGE AND ITS DISTRIBUTION

Cultural knowledge consists of things known (data) plus a general schema that stipulates what things count as data in the first place and how those data shall be organized. The data and the schema are mutually defining and change over time in a mutual progression: data are only 'data' because they are 'recognized' as data or potential data by a particular schema, while the schema itself evolves over time, as it is progressively challenged and changed by incoming data, which it needs either to accept or reject. This co-evolution can be thought of as the cumulative result of millions of individual thoughts and actions, transactions, and communications (all in the Barthian sense; see Barth 1976).

A system of geographical knowledge is never a simple 'picture' of the surface of the Earth, for the simple reason that the Earth is so big and differentiated, and human beings are so small and have such limited capacities for storing knowledge in the form of 'pictures.' Perhaps people can retain an overlapping series of more or less accurate pictures of a few square kilometres of landscape in the vicinity of their abode or home territory, but, beyond that, some mechanism for coding and referencing needs to be resorted to in order to have a sense of place. Today, of course, we use maps and tools like global positioning systems to locate ourselves in space.

But in non-literate and 'non-cartographic' societies, this sense of location on a scale needs to be achieved by other means of referencing. The most obvious means are the use of natural landmarks: coastlines, streams, rivers, drainage areas, mountain ranges, badlands, hills, forests, and/or deserts. But insofar as they are processed to fit within human knowledge systems, even these phenomena are 'constructed' – selected, filtered, framed, contextualized, and tweaked so that they are as much social and cultural data as 'natural' data. Thus reprocessed, they become, in the phrase of Lévi-Strauss, "good to think." They are 'semiotic' not because of anything inherent in them, but because of the way they have been incorporated into systems of signifiers. Because they remain stationary even as humans move about them, they are like so many drawing pins stuck on a blank sheet of paper – points of reference in terms of which movement, whether physical or notional, can be enacted or imagined. Taken all together, as a system, these bits of knowledge constitute a kind of map or cognitive grid.

Unlike printed maps, the 'data' of these shrine maps are distributed over the minds of tens of thousands, perhaps millions, of people who are, in turn distributed over space and time. No single individual ever has more than a partial picture of the whole, but there are two key attributes that make this a true system. First, the data sets contained in various peoples' minds overlap. Secondly, in the areas of overlap, there is a relatively high level of agreement on what constitute the data. That is, of all the possible attributes of a given saint, certain attributes become salient – that is, they are memorable and they are distinctive. By memorable, I mean they have a name and possess attributes that, to put it simply, stick in the memory and are readily recalled in association with the name. By distinctive, I mean they possess at least some attributes that contrast with the attributes of other saints or shrines in the general area in such a way that there are contexts in which they are 'like' the other saints, and other contexts in which they are 'unlike.' For example, the convention that Sdī Brahim u ʿAli and Sdī Ḥmad u Musa are putative cousins provides (like all kinship systems) a single nexus of simultaneous likeness and contrast. The convention that the two of them in turn share with Sdī Saʿīd u ʿAbd al Naʿīm (and others), namely the doctrinal tradition of being followers of Sīdī Muḥammad bin Slīmān al Jazūlī, provides another dimension of likeness-versus-contrast.

In distributed knowledge systems, all the data there are must be kept continually within the recall of living persons, although any single individual never knows all the data. The higher-order data, such as the shrines of Mulāy Idrīs the First and Second, and the shrine of Sdī Muḥammad the Fifth, and the names of the principal patron saints of cities and regions, are 'common knowledge' throughout Morocco. By contrast, lower-level data are, by their nature, 'local knowledge.' As a person travels throughout the country, these data are *accessible* on demand in the localities where they are significant. If I am travelling in a remote Anti-Atlas valley, I can access enough data necessary for my navigational purposes ("continue down the trail until you see a cemetery to your right with a saint's tomb with a blue dome, and turn left at the next crossroads") from the local stock of knowledge by speaking to local people. When I return to my home village, I may even regale my fellow villagers with accounts of the wonders I have beheld on my journey, and each mention of a saint of some other locality is greeted by *tslīms* from the audience. In this way, local knowledge, infused with the miracles of saints, is projected over distances and becomes subject to comparison and correction; but control over the knowledge remains overwhelmingly with the locality whose knowledge it is.

In this way, a virtual 'map' of the land is sustained, through verbal exchanges about the great religious lords of the land and their exemplary lives, exploits, and miracles, even though there may be no point in space or time in which all this geographical information comes together at once.[11] Such a map is at once useful, aesthetic, and editable – as it responds well to demographic changes. Moreover, within the traditional culture, it is well nigh indestructible – particular bits of data might be lost, but most often they can be reconstructed. Finally, by being cast in the idiom of Muslim ideals, the map embeds geographical knowledge within a matrix of Islamic identity.[12]

Every Moroccan saint's shrine is in its own way unique and has its own narrative and body of praxis. Most shrines possess both a corpus of ideas and practices that constitute the 'inner' knowledge, known by the shrine's community (whether this be a territory or a far-flung body of pilgrims), and a smaller corpus of external signifiers that are communicated to travellers. Strangers may be allowed access to some of the 'inner' knowledge at the community's discretion such as listening to the local legends of the 'saints of the land' – this is one of the most common forms of entertaining guests in a Berber village.

But, significant as this inner knowledge and practice may be in the dynamics and solidarity of village life, the exoteric face of this knowledge is just as important in its way. Through it, the village becomes part of something wider – certainly not quite a 'global' universe, as that term is understood today, but certainly a wider pattern of meaning and order that, among other things, enables a villager to travel freely about the land, finding fellow believers along the way who may provide shelter, food, and engagement in a narrative exchange of the 'saints of the land' (*rijāl lbləd*), in return for accounts of the saints of the land from whence the visitor hails.

As a system of knowledge, this system of 'orientation by saints' is not a rigid and tightly organized system like the periodic table of the elements. Rather it is a loosely structured system which, in its heyday, embraced an encyclopaedic quantity of information, organized by a small number of general principles, but distributed over millions of Moroccans, each an expert in a certain range of local knowledge, and able to access, when needed, other parts of the vast system.

THE POSTMODERN SHRINE

As I stated at the beginning, my analytical gaze in this paper is primarily retrospective. The 'system of distributed knowledge' I have been discussing certainly still exists but has been slowly loosening its grip for a half a century, consequent upon changes in the way in which Moroccans think about and move about their land. These changes are the standard transformations we associate with modernity and postmodernity. Though there are still many tribesmen, particularly in the mountainous areas, who continue to travel on foot or by donkey or mule along rugged trails, the vast majority of travel today is by bus, truck or automobile along paved roadways. Most men are, at least, rudimentarily literate and can read the road signs welcoming them to various districts and localities. Thus the habit of thinking of space in terms of the domains of the *rijāl lbləd* may not have quite the communicative power it once did. Today people tend to live in a more secularized, 'cartographic,' universe, consisting of officially demarcated provinces and city limits. Today, only the oldest men are apt to say, "I am going to visit Sdī u Sdī" (the patron saint of Tarudant) – most just say, "I have to make a trip to Tarudant." This is in no way to imply that the place of religion in peoples' thinking has declined or that the significance of the shrines has lessened. But rather, one system of *aides-mémoire* has been to some extent supplanted by another system, which is perhaps, given the change in material culture, more functional.

I noted earlier that modernity had favoured the minaret over the dome, the orthodox over the heterodox, and that, in the latter half of the twentieth century, government funding policies had led to a quantum increase in the number of minarets towering over villages in the rural areas. During this period there was little government funding available for the construction of saints' tombs, unless they happened also to be annexes to important mosques or madrasas, and thus their persistence is testimony to the generosity of private individuals. As a form of conclusion, I would like to speculate briefly on what a postmodern future holds in store for the saints' tombs that have been so distinctively a part of the Moroccan landscape for many centuries now.

There is already abundant evidence that the postmodern is not the opposite of the traditional. Indeed, nothing loves tradition more than postmodernity. But it does not passively transmit traditions in their classic 'low-grid' forms, full of inconsistencies, ambiguities, and overlapping realities. Rather, it selects and reprocesses the traditional, distilling a unitary text to suit it for mass communication.

One aspect of this concerns simple accessibility to transportation and iconic distinctiveness. Would the shrine of Sdī Bū Qnādīl have even the modest reputation that it possesses were it not located directly adjacent to the Ṭrīq al Sulṭān, the royal highway along the Atlantic coast, or if it were not of elegant and memorable architectural proportions? I do not think so. Likewise, at least some of the contemporary success of the *anəmugg^{w}ar* of Sdī Ḥmad u Musa is clearly due to its accessibility by bus and truck. A pilgrim can travel there in a day or less from almost anywhere in the Sūs for a modest bus fare, and even more cheaply if he is willing to ride standing up in the back of an overloaded truck. Meanwhile, the geographical remoteness in inaccessible mountains that once protected saint cults such as Sdī Brahim u 'Ali of the Idaw Tanan or Lalla 'Aziza of the Isəksawən (Berque 1955:35) from undue government intrusion, now makes them relatively less competitive for the fall-fair business.

I am not suggesting that the future of shrines and pilgrimages is likely to come down to nothing but the interplay of market forces and accidents of geography and accessibility. Local shrines will always convey their local meanings to their local constituencies. But as Moroccans increasingly develop wider social horizons, through education and exposure to mass media, local phenomena will find themselves increasingly competing against more cosmopolitan forces and may find themselves diminished simply because the range of choices has been widened. Just as the shrine of Sdī Ḥmād Lfāsī no longer stands out as distinctly from the other buildings of Timəkṭṭi as it once did, so, I suspect, will a great many saints' shrines as they cease receiving the attention they formerly did in times when people valued that which was local and particular over the world purveyed to them through global mass media.

NOTES

1 By 'national,' I do not simply mean Morocco in its modern sense as a nation-among-nations, but rather the 'Islamic nation,' the 'umma, seen from a western Arab (Maghribian) perspective.

2 In this paper, Berber (Tashelhait) words and names are transcribed without diacritics, whereas Arabic words are transcribed with diacritics. I use contemporary standard transliterations, with the following conventions: γ = gh, ḍ = dh, š = sh, j = dz, and x = kh. The symbol ẓ represents a velarized "j" phoneme peculiar to the Berber languages.

3 Shilha refers to a Berber-speaking ethnolinguistic group of southern Morocco. Called išəlḥain in their own language (Tašəlḥait), Šilḥa in Arabic, and Chleuh in French, the Shilha people number approximately three and a half million people spread out over the Western High Atlas and Anti-Atlas ranges, the adjacent piedmonts and intervening valleys, and the high plateaus between the mountain ranges and the Sahara. Their habitat covers a great variety of ecological settings. Some are transhumant nomads living part of the year in stone houses high in the mountains and living in tents near the highest pastures during July and August, and others are sedentary villagers practising mixed dry and irrigated cultivation with small livestock throughout the mountains. Those along the Atlantic coast also have a coastal fishery, which they combine with their mixed agriculture. In the Sūs Valley (the great plain between the High and Anti-Atlas ranges), some Shilha live in huge villages in conditions that approach peasantry, while in the desert others have semi-nomadic to fully nomadic adaptations, living in tents throughout the year. The classic ethnographic survey of the Shilha people is that of Montagne (1930).

4 In purely hagiographic terms, this saint cult is a minor one but, in this sense, is also quite typical, so that a brief account of it may be worthwhile. The saint himself, Aḥmad bin Ṣāliḥ al-Fāsī, came originally, as his laqab indicates, from Fez. He was a šrīf and progenitor of the inhabitants of the 'quarter' of the village immediately to the right of the tomb in the photograph. The annual musəm held to commemorate the saint is primarily attended by his own descendants, and so it is, in a sense, a kind of 'totemic' celebration on the part of a particular descent group, reuniting for a day many members who have moved away with those who have remained at home. At the same time, other residents of the village of Timəkṭṭi also attend the celebration, along with inhabitants of nearby settlements – Tišəkẓẓi, Aʷsdgəlt, Tagʷnit, and Targʷa – and so the event takes on something of the character of a local celebration in the heat of the summer. Non-members of the saintly family limit their religious observance to the paying of brief visits to the tomb, where they pay their respects.

5 An even more striking example of what might be termed nil architectural elaboration is the case of the shrine of Sdī Lḥajj Leḥsən, a twentieth-century saint of the Idaw Tanan-Iḥaḥan borderland. Because the man himself was, during his lifetime, the šaix lwird (initiator) in a religious order that actively opposed the popular saint cults, it would have been unseemly for a qubba to be erected over his grave. Today his simply marked grave is venerated and his agnatic descendants honoured in exactly the same manner that one sees in maraboutic cults. A detailed history of this case can be found in Hatt (1992a).

6 Šurfā and marabouts (igurramən) are quite distinct social categories, although both are based on patrilineal descent from revered ancestors, and both categories have tendencies toward endogamy. Šurfā exude baraka, although not in as intense a quantity as igurramən with whom one has a support relationship. Some saints are also šurfā, but most are not. Neither status implies any official

religious or clerical role, and neither *šurfā* nor marabouts have any licence, so to speak, to provide moral advice or religious interpretation (that is reserved for various grades of learned individuals, *ṭulba* and *'ulamā'*) or judicial services (reserved for judges, *quḍāt*).

7   The three tribes of thirds are Ait Wa'zzun, occupying the northeast, the Ait Tankərt, occupying the west, and the Axʷmas, occupying the south. The latter third is subdivided into four sub-tribes of unequal size, Ifəsfassən, Ait ʷAnukrim, Ait Awərga, and Ibərruṭən. For some purposes, Idaw Tanan emphasize the three-thirds organization and for other purposes the six tribes.

8   Most of the Idaw Tanan are agreed to be of Maṣmūda origin – the principal ethnic 'stem' of the High Atlas peoples – but there is also a significant admixture of Jazūla lineages among long-settled descent groups of all sectors of the confederation.

9   The term connotes the Bu Rəgrəg, one of the great rivers of Atlantic Morocco.

10 Actually, it would be more correct to say "under the leadership of the tribal chiefs of the Awrāba," for much of his accomplishment was achieved in an arrangement of regency (791–804) and reflected not the imposition of Arab ideas and styles but rather Berber notions of power and leadership.

11 A possible exception to this might be the fourteen-volume memoir of personal travels and pilgrimages by the great scholar Si Mukhtār al Sūsī, *Al Mas'ūl*. This work might be described as a meta-hagiography – as large a compendium as there is ever likely to be of Shilha saints and sufis and shrines, all set within a geographical frame that co-references place and sanctity in a distinctively Moroccan way.

12 A glance at the number of place names involving saints in Quebec or many other Christian lands might suggest this is a common phenomenon.

REFERENCES

Al Sūsī, Muxtār. 1958. *Al Ma'sūl*, 14 vols. Casablanca: Maṭbaʿ al Nidāh.

Barth, Frederik. 1966. *Models of Social Organisation*. London: Royal Anthropological Institute.

Bel, Alfred. 1938. *La religion musulmane en Berbérie*. Vol 1. Paris: Paul Geuthner.

Berque, Jacques. 1955. *Structures sociales du Haut-Atlas*. Paris: Presses Universitaires de France.

Borhek, James, and Richard F. Curtis. 1975. *Sociology of Belief*. New York: John Wiley & Sons.

Cenival, Pierre de. 1934. *Chronique de Santa-Cruz du Cap de Gué*. Paris: Paul Geuthner.

Dermenghem, Émile. 1954. *Le culte des saints dans l'Islam maghrébin*. Paris: Gallimard.

Doutté, Edmond. 1904. *Magie et réligion en Afrique du Nord*. Paris: Maisonneuve-Geuthner.

Douglas, Mary. 1996. *Natural Symbols: Explorations in Cosmology*. London: Routledge.

Geertz, Clifford. 1973. *The Interpretation of Cultures*. New York: Basic Books.

———. 1983. *Local Knowledge: Further Essays in Interpretive Anthropology*. New York: Basic Books.

Gellner, Ernest. 1969. *Saints of the Atlas*. London: Weidenfield and Nicholson.

Hatt, Doyle. 1981a. "Religious Institutions and Religious Establishments in a Tribal Region of Southern Morocco." In *Proceedings of Archaeological Association of the University of Calgary*, 12: 213–18.

———. 1981b. "Sainthood in Christianity and Islam." In *Proceedings of the XX Annual Canadian Ethnology Society Conference*, ed. Marie-Françoise Guédon and Doyle Hatt, 64–69. Ottawa: Canadian Ethnology Service.

———. 1992a. "A Tribal Saint of the Twentieth Century." In *An African Commitment: Papers in Honour of Peter Lewis Shinnie*, ed. Nicholas David and Judy Sterner, 3–30. Calgary: University of Calgary Press.

———. 1992b. "The Symbolic Landscape of the Berber Cemetery." *Culture* 12:29–38.

Julien, Charles-André. 1985. *Histoire de l'Afrique du nord, des origines à 1830*. 2 vols. Paris: Payot.

Justinard, Cmdt. 1954. *Un petit royaume berbère : Le Tazerwalt*. Paris: Maisonneuve.

Mason, John Paul. 1974. "Saharan Saints: Sacred Symbols or Empty Forms?" *Anthropological Quarterly* 47:390–405.

Montagne, Robert. 1930. *Les Berbères et le Makhzen dans le Sud du Maroc*. Paris: Alcan.

Sebeok, Thomas. 1979. *The Sign and Its Masters*. Austin: University of Texas Press.

Trimingham, J. Spencer. 1969. *The Sufi Orders in Islam*. London: Oxford University Press.

Westermarck, Edvard. 1926. *Ritual and Belief in Morocco*. Vol. 1. London: Macmillan.

———. 1935. *Survivances païennes dans la civilisation mahométane*. Trans. Robert Godet. Paris: Payot.

Index

A

Accra, 44, 73, 87–88, 91–92, 123, 148
acephalous, x, 87, 91, 98
African frontier thesis, ix–xi, 2, 17, 19–20, 35, 77–78, 122
Agadir, 165–66, 172, 174, 180, 182–86
'Ali u Ləhsən, 180–82, 186, 190
ancestors
    ethnicity,
    kinship, xii, 5–6, 11, 21, 82
    veneration (*See* ancestor shrines)
animals
    sacrificial, 8–9
Asante
    chiefdom, xi, xiv, 72, 76, 89, 92
    tribute, 76
Atlas mountains, 160–61, 165, 172–74, 177–78, 180, 197, 201–2
autochthony, v, viii, ix, xi–xiii, xvi–xvii, 71, 79, 90–91

B

Bagirmi, 21
Bakoteng, 128
baobab trees, ix, xii, 80, 82–83, 92
Bangwon, 123, 130–31, 133–34, 148
baraka, 155–56, 163–64, 172, 175, 183, 192, 201
Bawku, 44, 98
Bay Gudal, 1, 24, 26, 31–33, 35–36
beer
    brewing, 36
    offering, vii, 5, 7–9, 11, 13–15, 84, 87, 115
    ritual consumption, 23, 33, 109, 126

Bekpokpam, 72
Belgium, 162
birth, vii, xi, 7, 35, 53, 103, 106, 109–10, 113, 169
bləd, 159–61, 198
Bo'araam harvest festival, 58–59
Bonaab shrine, 45–46, 57–58, 60–61, 63–64
Britain, 36
Burkina Faso, xiii, xiv, 44, 71, 79, 98, 121–23, 130, 134, 136–37, 139, 147
Burkinabé, 79
Bwaba groups, 124

C

cairns, 48, 168
calabashes, 83–84, 87, 101, 104 (*See also* water vessels)
caterpillars, 23
ceramics, xii, 10, 16, 30, 42–43, 48, 53, 68, 96, 101, 103–4, 106, 109–11
chicken. *See* fowl
chieftaincy, 1, 3, 5, 9–10. 12–36, 43, 49, 71–72, 74–81, 87–89, 91–92, 136, 146, 187, 202
Christianity, 2, 4, 61, 68, 178
citizenship, vii, xii–xiv, 79
Colson, Elizabeth, xii, xv, 2
compound abandonment, xiv, 95–98, 101, 106–14 (*See also* dabog)
Côte D'Ivoire, viii, 136
curation, xiv, 45, 87, 95, 97, 107, 194
Cuvok chiefdom, 17

205

D

dabog, 100, 112
Dagara
   chiefs, 136
   earth priests, 140
   earth shrines, 124–27, 129, 133, 136, 138, 143–46
   farmers, 136
   frontiersmen, 124, 138, 142
   group fission,
   origins, 136
   relations with neighbours, 142–146
   ritual, 129
   speaking groups, xiii–xiv, 121–123
   territorial expansion, 129-32, 134-37, 143-49
   villages, 127, 129, 134, 138–39, 143–48
   youth associations, 92
Dagara-Lobr, 127
Dagbani chiefdoms, 72, 74, 76, 79–80, 88–89, 92
Dagomba chiefdom, 74–80, 82–83, 88–92
Dan Fodio, Usman, 17
depositional processes, 15, 46, 48–49, 96–97, 101, 106, 108
diaspora, 1, 17, 29
Dimeo chiefdom, 17
disease, 9, 11
divination, 4, 6, 10, 21, 33, 107, 147
diviners, 1, 6–11, 23, 28, 30–31, 34, 130, 142
Douglas, Mary, 171
Dyan groups, 124

E

earth priests, 20, 75, 81, 84, 122, 134, 136, 140, 142–43, 148
East Africa, 62
enstoolment, 72, 88, 92
Ethiopia, 61
ethnobotany, 63

F

femininity, 81, 163, 182
fertility, 19–20, 23, 33, 45, 53, 80, 84, 102, 106, 118, 122, 132, 138, 142–43, 194
firstcomer-latecomer dynamics, xiii, ix, 77, 81, 87, 90–91, 122, 125, 132–33, 139, 142, 144–45, 148

Fortes, Meyer, xiv, 42–43, 45, 51, 96
fowl, vii, 11, 84, 87, 92, 118
France, 36, 87, 162
frontier expansion. *See* firstcomer-latecomer dynamics
frontiersmen, ix, 122, 124, 126–27, 137–38, 141, 143, 145, 148 (*See also* firstcomer-latecomer dynamics)
Fulbe, 17, 19, 24, 29–30, 35
functionalist approach, 42

G

gawula, 8
Gazawa, 17
gbondaan, 84–85, 92 (*See also* earth priests)
Ghana
   house of chiefs, xiii
   northern, v, xiii–xv, xvii, 41–42, 44, 71, 74, 90–91, 96, 98, 118–19, 121
Gili, 28
Gilvawa chiefdom, 17
Gisega chiefdom, 17
golib festival, 45, 49–51, 58, 65
Gonja, xi
Goody, Jack, 62, 76, 117, 122, 125, 134, 147, 149
governance, xiv
granaries, 2, 7, 15, 103, 105, 109–11
gravesites, xii, 111–14, 156–58, 165
griots, 124
Gudal
   chiefdom, 5, 16–17, 19–36
Gudur
   chiefdom, 1, 5, 16–21, 17, 23, 24, 26, 28–36
   shrines, 20–29
guinea fowl, 87, 92
guinea fowl war, 92

H

halalay, 9, 16, 20 (*See also* spirits)
Higi people, 19 (*See also* Kamale)
homicide, 134
house of chiefs, xiii, 88–89
hri, 13, 15–16, 24, 33
hyrax, 21

I

Idaw Tanan, 157, 161, 163, 172–77, 181–83, 199, 201–2
identity
 ethnic, x, xii–xii, 80
immigrants, 6
Islam
 influence of, 4, 17, 61–62, 69, 76
 heterodox, 153–55, 159, 177, 199
 Moroccan, 153, 155, 156, 165, 169, 173, 174, 177, 187, 203
 orthodox, 153–55, 159 (*See also* minaret)
Islamic warriors. *See* Karantao; *see also* Zaberma
iron
 bloom, 16
 jewellery, 51, 53
 market, 16
 objects, 28–29, 36, 46, 51, 53, 56, 64–65, 96, 101, 104
 smelting, 1, 5, 10
 smithing, 5–6, 8, 10, 35–36
 vessels, 24
Ivory Coast. *See* Côte D'Ivoire

J

Jaffien, 130–31, 148
jars, 7–8, 11, 14, 20, 36
jihād, 173, 175, 178
jnūn, 162, 165
judicial power, 76, 155, 202

K

Kamale people, 14
Kapsiki people, 19, 28, 31
Karantao, 131–32
Katamsa chiefdom, 17, 23
Ketik, 80
Kilwo chiefdom, 17
kinkiriis, 102–3. (*See also* spirits)
kinship, ix, xvi–xvii, 11, 16, 23, 42, 45, 81, 84, 87, 89–91, 93, 100, 122, 124, 125, 126–27, 129, 131, 133, 136–37, 139, 141, 155, 170–71, 180, 201, 196
Kitāb Ghanjā, 75
knowledge systems, xv, 153, 168–71
 cultural, 195–96
 esoteric-exoteric, 168–70, 190

Konkomba
 ancestor shrines, 84–87
 Bimotiev tribe, 72–73, 78, 82, 84, 87–89
 ceremonial regalia. *See* kopanjok
 chieftaincy, 71, 87–90
 compounds, 77
 earth shrines, 80–83
 ethnography, 72
 Komba tribe, 72–73, 78, 82, 87–89
 people, xiii–xiv, 71–72
 relations with neighbours, 73–78
kopanjok, 84
Kopytoff, Igor, ix–xi, 2, 4, 17, 19–20, 35, 77, 122 (*See also* firstcomer-latecomer dynamics)
Kudoro, 58
kuley pots, 23, 33, 36
Kumasi, 91
Kusasi
 compounds, 96, 108–13
 ethnography, 98
 kinship, 98
 material culture, 106, 116
 people, xiv, 65, 95–96, 98, 112
 shrines, 6

L

Lālla Maryam Gʷugadir, 180–82, 186, 190
Lambussie, 123, 131, 133–34, 139, 148–49
land claims, vii, xiii
lateral cycling, 97, 107
Lekpokpam, 72
leopards, 7–8, 11, 15, 20, 23, 75
libation, 53, 81–85, 87, 89–90, 101–2, 107, 115
lions, 75, 181
littingbalm. *See* ntengbe
Lobi groups, 123–24, 147
locusts, 20, 24, 35–36 (*See also* shrines)
lqubt. *See* qubba

M

Maaca'b chiefdom. *See* Mosso
Mabas people, 14
Mafaw chiefdom. *See* Mofu
Mali, 67, 79, 131
Mālikī, 177 (*See also* Islam, orthodox)
Mambay chiefdom, 17

Mamprugu. *See* Mamprusi
Mamprusi, 42–43, 68–69, 72, 74, 88, 89, 119
Mandara
   mountains, 1–2, 17, 24, 28, 35, 53
   region, xv
   religious beliefs, 4
Mangzela chiefdom. *See* Minglia
maqām, 158, 181
ma'rūf, 158, 181, 184
marabouts, xvi, 155, 164, 174–75, 180, 183, 201–2 (*See also* saint descendants)
Marrakesh, 159–61, 172
maslaslam, 21
Mayo Tsanaga, 19
Mbesefwoy, 13, 16, 21, 30
metropoloes of power, ix, 2, 19, 90 (*See also* African frontier thesis)
millet, 7, 13–14, 23, 28, 76, 81, 84, 115
minaret, 159–60, 199
Minglia chiefdom, 17
miracles, 155, 177, 193, 197 (*See also* saints)
Mofu chiefdom, 17
Mofu-Diamaré chiefdoms, 17, 21, 31–32, 35
Mofu-Gudur
   chiefdoms, 5, 17, 29–31
   language, 5, 17
Mokong chiefdom, 17
Mole-Dagbani peoples, 74
Moroccan
   ministry of religious affairs, 154, 159
Mosso chiefdom, 17
Mowo, 17, 21, 23–24, 26, 31–32
Muláy Idrīs I, xvi, 166, 186–91
Muláy Idrīs II, 177, 187

N

Na-Yiri, 72, 85, 89
Nalerigu, 73, 88
Namoos, 43
Nanumba chiefdom, 74, 92
natural features
   bodies of water. *See* water
   mountain tops, xii, 13
   rock shelters, xii, 2, 9, 11, 28, 43, 45, 57–58, 62–63, 82
   trees, 9, 63–64
Ndeveley chiefdom, 17
Ngom, 19

Nigeria, xi, 3, 34, 48, 70, 74
ntengbe, 80 (*See also* earth shrines)
Nyoo shrine, 45–53, 56–58, 60–61, 63–65
Nyoor stones, 139–40, 149
Nzema, 79
Nzulezu, 79

O

oral traditions, 2, 24, 43, 78, 79, 124–25, 129, 136, 149, 175
Oti river, 72, 74, 76
Ouessa, 123, 128, 131, 143, 149

P

paramount
   chiefs, viii, xiii, 71, 74, 88–89, 146
   chiefdoms, 71
personhood, 51
Phuo speaking groups, 121–22, 127, 131, 138, 142–44, 148
pito, 84 (*See also* beer)
placentas, 8, 11
places of power, xii–xiii, xvi, 62
Portuguese, 162–63, 174–75, 178, 182, 184
potters, 6, 9–10, 35–36

Q

quartz, 6–8, 43, 46, 78, 53, 58, 60, 63
qubba, 166, 183–84, 201

R

rain sacrifice, 21, 24
rain stones, 21, 30, 32, 35–36
rainmaking, 1, 3, 14
Rattray, R.S., 72, 98, 177
rooster. *See* fowl

S

Saboba, 72–73, 77, 89, 91–92
sacred groves, 45–46, 63–64 (*See also* natural features)
sacrifice, vii, 4, 6–7, 9–11, 13, 21, 23–24, 26, 28, 29, 33, 35–36, 44, 45, 53, 59, 82, 84, 89–90, 101–2, 108, 115, 122, 125, 126–28, 138–39, 144, 158, 193

saints
   apostasy, 153–55, 159
   belief in, 155, 160–64
   cults, 155
   death, 155
   descendants, 155
   patron, xvi, 160–61, 191, 197
   sainthood, 155–56, 171
   saints of the land, 160–61, 197–98
   shrine architecture, 156–57, 167
   shrines, 154, 156–202
Sangur, 75, 77
scavenging, 97
Sdī Brahim u 'Ali, 161, 163–64, 172–77, 180–81, 196
Sdī Bū Qnādil, 184–86, 190
Sdī Ḥmad Lfāsī, 156–57, 171, 190, 200
Sdī Ḥmad u Musa, 161, 173–74, 177–81, 196, 199
Sdī Muhammad Laxamīs. *See* Sdī Muhammad V)
Sdī Muhammad bin Slīmān al Jazūlī, 173
Sdī Muhammad V, xvi, 173, 188, 190–91, 197
semiotics, 168–69, 190
Shilha
   people, 162, 164, 201
   saints, 202
   village, 156, 201
shrines
   ancestor, 6, 10–11, 45, 84, 101–2, 103–4, 113, 121, 125
   Bundi, 134
   chiefly, 14, 21, 104
   clan, 8–9, 11, 20
   communities, 9, 11–13, 20, 168, 170
   earth, xi, xiii, 45, 71, 74, 80, 82–83, 87, 90–91, 121–22, 124–25, 127, 129, 132, 134, 138–41, 143–44, 146
   household, 6, 11, 58
   locust, 24, 26–29, 31–33, 35
   Mixyrux, 13
   nature, 9, 11, 101, 162–65
   parish fission, 127, 129
   personal, 8, 101
   pilgrimages, 158, 191–93
   rain shrine. *See* suku yam; rain stones
   ritual protection, 124–25, 144, 161
   shrine of tears, 8
   symbolism, viii, 154
   water. *See* water, bodies of

Yendi earth shrine, 77
Sirak
   chiefdom, 1, 4–5, 10, 19–20, 30
   earth shrines, 5–11, 16, 20–21, 29, 32–34
Sisala
   chiefs, 136
   earth shrines, 124, 127, 129–36
   group fission, 151
   kinship, 129
   relations with neighbours, 143–46
   ritual, 133
   speaking groups, 121, 124, 127–29
   villages, 130–32
skins, 75–76
smith/diviners, 8
smith/potter caste, 6, 9–10, 35–36
sorghum, 7,
sorghum, 7, 15, 32, 77
spatial distribution
   lineage segments, 125
   shrines, 104, 116, 149
spirits
   ancestor, 4, 6, 11, 22, 35, 45, 84, 101–4, 113, 121, 125, 141
   bush, 124, 133
   dangerous, 2, 7–8
   earth, x, 101–2
   land, x, 102, 122
   nature, 9, 11, 14, 32–33, 80–81, 101–3, 105, 122, 124, 133
   of the dead, 13
   twin, 7, 8, 10–11, 33, 35, 84, 90, 103, 122
   venerated, vii, xii, 1, 4, 6–7, 11, 13, 33, 79, 102–4, 106–7
stones
   assemblages, 46–49, 51
   grinding, 11–12, 14–15, 35, 37, 46, 53, 58, 60, 105, 111
   kubile stones, 126–28, 138, 141, 143
   shrine, 129, 136–38, 145, 148, 183
suicide, 126–27, 134
suku juk, 11 (*See also* ancestor shrines)
suku yam, 14, 16
Sukur
   chiefdom, 1, 4–5, 10, 16, 19–20, 29–31
   shrines, 10–16, 21, 24–31, 33, 35–36
šurfā, 155, 164, 166, 174, 188, 201–2

T

Tallensi
    compounds, 42, 49
    elders, 56
    fertility, 53
    gender, 51
    initiation, 51
    kinship, 45
    material culture, 41, 43, 46, 48, 55, 58, 60–62, 65
    oral traditions, 43
    people, v, xiv–xvi, 41–43, 62, 65, 79, 96
    ritual practice, 41, 45–46, 49
Tamale, 73, 77, 83, 91
tendaana, 45 (*See also* earth priests)
tengan kube, 126
tengan kuur, 126–27
tengan tie, 126
tengansob, 126–27, 142
tengbana, 45, 102 (*See also* shrines)
territorial cults, 138
Timbuktu, 74
tlagama, 14
tlisuku, 14, 16, 21, 33
tluwala, 14
Togo, 55, 71–73, 76, 98
Tonga, xii
Tongnaab shrine, xii, xiv–xv, 42, 45–46, 57–59, 61–64, 149
Tongo hills, xiv–xv. 41–45, 57–58, 61, 63, 65, 69, 79
tson vwad, 14, 16

U

Udah, 28
Umbor, 80
utindaans, 74, 80–86, 88–90 (*See also* earth priests)

V

vegetation, 64, 172
Volta
    river, xii–xiii, 74, 98–99, 121
    region, 72, 122, 125, 127, 136–39, 144–45
    Upper. *See* Burkina Faso
    Voltaic region, xiv

W

Wandala state, 21, 26, 28
water
    bodies of, xii, 4
    shrine. *See* suku yam
    vessels, 103, 110–11, 114
Weberian sociology, 169
wise, 130–31, 148
witchcraft, viii, 45, 78, 83, 102, 142
World War I, 76, 182
World War II, 4
Wula, 10, 14, 28–29

X

xidi, 14

Y

Ya-Naa, 74–75, 77, 88–89, 92
Yaane. *See* Tongnaab
yams, 76–78, 81, 85, 87
Yendi, xiii–xiv, 73–78, 80, 82–83, 88–92
Yideng Bay, 23, 25, 36
Yiran, 49, 58
Yoruba, xi

Z

Zaberma warriors, 131–32
Zangina, 74–75 (*See also* Ya-Naa)
zāwīyas, 175, 178, 183
Zidim chiefdom, 17, 23, 36
Zimbabwe, xii
Zoku ceremony, 13
zong, 104, 109, 114
Zorse, 97–98, 100, 106–7, 116

www.ingramcontent.com/pod-product-compliance
Lightning Source LLC
Chambersburg PA
CBHW052059300426
44117CB00013B/2203